THE EXCEPTION
TO THE RULERS

THE EXCEPTION TO THE RULERS

Exposing Oily Politicians, War Profiteers, and the Media That Love Them

Amy Goodman
with David Goodman

HYPERION
New York

Ariel Dorfman, "Lessons of a Catastrophe," *The Nation*, September 29, 2003. Reprinted with permission of the author.

"Another Nameless Prostitute Says the Man Is Innocent" reprinted with permission of Martin Espada.

Excerpt from "Patriot Raid" by Jason Halperin reprinted with permission of the author.

Reprint of the statement on East Timor, as read on *Democracy Now!* on September 20, 1999, by Allan Nairn, reprinted with permission of Allan Nairn.

Samuel Gardiner, "Truth from These Podia," Self-published October 8, 2003. Website: *http://www.usnews.com/usnews/politics/whispers/documents/truth.pdf*. Used with permission of the author.

LIBRARY OF CONGRESS CATALOGING-IN-PUBLICATION DATA

Goodman, Amy L.
    The exception to the rulers : exposing oily politicians, war profiteers, and
    the media that love them / Amy Goodman with David Goodman.—1st ed.
        p. cm.
    Includes bibliographical references and index.
    ISBN: 1-4013-0131-2
    1. United States—Politics and government—2001- 2. Political corrup-
    tion—United States. 3. Mass media—Political aspects—United States.
    4. Journalism—Political aspects—United States. 5. War on Terrorism,
    2001- 6. War on Terrorism, 2001—Economic aspects. 7. Profiteering—
    United States. 8. Iraq War, 2003. 9. Goodman, Amy L. 10. Journalists—
    United States—Biography. I. Goodman, David. II. Title.

E902.G66 2004
973.931—dc22

2004040515

Hyperion books are available for special promotions and premiums. For details contact Michael Rentas, Manager, Inventory and Premium Sales, Hyperion, 77 West 66th Street, 11th floor, New York, New York 10023, or call 212-456-0133.

FIRST EDITION

Book design by Richard Oriolo

10   9   8   7   6   5   4   3   2   1

Contents

To our Parents,
George (1928–1998)
and
Dorothy Goodman

Who taught us to listen
To learn
To laugh
To love

Acknowledgments

There would be no *Democracy Now!* without the many incredibly dedicated people who have helped to transform it from a daily election show in 1996 to the largest public media collaboration in the country.

A huge thank-you to those who have taken that daily journey with me, especially my cohost Juan Gonzalez, who has been there from the beginning, and longtime senior producers Kris Abrams and Maria Carrion. The current magicians that keep us on the airwaves every day include Mike Burke, Sharif Abdel Kaddous, Denis Moynihan, Ana Nogueira, Elizabeth Press, Karen Ranucci, Jeremy Scahill, and Mike Di Fillippo.

Endless gratitude to those who help and have helped broadcast *Democracy Now!* over the years: Gillian Aldrich, Terry Allen, Angela Alston, Jim Bennett, Larry Bensky, Russell Branca, Dominique Bravo, Verna Avery Brown, Hesu Coue, Dan Coughlin, Rafael de la Uz, Julie Drizen, Deepa Fernandes, Jenny Filippazzo, Matthew Finch, Laura Flanders, Uri Gal-Ed, Nell Geiser, Linda Greco, DeeDee Halleck, David Isay, Rachel Jones, Rick Jungers, Angie Karan, Miranda Kennedy, Rich Kim, Emily Kunstler, Tia Lessin, David Love, Carmen Mitchell, Fatima Mojaddidy, Salim Muwakkil, Lenina Nadal, Smitha Parigi, Isis Phillips, Chase Pierson, Karen Pomer, Noel Rabinowitz, Lizzy Ratner, Mark Read, Noah Reibel, Orlando Richards, Anthony Riddle, Rick Rowley, Simba Russeau, Eric Rweyemamu, Jonny Sender, Parvez Sharma, Brad Simpson, Anthony Sloan, Jacquie Soohen, Julie Spriggs, George Stoney, Vilka Tzouras, Jayana Verderosa, Warcry, Gabriel

Weiss, Alex Wolfe, Ben Zipperer, Chris Zucker, and all of those staff and volunteers unnamed yet so appreciated.

Among my WBAI colleagues at *Wake Up Call,* a special thanks to Bernard White, Janice K. Bryant, Sharan Louise Harper, Dred Scott Keyes, Robert Knight, Errol Maitland, Mario Murillo, and Don Rojas and all the crew for the many magic moments over this last decade.

A very special thanks to:

Valerie Van Isler and the late great Samori Marksman for leading the way;

All my colleagues at WBAI, KPFK, WPFW, KPFT, and KPFA and the network of community radio stations for continuing to believe in this noble experiment that is Pacifica Radio;

Free Speech TV, Downtown Community Television, Manhattan Neighborhood Network, and all public access TV stations, Openflows, and Indymedia centers around the world that continue to build the legacy in the wider independent media movement;

Jon Alpert, Laurie Betlach, Diana Cohn, Jaune Evans, Ken Freedman, Mark Friedberg, Richard Hoover, Patrick Lannan, Michael Moore, Tim Robbins, David Rosenmiller, Alex Tager, Israel Taub, Keiko Tsuno, and Andy Tuch.

Viewers and listeners everywhere. You are our lifeline.

This book would not have been written if it weren't for my brother David Goodman, who encouraged me to undertake this project and didn't look up until it was finished. I thank him for his patience, sensitivity, incredible good humor, and intelligence. And I thank Sue, Ariel, and Jasper for sharing him.

I am particularly grateful to my friend and colleague Allan Nairn. His friendship, his dedication to human rights, and his tireless determination to expose injustice humble and strengthen me.

David and I have tried to steer this runaway train as best we could. We had crucial help in keeping it on the rails. Thanks to Michael Ratner, Julie, Bill Hoynes, and Mike Burke, all of whom commented on parts of the book. We benefited from the editorial talents of Bob Moser and the research skills of Elaine Zelmanov. Jeremy Scahill, my colleague and friend, spent sleepless nights helping to edit this book.

Thanks to C. M. Choy and Silk Road Mocha in Chinatown, Robert Kim, Amy Graf, and Kim and Jane Brown for their contributions.

Our agent, Luke Janklow, found the right home for this book and gave us helpful advice. And thanks to our editor at Hyperion, Bill Strachan, for his many suggestions, his encouragement and patience, and his shepherding of this project to completion; and to Hyperion president Bob Miller and editor in chief Will Schwalbe for their enthusiastic support for this project from the outset. Thanks also to Ben Loehnen and Christine Ragasa at Hyperion.

Thanks to our brothers Steve and Dan Goodman for their insights and support, and to Ruth Levine, Anna, Sarah, and Eli. And to Caren Spruch, Elisabeth Benjamin, and Brenda Murad for their friendship.

We are grateful to Denis Moynihan for his remarkable array of talents: researching, writing, editing, humoring, and prodding us over the finish line. We couldn't have done this without him.

From David: A special thanks to Jasper and Ariel Goodman for letting me spend long days writing at home and away, while simultaneously driving me crazy and making me laugh with their fantastic interruptions. They gave me all the incentive I needed to finish. To my wife, teammate, and love, Sue Minter, I offer my heartfelt gratitude. She has shared the vision for this book and a passion for me and the cause, and she has shouldered the considerable burden to help make all of this happen. Any good I do is a result of her love and support.

I am grateful to Bill, Dawn, Bob, and Evelyn Minter for the countless ways that they help. Thanks also to David Weber for musical inspiration.

And from both of us: Our grandmother Sonia Bock, at 106, is our model for wisdom, endurance, and optimism.

This book is dedicated to our parents. Our late father, George Goodman, and our mother, Dorrie Goodman, would be amazed that years of childhood pillow fights would one day morph into a book. As children always do, we blame our parents for everything: They taught us by wonderful example how to care, love, laugh, and fight like hell for what we believe in. For that, and so much more, we thank them. Their dedication to us makes this dedication easy.

The Silenced Majority

THE TROOPS MARCHED SLOWLY up the road, their U.S.-made M-16s in the ready position. It was November 12, 1991, a day that would forever be seared into my memory, and into history. I was in Dili, the capital of East Timor, a small island nation 300 miles north of Australia. East Timor had been brutally occupied by Indonesian troops for sixteen years, since they invaded in 1975. The Indonesian military had sealed off East Timor from the outside world and turned it into their private killing field. A third of the population—200,000 Timorese—had died. It was one of the worst genocides of the late twentieth century.

I had just attended mass at the main church in Dili with Allan Nairn, journalist and activist, then writing for *The New Yorker* magazine. After the service, thousands marched toward the Santa

Cruz cemetery to remember Sebastião Gomes, yet another young man killed by Indonesian soldiers. The people came from all over: workplaces, homes, villages, and farms. They traveled through a geography of pain: In almost every other building, Timorese had been held or tortured, disappeared or killed. Whether it was a police station or a military barracks, a hotel or an officer's house, no place was beyond reach of the terror. Not even the church was safe. It was about 8 a.m. when we reached the cemetery.

We had asked people along the way: "Why are you marching? Why are you risking your lives to do this?"

"I'm doing it for my mother," one replied. "I'm doing it for my father," said another. "I'm doing it for freedom."

In the distance, we heard an eerie, synchronized beat. Suddenly we saw them. Many hundreds of Indonesian troops coming up the road, twelve to fifteen abreast. People grew very quiet.

We knew the Indonesian military had committed many massacres in the past, but never in front of Western journalists. Allan suggested we walk to the front of the crowd, hoping that our presence could head off what looked like an impending attack. I put on my headphones, took out my tape recorder—I usually kept these hidden so as not to endanger Timorese caught talking to us—and held up my microphone like a flag. Allan put his camera above his head, and we went and stood in the middle of the road, about fifteen yards in front of the crowd. By visibly showing the tools of our trade, we hoped to alert the troops that this time they were being watched.

A hush fell over the Timorese. Those in the back could run, but the thousands of people in front were trapped by the cemetery walls that lined both sides of the road. The main sound was the rhythmic thump of boots hitting the road as the troops marched in unison toward the people. Children whispered behind us. Then, without any warning or provocation, the soldiers rounded the corner, swept past us, raised their U.S.-made weapons, and opened fire.

People were ripped apart. The troops just kept shooting, moving their guns from left to right, killing anyone still standing.

A group of soldiers surrounded me. They started to shake my microphone in my face as if to say, *This is what we don't want.* Then they slammed me to the ground with their rifle butts and started to kick me with their boots. I gasped for breath. Allan threw himself on top of me to protect me from further injury.

The soldiers wielded their M-16s like baseball bats. They slammed them against Allan's head until they fractured his skull. For a moment, Allan lay in the road in spasm, covered in blood, unable to move. Suddenly, about a dozen soldiers lined up like a firing squad. They put the guns to our heads and screamed, *"Politik! Politik!"* They were accusing us of being involved in politics, a crime clearly punishable by death. They also demanded, "Australia? Australia?"

We understood what was at stake with this question. In October 1975, Indonesian soldiers had executed five Australia-based television journalists in an attempt to cover up a military incursion leading up to the December 7, 1975, invasion of East Timor. On December 8, Australian journalist Roger East, the only other Western reporter left in East Timor, was dragged out of a radio station in Dili down to the harbor and shot.

Almost exactly sixteen years later, as Allan and I lay on the ground surrounded by Indonesian soldiers, we shouted, "No, we're from America!" They had stripped us of our possessions, but I still had my passport. I threw it at them. When I regained my breath, I said again, "We're from America! America!"

Finally, the soldiers lowered their guns from our heads. We think it was because we were from the same country their weapons were from. They would have to pay a price for killing us that they never had to pay for killing Timorese.

At least 271 Timorese died that day, in what became known as the Santa Cruz massacre. Indonesian troops went on killing for days. It was not even one of the larger massacres in East Timor, and it wouldn't be the last. It was simply the first to be witnessed by outsiders.

"A Sanctuary for Dissent"

GOING TO WHERE the silence is. That is the responsibility of a journalist: giving a voice to those who have been forgotten, forsaken, and beaten down by the powerful. It is the best reason I know to carry our pens, cameras, and microphones into our own communities and out to the wider world.

I am a journalist from Pacifica Radio, the only independent media network broadcasting in the United States. It was founded in 1949 by a man named Lew Hill, a pacifist who had refused to fight in World War II. When he came out of a detention camp after the war, he said the United States needed a media outlet that wasn't run by corporations profiting from war. His vision was of an independent network run by journalists and artists—not by "corporations with nothing to tell and everything to sell that are raising our children today," in the words of journalism professor George Gerbner, founder of the "cultural environment" movement.

KPFA, the first Pacifica station, began in Berkeley, California. FM radio was in its infancy at the time, so KPFA had to make and give out FM radios in order for people to hear the station. As would happen so many times in the decades that followed, Pacifica Radio tried something no one thought would work—building a network based on the financial support of individual listeners. This marked the birth of listener-sponsored media in this country, a model later used by National Public Radio and public television.

The Pacifica network grew to five stations: KPFA in Berkeley, KPFK in Los Angeles, WBAI in New York, WPFW in Washington, and KPFT in Houston. In 1970, KPFT became the only radio station in the United States to have its transmitter blown up. The Ku Klux Klan did it. In 1981, the KKK's Grand Wizard claimed that his greatest act "was engineering the bombing of a left-wing radio station," because he understood how dangerous Pacifica was.

Pacifica is a sanctuary for dissent. In the fifties, when the legendary singer and African-American leader Paul Robeson was whitelisted during Senator Joseph McCarthy's witch hunts, banned from almost every public space in the United States but for a few black churches, he knew he could go to KPFA and be heard. The great writer James Baldwin, debating Malcolm X about the effectiveness of nonviolent sit-ins in the South, broadcast over the airwaves of WBAI.

Today, Pacifica continues that tradition. My colleagues at WBAI, including Elombe Brath and the late Samori Marksman, have taught me how a local radio station can be the gateway to a rich world. Samori was a pan-Africanist who taught me so much about the history of Africa and the Caribbean. Elombe Brath has long provided a voice for leaders of African liberation movements. These men made the whole world our community. Great African leaders such as Kwame Nkrumah, Sékou Touré, and Julius Nyerere were local voices to WBAI's listeners. In his role as WBAI program director, Samori would call me into his office under the pretext of discussing some bureaucratic minutiae. I would emerge three hours later, newly educated about a liberation movement in Africa or the Caribbean.

It's still much the same. On any given day, you can listen to the news on CNN or National Public Radio, then tune in to a Pacifica station. You would think you were hearing reports from different planets.

We inhabit the same planet, but we see it through different lenses. On community airwaves, color isn't what sports commentators provide, and it isn't the preserve of a "diversity" reporter. We are a cross section of races, ethnicities, and social classes explaining the world we see around us.

Take, for example, my WBAI colleague Errol Maitland. In March 2000, while he was reporting live from the funeral of Patrick Dorismond—a Haitian-American who was shot and killed by police—Errol attempted to interview New York City police who were moving in on the crowd of mourners. We listened as he tried to question police, who then threw him to the ground. Errol was beaten by New York City police officers and had to be hospitalized for weeks. When I visited him in the hospital, I found him handcuffed to his bed. All for what? For reporting while black.

It was stories like Errol's, in New York and around the world, that my WBAI colleague Bernard White and I took on each day for a decade on the morning show *Wake Up Call*. We heard people speak for themselves, instead of hearing them defined by officialdom. Bernard, a former New York City schoolteacher, has deep roots in the community. Whether in the classroom, on air, or as Samori's successor as WBAI program director, Bernard's idea of education is to have people tell their own stories, document their own lives.

I began hosting *Democracy Now!* in 1996, when it was launched as the only daily election show in public broadcasting. Listener response was enormous. Suddenly the daily struggles of ordinary people—workers, immigrants, artists, the employed and the unemployed, those with homes and those without, dissidents, soldiers, people of color—were dignified as news. I call it trickle-up journalism. These are the voices that shape movements— movements that make history. These are people who change the world just as much as generals, bankers, and politicians. They *are* the mainstream, yet they are ignored by the mainstream media.

After the 1996 election, we decided to continue the show as a daily grassroots political newshour. When the media began beating the drums of war after September 11, 2001, *Democracy Now!* expanded to television and became the largest public media collaboration in the country. We now broadcast on hundreds of community radio and public access TV stations. We beam out over satellite television and stream on the Internet at www.democracy now.org.*

Why has *Democracy Now!* grown so quickly? Because of the deafening silence in the mainstream media around the issues—and the people—that matter most. People are now confronting the most important issues of the millennium: war and peace, life and death. Yet who is shaping the discourse? Generals, corporate executives, and government officials.

In a media landscape where there are more channels than ever, the lack of any diversity of opinion is breathtaking—and boring. As my colleague Juan Gonzalez often says, "You can surf through hundreds of channels before you realize there is nothing on TV." In a society where freedom of the press is enshrined in the Constitution, our media largely acts as a megaphone for those in power.

That's why people are so hungry for independent media—and are starting to make their own.

Democracy Now! can be seen on Free Speech TV (Dish Network channel 9415). It can currently be heard on Pacifica and NPR stations around the United States, on Sirius satellite radio, on public access TV, and on community radio stations across Canada, Australia, Europe, and on shortwave (Radio for Peace International).

Muzzling Dissent

VIBRANT DEBATE AND dissent exist in this country, but you are not reading or hearing about this in the mainstream press.

If you are opposed to war, you are not a fringe minority. You are not a silent majority. You are part of a *silenced* majority. Silenced by the mainstream media.

After 9/11 the media personalities on television—you can't call many of them journalists—kept saying that 90 percent of Americans were for war.

Were you ever called and asked your views? And if you were, what were you asked? Because if someone called and asked, "Do you believe the killing of innocent civilians should be avenged by the killing of innocent civilians?" I'm sure that 90 percent of Americans would say no. We are a compassionate people. But people cannot take action if they don't have accurate information.

Politicians who never met a war they didn't like (and in the case of Bush, Cheney, and Rumsfeld, never fought in any of them) began to beat the drums of war after 9/11. Corporations chimed in, knowing they could make a killing off of killing. And then came the mainstream media to manufacture consent, as Noam Chomsky puts it.

To understand how the media shape the message, look at who the messengers are. The media watch group Fairness and Accuracy in Reporting (FAIR) did a study of the "experts" who appeared on-camera on the major network news shows during the critical week before and week after February 5, 2003—the day Secretary of State Colin Powell made his case to the UN Security Council for invading Iraq. This was at a time when 61 percent of Americans supported more time for diplomacy and inspections. The FAIR study found only 3 of 393 sources—fewer than 1 percent— were affiliated with antiwar activism.[1]

Three out of almost 400 interviews. And that was on the "respectable" evening news shows of CBS, NBC, ABC, and PBS.

So if you ran to the bathroom while watching TV during that critical two-week period—sorry! You might have missed the only dissenting viewpoint the network news offered.

This is not a media that is serving a democratic society, where a diversity of views is vital to shaping informed opinions. This is a well-oiled propaganda machine that is repackaging government spin and passing it off as journalism.

Why does it matter? Well, consider the alternative: Imagine if instead of 3 voices against the war, the networks allowed 200 war skeptics on the air—roughly the proportion of the public opposed to war.

And imagine if the U.S. media showed uncensored, hellish images of war—even for one week. What impact would that have? I think we would be able to abolish war.

Instead, after our loved ones and neighbors followed orders and marched off to war (unlike the children of the top warmakers), the networks showed us a colorful, video-game version of what was going on.

In Iraq, the U.S. government discouraged independent coverage of the war—sometimes at gunpoint. And when the remains of dead soldiers began coming back, the Bush administration ordered curtains to be erected when the planes off-loaded the flag-draped coffins at Dover Air Force Base. In fact, the administration has enforced a ban on any filming of returning caskets. As of early 2004, with more than 500 dead Americans and over 11,000 wounded or medically evacuated, Bush had not attended a single funeral for a soldier killed in action during his presidency, either from Afghanistan or Iraq.[2] The Bush team has invoked a basic principle of propaganda: Control the images and you control the people.

The lesson had been learned from Vietnam—a lesson in manipulation. In Iraq, there would be no daily television images of the human toll of war. The government and the media would portray a clean war, a war nearly devoid of victims.

Breaking the Sound Barrier

IT IS ABSOLUTELY critical right now to break the sound barrier when it comes to dissent. The U.S. government has used the war on terror as its rationale for the biggest crackdown on civil liberties since the McCarthy era of the 1950s. Right now, people are being thrown in jail without charges. Men from the Middle East and South Asia are being singled out as enemies. Lawyers defending dissidents are under attack.

These are the first warnings. You could be next.

The U.S. Constitution has been swept aside by myriad draconian measures that are part of the USA PATRIOT Act. When George W. Bush and his foot soldiers can't build an airtight legal case, suspicion and xenophobia will suffice. Prisoners classified by the U.S. president as "enemy combatants" can now be tried by military tribunals on ships docked in foreign waters, beyond the protective reach of the Bill of Rights. Some are being tortured to pry information out of them. Hundreds of foreign nationals are presently being detained by the United States—at Guantánamo Bay, Cuba, and Bagram Air Base in Afghanistan—without knowing the charges against them. We don't know the defendants' names or their purported crimes, and they don't hear the evidence against them. According to a November 13, 2001, presidential order, their trials can be held in secret and they can be found guilty by a tribunal of military judges chosen by the secretary of defense. If the tribunal unanimously sentences the prisoner to death, he or she can be executed. We would know nothing of the case, and those with knowledge of the tribunals' actions are forbidden to speak about them.[3]

If there was an honest discourse in the mainstream media, if we really did present alternatives to kangaroo court justice and war, people would be able to imagine a much wider range of options. That is one of the media's most serious responsibilities, to open up the discussion.

The silenced majority is chafing behind the corporate media muzzle. Lines are breaking down between Democrats and Republicans, conservatives and liberals. Conservatives, like progressives, care deeply about privacy, about corporate control of their lives. People across the political spectrum are outraged by the profiteering corporations—Bush's corporate criminal sponsors, including Enron, WorldCom, and Halliburton—robbing our treasury, raiding our pensions, ravaging our wilderness areas, and running away with the loot.

More and more people are saying *no* to government lies, corporate greed, and a slavish media.

The silenced majority is finding its voice.

1

Blowback

Those who do not remember the past are condemned to repeat it.

—George Santayana[1]

THE MORNING STARTED LIKE every other. It ended like no other.

It was September 11, 2001. At about 6 a.m., I raced out of my apartment to get a stack of newspapers and hopped in a cab on that brilliant Tuesday, headed to the firehouse.

A dozen blocks past the World Trade Center, I arrived at the century-old decommissioned home of Engine Company 31. The building, with its large red doors in front of the fire truck bays, continues to serve the larger neighborhood with a community media center and the studio of *Democracy Now!* For the next several hours, we went about our normal routine. We prepared copy, researched stories, checked facts, and wrote leads. We were wedged into a small space with angled ceilings. As the clock ticked toward airtime, the mayhem grew louder. We are constantly shouting, debating, and discussing how we are going to cover the news of the day. To move between floors, we go up and down the old brass fire pole. (Well, I slide down it; only Anthony Sloan, our engineer, is able to shimmy up it.)

As our daily broadcast time of 9:00 a.m. approached, we checked the mikes and connected to the Pacifica Radio satellite. Unbeknownst to us, as we went about our morning rituals, the first plane hit the World Trade Center. It was 8:47 a.m. We were minutes from airtime, unaware that a global calamity was unfolding a few blocks away.

Just before nine, my pulse instinctively quickened as I heard the familiar countdown: "Five . . . four . . . three . . . two . . . one . . ."

"From Pacifica Radio, this . . . is *Democracy Now!*" I began my daily refrain. Once I utter those words, I quietly breathe a sigh of relief—we have made it to another day's show.

But this day, three minutes into the show, as I was presenting the news headlines, I heard a muffled explosion outside. It was the second plane hitting the World Trade Center. Listeners soon heard sirens wailing outside the studio.

Moments later, Keiko Tsuno, codirector of Downtown Community Television, the nonprofit television production and training facility that owns the firehouse, burst into our studio. She shouted, "A plane has hit the World Trade Center!" She told us that they were opening the firehouse to help people fleeing the disaster.

I stared at her in disbelief. A plane? She must be mistaken.

We'd just begun playing a taped interview from the World Conference on Racism in Durban, South Africa, so I was able to take a moment to switch on the television. The four of us in the studio crowded around the TV in horrified silence as we saw the images of the burning towers.

I broke into the program to announce what had happened. We grabbed wire reports and continued to monitor the TV. I was now on live. "It appears that planes crashed into upper floors of both World Trade Center towers in a horrific scene that left gaping holes in both buildings. President Bush has said it is the result of a terrorist attack. Possibly a plane has hit the Pentagon, and there is a fire on the mall [in Washington, D.C.] and a fire behind the Old Executive Office Building. The White House and Pentagon are being evacuated," I said. The initial stories about fires in and around Washington were confusing; it turned out later that the Pentagon plane crash was responsible for the smoke over the city.

I continued: "You may hear the sirens in the background. We heard the explosion just a little while ago. Emergency vehicles are racing to the World Trade Center."

Within hours of the attack, evidence began emerging that suggested that this was yet another case of what has come to be known as *blowback*—how backing despots in far-off places inevitably comes back to haunt us at home. If we learn anything from September 11 and the wars on Iraq and Afghanistan, it should be that there will be a price to pay every time our government backs thugs and torturers abroad—or becomes one of them. But on that terrible morning, we were more concerned with grappling with the disaster unfolding in our own neighborhood.

Downstairs, our colleagues opened the old firehouse doors onto the street. They offered water and use of telephones to the people streaming uptown. *Democracy Now!* producer Brad Simpson ran outside and brought in people stumbling away from the horror, like a man who came with his boss. A wave of rubble had overcome them, but miraculously they were still standing. They shared their story. We continued to broadcast throughout the day.

At 5:00 p.m., producer Miranda Kennedy and I walked outside and watched Building 7 go down. Seeing this forty-seven-story building just north of the Twin Towers crumple like a dollhouse was a surreal, sad moment. The building housed the mayor's multimillion-dollar eighth-floor bunker, built after the 1993 attack on the World Trade Center. The command center included 130,000 gallons of oil. As many pointed out—and objected to—at the time, if the World Trade Center was attacked again, Mayor Giuliani's command center would blow up, endanger everything around it, and poison Lower Manhattan with PCBs. That's exactly what happened.

Lower Manhattan was declared an evacuation zone. The line was drawn at Canal Street, two blocks north of us. The *Democracy Now!* crew decided to stay in the firehouse so that we could be assured access to our broadcast facilities. We slept on the floor for three nights, as the military rapidly occupied Lower Manhattan.

In the days following 9/11, I felt like a ghost walking among ghosts. The only place to get food was a deli over on Broadway and Leonard. Late one night I ventured out from the *Democracy Now!* studio. Rescue workers were straggling in. I knew all these guys were heroes, desperately trying to save anyone they could, but they didn't look larger than life. They were skinny and fat, some in coveralls, some in T-shirts and jeans.

Rescue workers poured in from everywhere. A group from Buffalo, that group from around the corner, all covered in ash. There were no perfunctory smiles or greetings; the group members were just trying to get some nourishment to keep going. I couldn't bring myself to eat any of the usual foods from the salad bar because I kept thinking of the deathly ash, so I confined myself to canned goods. It was like wartime rations.

As I walked back to our firehouse one evening, the acrid air got worse. I kept my head down and heard my breathing in the flimsy dust mask I was wearing. When I looked up, I saw a car smashed to half its height. How had it gotten there? I ran my finger along the ash-covered hood, like drawing pictures in snow. But this was September.

When engineer Anthony Sloan went out to get us some food up north, he couldn't get back across the evacuation line. We were down to three people the next day, engineering the show ourselves. I was careful not to venture too far from our studio, afraid of being thrown out of the evacuation zone entirely. We had to do the program. We were the closest daily national broadcast to Ground Zero. We heard the reports that dozens of firefighters had died, then that the number was more than a hundred, then two hundred. My God, then it was more than three hundred.

On Thursday night, I went to Ground Zero with a friend and colleague, Denis Moynihan. Once again I put on a mask, trying not to breathe in all the dust. As we walked down Lafayette Street, we passed a park where people had earlier been hammering together makeshift pine pallets to carry out bodies. All day, pounding away. The only thing worse was when the hammering stopped. That awful silence. There was no need for the pallets. They weren't finding bodies.

On Saturday, we walked past Wall Street to Battery Park. Manhattan's southernmost tip had become a bustling military camp. Olive green vehicles of all sizes circled the park. Signs with billeting instructions and security detachment schedules were everywhere, all in the military's inscrutable jargon. It was still hours before dawn, but hundreds were awake and at work. We approached a woman in green camouflage fatigues, a helicopter pilot in the National Guard from upstate New York. She had just arrived and was likely to be assigned to guard duty, protecting access to Ground Zero.

I asked her what she thought was going to happen in the aftermath of the week's attack. She first talked about how horrified she was at the scene of devastation. Then she paused, and looked around to see who might overhear. She turned back and looked directly at me, eyes sad.

"My mother recently died. And now this. I don't want to see any more suffering. I hope there won't be a military response to this. I'm a mother, and I don't want to see more death coming from this."

I asked if she would come in and speak on our show. She declined, but her words stayed with me.

Three thousand people incinerated in a moment. We will never know exactly how many people died on September 11, 2001. Those who were uncounted in life go uncounted in death. Numerous undocumented immigrants who worked in and around the World Trade Center simply vanished. Their families are still afraid to come forward because of what could happen. They could be detained or even deported because of the increasingly close relationship between police and immigration authorities. Some companies were not willing to come forward to name the undocumented workers they had employed for decades. We will never know the names of these missing.

Not in Our Name

HOLED UP IN our studio, we felt it was critical to continue to bring out the diverse views of people trying to make sense of this senseless act. We understood only too well that the war machine was gearing up in Washington. We wanted to make sure that *all* voices were heard, not just those calling for military retribution.

There was Rita Lasar, a 70-year-old woman who lost her brother Abe Zelmanowitz, 55, who worked on the twenty-seventh floor of the World Trade Center. On September 11, Rita heard that something had happened at the Twin Towers. She went up on her roof, where she watched the towers collapse. "It was like a movie," she told me later. That is, until she realized that her brother was inside.

Her other brother had been screaming at Abe on his cell phone. "Get out of the building! Get out of the building now!"

But Abe wouldn't leave. He was waiting until emergency workers came to help his best friend, Ed, a quadriplegic who worked next to him. And so Abe stayed, and died with Ed and so many others.

Rita immediately began the 9/11 death ritual. She went from hospital to hospital, hoping against hope that she would find Abe. Later, she provided samples of her own DNA in order to identify Abe's remains.

On September 14, President Bush invoked Abe Zelmanowitz's story in his speech at the National Cathedral in Washington. Rita quickly understood how her brother's gentle heroism was being used. She wrote a letter that appeared in *The New York Times* on September 18, 2001. "It is in my brother's name and mine," she wrote, "that I pray that we, this country that has been so deeply hurt, not do something that will unleash forces we will not have the power to call back."

That was also the prayer of Phyllis and Orlando Rodriguez, who lost their son. Greg Ernesto Rodriguez, 31, worked for Cantor Fitzgerald, which lost 658 of its 1,050 employees above the hundredth floor of the World Trade Center that day. As the Rodriguez family gathered to remember Greg, Phyllis and Orlando wrote a letter that circulated widely on the Internet:

> We read enough of the news to sense that our
> government is heading in the direction of violent revenge,
> with the prospect of sons, daughters, parents, friends in
> distant lands, dying, suffering, and nursing further

grievances against us. It is not the way to go. It will not avenge our son's death. Not in our son's name.

Nor in Jim Creedon's. I met him on October 7, 2001, the day the bombs started to fall on Afghanistan. Thousands of people gathered in Manhattan to protest the war, marching several miles from Union Square to Times Square, site of the armed forces recruiting station (not to be confused with *The New York Times* nearby). They held signs with messages such as "Our grief is not a cry for war."

Jim Creedon stood on a pickup truck and spoke through a loudspeaker about his experience as an emergency worker. He was injured on September 11, but he went back to try to help other people. "I lost four men in my squad," he said. "War is not going to bring our loved ones back. . . . Today the U.S. government began bombing in Afghanistan. We've seen what happens when they bomb: Hundreds and thousands of people lose their lives."

I thought there would be a long line of reporters who would want to interview him. He met all the important criteria for a story. He was a heroic first responder. They were so hard hit.

I raced over to invite him on the program, but there was no need to run. I was first and last in line to interview him. He told me, "As a rescue worker, I can't say, 'We lost six thousand people, so let's kill six thousand more.' We need to stand together today and say, 'No more destruction of innocent lives.'"

Creedon was part of a movement that started in New York called September 11th Families for Peaceful Tomorrows (www.peacefultomorrows.org). These are people who have lost loved ones and said, "Not in our name." We watched over and over again on television as family members told the sad stories of the people who had died. But when Rita and Phyllis and Orlando and Jim and others who were opposed to war wanted to get to the second part—from description to prescription—and say, "We don't believe that war is the answer," the media would cut away. They would turn to the so-called terrorism experts, people like Oliver North and Henry Kissinger.

Maybe the corporate media got it right for once. Those guys are experts in terrorism—after all, it takes one to know one.

IRONICALLY, ONE OF THE topics we were covering as the planes were hitting the World Trade Center was the connection between September 11 and terror—September 11, 1973. It was on this day that Salvador Allende, the democratically elected leader of Chile, died in the presidential palace in Santiago as General Augusto Pinochet and the Chilean military seized power. The Pinochet forces were backed by then President Richard Nixon and Secretary of State Henry Kissinger,[2] and had financial support from two major multinational corporations operating in Chile, Anaconda Copper and ITT, both of which were closely tied to the Republican administration. We were doing the show because declassified documents had come out that further implicated Kissinger and Nixon in that coup and in the rise to power of Pinochet, who led a seventeen-year reign of terror.

Kissinger once commented that he saw no reason why Chile should be allowed to "go Marxist" simply because "its people are irresponsible."[3] The result? As Peter Kornbluh of the National Security Archive, the guest on our show that day, has recounted, "Pinochet murdered more than 3,100 Chileans, disappeared 1,100, and tortured and jailed thousands more. He closed the Chilean Congress, banned political parties, censored the press and took over the universities. Through decree, the barrel of the gun and the touch of the electrode, he imposed a seventeen-year dictatorship that became synonymous with human rights abuses at home and terrorist atrocities abroad."[4]

The Circle Closes

AS I WALKED around those first days after 9/11, I saw pictures going up everywhere. People posted color copies of photographs of their loved ones. There were pictures of a woman with her child, a man holding his cat. Signs would plead silently from lampposts, "If you have seen my son, please call his mother. He was last seen on the 77th floor of the World Trade Center. My number is . . ."

Thousands of these photographs went up all over the city—on telephone poles, on the walls of hospitals, in the parks. I thought of how similar those pictures were to the images carried by the mothers of the disappeared in Argentina. Since the late 1970s, these heroic, tenacious women have stood in silent witness in the Plaza de Mayo in Buenos Aires demanding to know the truth about their loved ones who disappeared in Argentina's "dirty war" against alleged dissidents. The mothers stand holding pictures and placards reading "Have you seen my son?" "Have you seen my granddaughter?" Between 1975 and 1983, the Argentine military killed 30,000 of its own people. In October 1976, then Secretary of State Henry Kissinger told an Argentine Navy admiral, "The quicker you succeed, the better."[5]

September 11 united Americans with people around the world who have been victims of terror. In my years working as a reporter, I have covered many horrors: war, torture, bombings, genocide. In most cases, I have had to fight to tell the stories of the victims because doing so often implicated the U.S. government and its al-

September 11 Around the World

September 11 has now become synonymous with the tragic events of 2001. But for others around the world, this date evokes different images and memories of terror:

September 11, 1973, Chile. President Salvador Allende, democratically elected leader of Chile, died in a CIA-backed military coup.

September 11, 1977, South Africa. Antiapartheid leader Stephen Biko, unconscious on the floor of a police van after being beaten by police, was driven 1,000 kilometers to Pretoria, where he would die the following day.

September 11, 1990, Guatemala. Guatemalan anthropologist Myrna Mack was murdered by U.S.-backed military.

September 9–13, 1971, New York. The Attica prison uprising occurred, in which New York state troopers killed thirty-nine men and wounded eighty-eight others.

lies. From Timor to Iraq to Haiti, there always had to be a reason, a false balance to explain away the atrocities. "It's more complicated than that . . ." goes the official response. "Collateral damage is part of war . . ."

But in the case of 9/11, there was an unequivocal collective revulsion at the mass killing. The model for media coverage was to find the families who had lost loved ones, telling their stories, naming names. Those are the details that dignify a life; that's what makes us feel the loss. The portraits of grief, profiles of the children left without a parent, the deeds of unsung heroes—these should be the models for how all atrocities are covered. Because when people learn of others' pain, they are moved to act.

Our Guy: Putting the U-S-A in "Usama"

IN A TRAGIC closing of the circle, the terror that has for so long been out of view in faraway lands has come back to us with terrible ferocity. The CIA calls it blowback—when U.S. support for repressive militaries or armed insurgencies somewhere else boomerangs back at the United States.

After 9/11, Osama bin Laden became a household name across the globe. But for two decades before the attacks, his name was familiar to a small, powerful group in Washington. The reason? Osama bin Laden was financed and trained by the United States.

A leader of militant Islamic fundamentalist groups, bin Laden was the answer to Washington's prayers in the 1980s as the U.S. government tried to lure the Soviets into Afghanistan. In the words of President Carter's national security advisor, Zbigniew Brzezinski, the aim was to give "the USSR its Vietnam war." Between 1982 and 1992, the CIA spent $3 billion training and arming Islamist radicals to fight the Soviets in Afghanistan (an amount matched by the Saudis bill for bill, according to a CIA official).[6] It was the largest U.S. covert operation since World War II.

Brzezinski later revealed that the U.S. covert program to aid and train the Afghan mujahedeen, or holy warriors, had begun six months *before* the Soviets invaded.[7] Some 35,000 Muslims from forty-three countries fought with the mujahedeen, while another 100,000 were influenced by the war either through military training or by attending militant Islamic schools.[8]

"[T]he whole country is a university for jihad," or holy war, said Afghan commander Noor Amin.[9]

Asked in 1998 if he had any regrets, Brzezinski replied: "Regret what? That secret operation was an excellent idea. It had the effect of drawing the Russians into the Afghan trap, and you want me to regret it?"

Did he have any second thoughts about arming and advising future Islamic terrorists? "What is most important to the history of the world?" Brzezinski shot back. "The Taliban or the collapse of the Soviet empire? Some stirred-up Moslems or the liberation of Central Europe and the end of the cold war?"[10]

Brzezinski got his answer on 9/11.

Osama bin Laden was a paymaster for the Afghan mujahedeen. His father was a wealthy Yemeni construction magnate who had moved his family to Saudi Arabia. The bin Laden family business is now worth some $5 billion. According to Milton Bearden, the CIA station chief in Pakistan from 1986 to 1989, Osama and his family were crucial in fighting the Soviets. "There were a lot of bin Ladens who came to do jihad, and they unburdened us a lot," Bearden told *The New Yorker*. "These guys were bringing in up to $20 to $25 million a month from other Saudis and Gulf Arabs to underwrite the war. And that is a lot of money. It's an extra $200 to $300 million a year."[11]

The United States was only too happy to foment an Islamic revolution so long as Washington's proxies waged war on its chosen enemy. But following the devastation of Afghanistan and the breakup of the Soviet Union, the Islamic groups were predictably discarded by their U.S. patrons. The orphaned warriors then set their sights on their next enemy.

Osama bin Laden's target was dressed in a U.S. military uniform. To Muslims around the globe, the arrival of 540,000 U.S. troops in Saudi Arabia in 1991 to wage the Persian Gulf War was sacrilege. The country is home to Mecca and Medina, the two holiest sites in Islam. Both the United States and the corrupt Saudi regime that invited the troops became the new infidels to bin Laden.

And so Washington's guy fell out of favor. He had returned to Saudi Arabia after the defeat of the Soviets in Afghanistan, but he was soon driven into exile, first to Sudan and then to Afghanistan, where he became patron to the Taliban. He spent the 1990s training and financing Afghan Arab fighters, scheming how to murder as many Americans as possible.

Our Shah

REMEMBER THE SHAH of Iran? Most Americans don't, but Iranians remember him well. They remember how in 1953, the United States, with British backing, overthrew the popularly elected Prime Minister Mohammad Mosaddeq and brought the shah to power. Mosaddeq had the audacity to nationalize Iran's oil industry, which was then owned by the Anglo-Iranian Oil Corporation, later renamed British Petroleum. The British, who had been helping themselves to some 85 percent of Iran's oil profits at the time, leaned on the United States to intervene.

So President Dwight Eisenhower dispatched some familiar American names to do the dirty work for the multinational oil companies: Kermit Roosevelt, Teddy's grandson, was the CIA operative who hired mobs to attack the prime minister's residence, resulting in the deaths of hundreds of Iranians. Norman Schwarzkopf Sr., father of Stormin' Norman, the American general who led the 1991 Persian Gulf War, was an old Iran hand who leaned on the shah to issue a decree firing the prime minister, which the shah had no legal authority to do.

Brimming with cash and weapons, Kermit Roosevelt took about three weeks to topple the democratic leadership of Iran, whereupon the shah, Mohammad Reza Shah Pahlavi, who had days earlier fled the country, was brought back into Iran by the United States. It took a quarter century of U.S.-backed repression under the boot of SAVAK, the shah's secret police, to spawn Iran's Islamic revolution of 1979. That ushered in the fundamentalist reign of Ayatollah Ruhollah Khomeini and sparked a long-suppressed anti-American backlash.

Then Henry Kissinger threw fuel on the flames. He coaxed then President Jimmy Carter in 1979 to allow his good friend, the ailing shah, into the United States for medical treatment. Iranian students vented their rage and fear by overrunning the U.S. embassy in Tehran and taking the staff hostage. They were afraid that the United States would bring Our Guy back to power in a cruel recap of 1953. In subsequent accounts of the embassy takeover, the American media rarely mentioned the 1953 coup.

In a scandal that came to be known as the "October surprise," it was later revealed that officials of Ronald Reagan's 1980 presidential campaign, including Kissinger, had secretly struck an arms-for-hostages deal with the Iranians. The deal ultimately ensured that the Iranians would hold the fifty-two Americans hostage through the elections, helping to humiliate and defeat Carter. The hostages were finally released on January 20, 1981, the day of Ronald Reagan's inauguration.

We are still dealing with the blowback from Washington's Iran policy. "When we overthrew a democratic government in Iran fifty years ago, we sent a message not only to Iran, but throughout the entire Middle East," Stephen Kinzer, author of *All the Shah's Men: An American Coup and the Roots of Middle East Terror*, explained on *Democracy Now!* "That message was that the United States does not support democratic governments and the United States prefers strong-man rule that will guarantee us access to oil. . . . A lot of people in the Middle East got that message very clearly."

Our Saddam

THEN THERE WAS Saddam Hussein. In 2002, Defense Secretary Donald Rumsfeld declared, "The regime of Saddam Hussein is so vicious, and killed so many of their own people, and used chemical weapons against their own people . . . it's one of the most vicious regimes on the face of the earth." None of which seemed to matter years before, when Saddam was Rumsfeld's favored Middle Eastern dictator.

Saddam Hussein had come to prominence following a 1968 Baath Party coup in Iraq, and became president in 1979. Washington's relations with Baghdad had been strained since the 1967 Arab-Israeli War. But in the mid-1980s, the U.S. attitude changed.

In August 2002, as the administration began its major push on Capitol Hill to win support for an attack on Iraq, *Democracy Now!* correspondent Jeremy Scahill reported how the United States had helped shore up Saddam Hussein at a time when he was actively using chemical weapons. "Five years before Saddam Hussein's now-infamous 1988 gassing of the Kurds, a key meeting took place in Baghdad that would play a significant role in forging close ties between Saddam Hussein and Washington," Scahill reported. "It happened at a time when Saddam was first alleged to have used chemical weapons. The meeting in late December 1983 paved the way for an official restoration of relations between Iraq and the U.S."[12]

It was Reagan's Middle East envoy, Donald Rumsfeld, who traveled to Baghdad "with a handwritten letter to Iraqi President Saddam Hussein and a message that Washington was willing at any moment to resume diplomatic relations." Just twelve days after the meeting, on January 1, 1984, *The Washington Post* reported that the United States, "in a shift in policy, has informed friendly Persian Gulf nations that the defeat of Iraq in the three-year-old war with Iran would be 'contrary to U.S. interests' and has made several moves to prevent that result."[13]

Rumsfeld returned to Baghdad in March 1984 for meetings with then Iraqi Foreign Minister Tariq Aziz. On March 24, 1984, the day of Rumsfeld's visit, UPI reported: "Mustard gas laced with a nerve agent has been used on Iranian soldiers in the 43-month Persian Gulf War between Iran and Iraq, a team of UN experts has concluded. . . . Meanwhile, in the Iraqi capital of Baghdad, U.S. presidential envoy Donald Rumsfeld held talks with Foreign Minister Tariq Aziz . . . before leaving for an unspecified destination."[14] The U.S. State Department had also concluded that Iraq was using chemical weapons in a report on March 5, 1984.

In 2003, Rumsfeld cited Iraq's use of poison gas as a reason to attack Iraq. But in 1984, he was mum about the gas attacks. According to a *New York Times* report from Baghdad on March 29, 1984, "American diplomats pronounce themselves satisfied with relations between Iraq and the United States and suggest that normal diplomatic ties have been restored in all but name."

In November 1984, full diplomatic relations between Iraq and the United States were restored.

On August 27, 2002, I questioned Pentagon spokesperson Lieutenant Colonel David Lapan on Rumsfeld's 1983 meeting with Saddam. "It is my understanding that Secretary Rumsfeld was in Syria at the time," Lapan said. "There was no evidence that he met with the Iraqis."

"No," I corrected Lapan. "He went to Iraq and it was widely reported, both times. . . . He met with Saddam Hussein, and afterwards the Reagan-Bush administration normalized relations with Iraq and . . . allowed the sale of goods to Iraq."

Lapan then backed off. "I'm just not well versed in that aspect of things," he said.[15]

A month later, the story became impossible to deny when CNN confronted Rumsfeld with the videotape of his now-famous hearty handshake with Saddam from December 1983. An embarrassed Rumsfeld went on the attack. "Where did you get this video? From the Iraqi television?" As the video rolled, Rumsfeld then remarked, "Isn't that interesting? There I am."[16]

CNN's Jamie McIntyre then pressed Rumsfeld on whether Washington had aided Saddam's chemical weapons program. "I had no knowledge. I have no knowledge today," Rumsfeld said. He said it "was most unfortunate that even the implication of that would be raised simply because of some article that somebody wrote. I cannot believe that that would be true, and certainly I would have had absolutely nothing do with it."

But it was true, and it remained true from the Reagan-Bush years to the eve of President Bush's 1991 Gulf War.

Rumsfeld helped facilitate Iraq's buying spree from American firms. As the *Los Angeles Times* reported, the U.S. government approved the sale of "a whopping $1.5 billion worth" of high technology to Iraq between 1985 and 1990. There was ample evidence that the equipment had dual military applications.[17]

In 1984, shortly after Rumsfeld's meeting with Saddam, the State Department—in the name of "increased American penetration of the extremely competitive civilian aircraft market"—pushed through the sale of forty-five Bell 214ST helicopters to Iraq. The helicopters, worth some $200 million, were originally designed for military purposes. *The New York Times* later reported that Saddam "transferred many, if not all [of these helicopters] to his military."[18]

What followed from this lethal shopping spree was hardly surprising. In 1988, Saddam's forces allegedly attacked Kurdish civilians in the northern city of Halabja with poisonous gas from Iraqi helicopters and planes. The *Los Angeles Times* reported that U.S. intelligence sources "believe that the American-built helicopters were among those dropping the deadly bombs." In all, some 5,000 people are estimated to have died in the Halabja attacks.*

In response to the gassing, sweeping sanctions were unanimously passed by the U.S. Senate that would have denied Iraq access to most U.S. technology. The measure was killed by the Reagan-Bush White House. The reason? There was money to be made in Iraq.

In December 1988, with the graves in Halabja still fresh, Dow Chemical sold $1.5 million worth of pesticides to Iraq, despite concerns expressed by some in the U.S. government that they could be used as chemical warfare agents. According to *The Washington Post*, "An Export-Import Bank official reported in a memorandum that he could find 'no reason' to stop the sale, despite evidence that the pesticides were 'highly toxic' to humans and would cause death 'from asphyxiation.'"[19]

Former Senator Bob Dole was especially eager to dance with the dictator. Described by *The Washington Monthly* as President George Bush I's "goodwill ambassador" to Saddam Hussein, Dole was assigned the task of derailing sanctions against Iraq. In 1989, less than a year after the Halabja gas attacks, Dole traveled to Iraq to meet with Saddam Hussein, along with Senators Howard Metzenbaum, Frank Murkowski, Jim McClure, and Alan Simpson. Dole proclaimed the dictator "an intelligent man" and insisted there was real "potential for improving our relationships."[20] What he did not say was that U.S. loan guarantees approved by President Bush had made Iraq one of the largest overseas importers of American rice, corn, and wheat—some of which was grown in Dole's home state of Kansas.[21]

---

*There is some dispute over whether the 1988 gassing of Halabja was done by Saddam Hussein against the Kurds, or by Iranian soldiers fighting in the area. The third possibility raised by CIA analysts is that Iraq did it, but its intended target was Iranian soldiers.

As one congressman observed of the U.S. government policy toward Iraq, "Their attitude is 'Business *über alles.*'"[22]

That logic also helps to explain why the United States was double-dealing with Iraq's mortal enemy, Iran. In 1986, the United States illegally sold $30 million in arms to Iran. The Reagan-Bush White House was forced to disclose that it used the money from the Iran arms sales to illegally finance the Nicaraguan Contras. This became the biggest scandal of the Reagan-Bush years—the Iran/Contra affair.

When the Bush administration offered its reasons for invading Iraq in 1991, the Halabja gas attack barely merited a mention. It would have been awkward, after all, to complain about an atrocity that occurred while the United States was a key backer of Iraq. But with the 2003 Iraq war, the memory of Halabja was revived. As Sheldon Rampton and John Stauber chronicle in *Weapons of Mass Deception,* Halabja went from being mentioned in news articles only 20 times in 1989 to 145 times in March 2003.[23] Fifteen years after the fact, the United States became outraged.

In the aftermath of the invasion of Iraq, a new era of blowback has been inaugurated. Iraq seethes as American companies divide the spoils of war, and as American troops prowl the country arresting and shooting civilians—whether out of fear or aggression. One Baghdad veterinarian who was imprisoned with his 16-year-old son for sixty-six days fumed, "When the Americans first came to Baghdad I was happy, but I don't want to speak about my feelings towards them now."[24]

"Many of the people say they didn't like Saddam Hussein," reported Robert Fisk of the London *Independent*. "But they are adamant the Americans must leave and are beginning to truly hate the Americans."

Iraq's Death Machine: Made in the USA

A JOKE WENT around during the invasion of Iraq:

"Iraq has weapons of mass destruction!" bellows U.S. Secretary of Defense Donald Rumsfeld to anyone who will listen.

"How do you know?" asks a skeptical observer.

"Because I have the receipts!"

On December 18, 2002, *Democracy Now!* was one of the first American media outlets to reveal where those receipts came from. We interviewed Andreas Zumach, a Geneva-based UN correspondent with the German daily newspaper *Die Tageszeitung.* Zumach had obtained portions of Iraq's report to the United Nations detailing its weapons programs. What Zumach had was a collector's item: He had the parts of Iraq's 12,000-page report that the United States had redacted.

You might think the United States deemed this material dangerous because it could be misused by terrorists. Try again: The material was dangerous because if it got out, it would expose corporate and official complicity in arming Iraq, which might dampen global enthusiasm for war.

The portions of the UN report censored by the United States identified at least twenty-four U.S. corporations that helped Iraq build its pre–Gulf War weapons programs and rockets. The list includes

Bechtel (conventional)

DuPont (nuclear)

Eastman Kodak (rocket)

Hewlett-Packard (nuclear, rocket, conventional)

Honeywell (rocket, conventional)

International Computer Systems (nuclear, rocket, conventional)

Rockwell (conventional)

Sperry Corp. (rocket, conventional)

Tektronix (rocket, nuclear)

Unisys (nuclear, conventional)

Die Tageszeitung also reported that the U.S. Department of Energy delivered essential nonfissile parts for Baghdad's nuclear weapons program in the 1980s. The Reagan and Bush I administrations also authorized sales of deadly chemical and biological agents to Iraq, including anthrax and bubonic plague.[25]

How did this essential information go missing?

In December 2002, the rotating presidency of the UN Security Council was held by Colombia. The twelve-member UN Security Council agreed on December 6 to provide copies of the full report to all members of the Security Council, minus a section that contained information on how to build a nuclear bomb.

But U.S. Secretary of State Colin Powell secretly leaned on Colombia's UN ambassador to provide the original copy of Iraq's report exclusively to the United States. So when Iraq's report arrived at the UN on December 8, the Colombian ambassador, in his capacity as president of the Security Council, dutifully ordered that it be handed over immediately and exclusively to U.S. diplomats. U.S. officials then took the report to Washington, D.C., keeping it to themselves for twenty-six hours. The official reason for this: There were better copying machines in Washington, D.C.[26]

When Security Council members finally received their copies, the massive report had shrunk to roughly 3,500 pages.

What was in the missing 8,500 pages? Information embarrassing to U.S. companies and the Bush administration.

The result: The nonpermanent members of the UN Security Council—and the public—received only the Bush administration's sanitized version of Iraq's weapons programs. The censored document made no mention of U.S. complicity with arming Saddam Hussein.

This is freedom, Bush style: freedom to know what they want us to know.

Colin Powell dismissed Iraq's report as a "catalogue of recycled information and flagrant omissions." Why, then, was he so intent on keeping everyone, including UN weapons inspectors, from finding out the truth for themselves?

UN Secretary-General Kofi Annan declared that it was "unfortunate" that the United States hijacked the report. Hans von Sponeck, the former assistant secretary general of the UN and the UN's humanitarian coordinator in Iraq until 2000, charged, "This is an outrageous attempt by the U.S. to mislead."[27]

You would think that Andreas Zumach's investigative exposé would be major news here, right? Wrong. "This knowledge about our responsibility or co-responsibility for the problem now called Saddam Hussein has been suppressed, has been wiped out of our memory," says Zumach. "The big papers [in the United States] were not interested at all. The European papers, the British, the Scandinavian, the French papers, the Italian, Japanese, Brazilian— they were all on the telephone with me asking for information and doing huge stories. There was silence on this side of the Atlantic."[28]

The Bush Wars

THE BUSH REGIME has shamelessly exploited 9/11. It has revived everything that Washington loved about the cold war. Substitute "fighting communism" with "fighting terrorism," and you have the justification for many of the items on the Bush administration wish list. From tax cuts for the rich to pushing to drill in the Arctic National Wildlife Refuge to the failed "war on drugs" to war on the world—it's all just part of keeping America safe from terrorists.

The blueprint for what has happened since 9/11 was drawn up years earlier, by the Project for the New American Century (PNAC), a think tank formed in 1997 "to promote American global leadership." Its founders are a who's who of the neoconservative movement, which seamlessly morphed into the top officialdom of the Bush II administration: Secretary of Defense Donald Rumsfeld, Vice President Dick Cheney, Cheney's chief of staff L. Scooter Libby, Deputy Secretary of Defense Paul Wolfowitz, Defense Policy Board member Richard Perle, and National Security Council staff member (and convicted liar) Elliot Abrams,* among others.

The PNAC members had a reputation around Washington, explained Ray McGovern, a retired CIA analyst with twenty-seven years' experience. A former intelligence briefer for Vice President George Bush, McGovern observed, "When we saw these people coming back in town, all of us said . . . 'Oh my God, the crazies are back.'" McGovern said their wild-eyed geopolitical schemes would typically go "right into the circular file."[29]

In September 2000, PNAC issued a report that called upon the United States to dominate global resources and, well, the globe. The key to realizing this was "some catastrophic and catalyzing event—like a new Pearl Harbor."[30]

As investigative reporter John Pilger has written, "[PNAC]

---

*Elliot Abrams pleaded guilty to two counts of withholding information from Congress in 1991. President George Bush pardoned Abrams on Christmas Eve 1992, along with Reagan-Bush Defense Secretary Caspar Weinberger and National Security Advisor Robert McFarlane.

recommended an increase in arms-spending by $48 billion so that Washington could 'fight and win multiple, simultaneous major theatre wars.' This has happened. It said the United States should develop 'bunker-buster' nuclear weapons and make 'star wars' a national priority. This is happening. It said that, in the event of Bush taking power, Iraq should be a target. And so it is."[31]

Weapons of mass destruction and Iraq itself were mere pretexts for larger schemes. According to PNAC: "While the unresolved conflict with Iraq provides the immediate justification, the need for a substantial American force presence in the Gulf transcends the issue of the regime of Saddam Hussein."[32]

And so on the morning of September 12, 2001, Donald Rumsfeld reacted to the World Trade Center and Pentagon attacks by declaring to Bush's cabinet that the United States should immediately attack Iraq.[33] It didn't matter then or later that Iraq had no connection to Al Qaeda or the 9/11 attacks. The neoconservatives, annoyed that we merely owned the pumps and not the oil, were itching to dominate the world. The facts could be molded to fit their designs.

Meanwhile, the Bush team saw 9/11 as a potential boon to its cronies. All that was needed was a plan—and the PNAC blueprint was conveniently available. National Security Advisor Condoleezza Rice told senior National Security Council staff "to think about 'how do you capitalize on these opportunities?'" She compared the situation with "1945 to 1947," the start of the cold war.

The Bush people were eager to respond to the call. "Since 11 September," reports Pilger, "America has established bases at the gateways to all the major sources of fossil fuels, especially central Asia. The Unocal oil company is to build a pipeline across Afghanistan. Bush has scrapped the Kyoto Protocol on greenhouse gas emissions, the war crimes provisions of the International Criminal Court, and the anti-ballistic missile treaty." And that's just the start. "[T]he Bush regime is developing new weapons of mass destruction that undermine international treaties on biological and chemical warfare."[34]

So useful have terrorist attacks been to advancing the neocon agenda that hawks are intent on provoking more. As William Arkin wrote in the *Los Angeles Times,* Rumsfeld's Defense Science Board recommended in 2002 the creation of a supersecret "Proactive, Preemptive Operations Group (P2OG) to bring together CIA and military covert action, information warfare, intelligence, and cover and deception. Among other things, this body would launch secret operations aimed at 'stimulating reactions' among terrorists and states possessing weapons of mass destruction—that is, for instance, prodding terrorist cells into action and exposing themselves to 'quick-response' attacks by U.S. forces. Such tactics would . . . 'signal to harboring states that their sovereignty will be at risk.'"[35]

An estimated 4,000 Afghan civilians have died, and up to 9,600 Iraqi civilians have been killed in pursuit of this pipe dream of global military hegemony. But the worldwide war plan is far more ambitious. As General Wesley Clark notes in his book *Winning Modern Wars: Iraq, Terrorism, and the American Empire,* he was informed privately by a top Pentagon colleague that the war on terror was part of "a five-year campaign plan, he said, and there were a total of seven countries, beginning with Iraq, then Syria, Lebanon, Libya, Iran, Somalia, and Sudan." Clark, a former NATO Supreme Allied Commander, recounted, "I left the Pentagon that afternoon deeply concerned."

Across the Atlantic, Michael Meacher, Tony Blair's environment minister from May 1997 to June 2003, wrote in the British newspaper *The Guardian* that the PNAC report is "a blueprint for U.S. world domination." September 11 was the perfect excuse for turning the blueprint into reality, Meacher says. But to what end?

"The overriding motivation . . . is that the U.S. and the UK are beginning to run out of secure hydrocarbon energy supplies. By 2010 the Muslim world will control as much as 60% of the world's oil production and, even more importantly, 95% of remaining global oil export capacity. As demand is increasing, so supply is decreasing, continually since the 1960s."

The "global war on terrorism," Meacher concludes, "has the hallmarks of a political myth propagated to pave the way for a wholly different agenda—the U.S. goal of world hegemony, built around securing by force command over the oil supplies required to drive the whole project."[36]

USA! USA! . . . USA?

A FEW DAYS after the Twin Towers fell, President Bush came to Ground Zero. I watched as a chilling cheer went up around him: "U-S-A! U-S-A!" chanted the crowd in unison. Among those who set up this Ground Zero photo op—a defining moment in Bush's presidency—was Jim Wilkinson, who went on to become the media point man in Qatar spinning the Jessica Lynch story and was then appointed communications czar of the 2004 Republican National Convention.[37]

I don't think rallying around the flag is the answer to what happened on September 11. The answer is a global community united against terror, determined to rout it out wherever it originates—including the White House and the Pentagon.

The answer is institutions such as the International Criminal Court (ICC), where people who commit crimes against humanity can be tried. But who is the primary force opposing this court? The United States. A reluctant President Clinton waited until the last moment to sign the treaty to recognize the authority of the ICC.

Then Bush came in and *un*signed the treaty. In mid-2003, Bush strong-armed the UN Security Council to pass a resolution that would exempt U.S. officials and soldiers from being held account-able in the same way as others around the world. And the Bush ad-ministration has pressured countries, at the risk of losing U.S. aid, to sign bilateral agreements that would prohibit them from bring-ing charges against U.S. citizens before an international court.

Of course I think that Osama bin Laden and his accomplices should be tried for what happened on September 11. But when you look at where bodies have stacked up around the world—from Chile and Argentina to Cambodia, Vietnam, Laos, and East Timor—I think Henry Kissinger should also be tried for crimes against humanity.

If we have any hope of routing out terror and breaking the cy-cle of blowback, we must have a universal standard of justice.

2

OILYgarchy

OILYgarchy Cast of Characters

George Bush, president: Failed oilman.

Dick Cheney, vice president: Former CEO of Halliburton, the largest oil services company in the world.

Condoleezza Rice, national security advisor: Former member of Chevron board of directors for a decade. Had an oil tanker named after her.

Spencer Abraham, secretary of energy: Former top recipient of campaign contributions from the automotive industry while a one-term senator.

Don Evans, secretary of commerce: Ex-CEO and chair of Tom Brown Inc., a billion-dollar oil and gas company.

Gale Norton, secretary of interior: Former lawyer for Delta Petroleum.

Andrew Card, chief of staff: Former chief lobbyist, General Motors.

oligarchy *n* a small group of people who together govern a nation or control an organization, often for their own purposes.[1]

OILYgarchy *n* a bunch of guys from the oil industry who take over the political leadership of a nation, then hijack its military to attack and occupy a vast oil-producing region of the world, lavishly enriching themselves and ensuring perpetual control of global oil. In order to survive, OILYgarchies typically require the abrogation of civil liberties, depict self-enrichment as a patriotic duty, and rely on the cooperation of a slavish press.

For Sale: A fertile, wealthy country with a population of around 25 million . . . plus around 150,000 foreign troops and a handful of puppets. Conditions of sale: should be either an American or British corporation (forget it if you're French) . . . preferably affiliated with Halliburton. Please contact one of the members of the Governing Council in Baghdad, Iraq, for more information.[2]

This is how Iraq's "girl blogger"—an Iraqi running a website from Baghdad—captured a bitter truth of the post-9/11 American adventure. Like Afghanistan, Iraq has certainly been "freed"—it's being given away and auctioned off to U.S. corporations, big and small. But not just any corporations—these are corporations with the closest of ties to the Bush administration.

The feeding frenzy began the morning of 9/11. As my neighbors and coworkers were choking on the debris of the World Trade Center, a windfall awaited a powerful group gathered at the Ritz-Carlton hotel in Washington, D.C. The secretive Carlyle Group was holding its annual investors' conference. The private investment company, named for the swank Manhattan hotel where the group was formed in 1987, has tentacles in both the Washington power elite and the Saudi ruling class. In town for the meetings was former President George H. W. Bush, then a senior adviser to Carlyle. He was joined by a cast of characters who have been fixtures in Bush regimes over the years.

There was Reagan's former secretary of defense Frank Carlucci, then head of the Carlyle Group. James Baker III, secretary of state under Bush Sr.—better known as the choreographer of Bush Jr.'s theft of the 2000 election—was also there in his capacity as Carlyle's senior counsel. But it wasn't just Bush's inner circle gathering that day. They were joined by a man by the name of Shafiq bin Laden, brother of Osama bin Laden. It wasn't the first time a bin Laden had worked with Washington's power elite, and this particular bin Laden was a longtime friend and benefactor of the Bush clan. Bush Sr. left the meetings early, but the rest of the men were just finishing breakfast when Shafiq's brother's plot culminated in airplanes slamming into the World Trade Center and the Pentagon.

A bizarre coincidence? No, the meeting was just business as usual for the Bushes, whose family fortunes have been greased by Saudi oil money for decades. That helps explain why, when the United States grounded all aircraft on that terrible day, one exception was made: Top White House officials authorized planes to pick up 140 Saudis, including two dozen members of the bin Laden family, from ten cities and spirit them back to Saudi Arabia. Dale Watson, the former head of counterterrorism at the FBI, conceded in *Vanity Fair* that the departing Saudis "were not subject to serious interviews or interrogations."[3]

Tom Kinton, director of aviation at Boston's Logan Airport, was incredulous, according to *Vanity Fair*. With the airport still closed and reeling from the 9/11 attacks, Kinton received the order to allow the bin Ladens to fly. "We were in the midst of the worst terrorist act in history and here we were seeing an evacuation of the bin Ladens!" he exclaimed. "The federal authorities knew what it was doing. And we were told to let it come."[4]

Virginia Buckingham, then head of the Massachusetts Port Authority, which oversees Logan Airport, was similarly stunned. "Does the FBI know?" she wrote of the order to allow up to fourteen members of the bin Laden family to fly in a private plane from Logan. "Does the State Department know? Why are they letting these people go? Have they questioned them? This was ridiculous."[5] Even a plane carrying a heart for transplant to a deathly ill patient in Seattle was forced to land, nearly costing the patient his life.[6] But free passage for the bin Ladens was mysteriously approved—no questions asked.

The actions of the Bush administration led Senator Charles Schumer to charge in September 2003, "This is just another example of our country coddling the Saudis and giving them special privileges that others would never get."[7]

That's the fateful conclusion that FBI counterterrorism chief John O'Neill drew. All his efforts to investigate Saudi links to terror were stymied by the Bush administration. "The main obstacles to investigating Islamic terrorism were U.S. oil corporate interests and the role played by Saudi Arabia in it," he said. O'Neill, who led the FBI investigations into the 1998 African embassy bombings and the USS *Cole* bombing in 2000, charged that the intelligence agencies were told to back off from investigations involving other members of the bin Laden family, the Saudi royals, and possible Saudi links to the acquisition of nuclear weapons by Pakistan.[8]

O'Neill finally quit the FBI in disgust in July 2001 and took a job as head of security at the World Trade Center. He died in the September 11 attack. Fifteen of the nineteen hijackers on 9/11 were from Saudi Arabia.

About Saudi terror links, Schumer concluded, "It's almost as if we didn't want to find out what links existed."[9]

Small wonder. For the Bush family, taking care of business—and its billionaire friends—has always come first, and these friends have always repaid the favor by taking very good care of the Bushes. George W. Bush made his first million dollars twenty years ago from Arbusto Energy (*arbusto* is Spanish for bush), a company partially financed by Osama bin Laden's elder brother Salem.[10]

When George W. Bush was in need of a job in 1990, he looked no further than the Carlyle Group, where he found a lucrative seat on the board of Carlyle subsidiary Caterair, an airline catering company. As governor of Texas in 2000, Bush tipped his hat to his former meal ticket (and his father's company) when the Texas teachers' pension fund invested $100 million with the Carlyle Group.[11] And after Bush playacted his fighter jet landing on the USS *Abraham Lincoln* on May 1, 2003, where he stood beneath a "Mission Accomplished" banner, he traveled to terra firma in Santa Clara, California, for yet another photo op. This time, he stood beneath a banner for United Defense Industries, showcasing a Carlyle Group weapons manufacturer.

Although Bush was paying his respects to a former paymaster, not everyone at Carlyle was happy with the relationship. In a rare public appearance, on April 23, 2003, Carlyle founder and managing director David M. Rubenstein tried to convince the Los Angeles County Employees Retirement Association not to divest from his company. In an effort to downplay Carlyle's political connections to the current administration, Rubenstein told the association a story:

"When we were putting our board together, somebody came to me and said, 'Look, there is a guy who would like to be on the board. He's kind of down on his luck a bit. Needs a job. Needs some board positions. Could you put him on the board? Pay him a salary and he'll be a good board member and be a loyal vote for the management and so forth.'"

Rubenstein continued, "We put him on the board and he spent three years. Came to all the meetings. Told a lot of jokes. Not that many clean ones. . . . I kind of said to him after about three years, 'You know, I'm not sure this is really for you. Maybe you should do something else because I don't think you're adding that much value to the board. You don't know that much about the company.' He said, 'Well, I think I'm getting out of this business anyway and I don't really like it that much. So I'm probably going to resign from the board.' And I said, 'Thanks.' Didn't think I'd ever see him again.

"His name is George W. Bush. He became president of the United States. So, you know, if you said to me, 'Name twenty-five million people who would maybe be president of the United States,' he wouldn't have been in that category. So you never know."[12]

Making a Killing off the Killings

A MONTH AFTER the terror attacks, the Carlyle Group took its subsidiary, United Defense, public. It noted in its financial filings that "the Bush administration's recently published Quadrennial Defense Review calls for . . . increasing investment . . . to enable U.S. military forces to more effectively counter emerging threats."

Translation: We just got check-writing privileges at the U.S. Treasury.

Carlyle netted profits of $237 million in that one day, making three times as much on paper. The old adage has never been truer: It pays to have friends in high places.

Stroking the Saudis

The Bush family has had a long and mutually profitable connection with the corrupt Saudi oil dictatorship. Prince Bandar, Saudi ambassador to the United States, has been an honored guest both at the Bush I summer home in Kennebunkport, Maine, and at Bush II's getaway in Crawford, Texas (hence his nickname, "Bandar Bush"). Bandar expressed his gratitude to Bush I by donating $1 million to the Bush Presidential Library in Texas. And Bandar's prodding prompted Saudi King Fahd to send another $1 million to Barbara Bush's campaign against illiteracy.[13]

Saudi Prince al-Walid contributed half a million petrodollars to help launch the George Herbert Walker Bush Scholarship Fund at Phillips Academy, the alma mater of both Bush presidents.[14] The depth of these connections was highlighted when the former president visited the Saudis to "discuss U.S.-Saudi business relations" with Crown Prince Abdullah during his son's 2000 presidential campaign.[15]

And then there is the bin Laden problem. The bin Laden family, a key Carlyle investor, stood to make millions of dollars from the war on terror—a war that has as its chief villain a member of their own family. The bin Ladens withdrew from the Carlyle Group in late October 2001, but it's not just the bin Laden family proper that was problematic for the Bushes. It turns out that Prince Bandar's wife, Princess Haifa, had made charitable contributions that may have helped finance two of the 9/11 hijackers.

It would be reasonable to think that U.S. investigators would have great interest in getting to the bottom of all these possible Saudi terror connections. But in mid-2003, the Bush administration withheld 28 pages relating to Saudi Arabia's role in the attacks from the 800-page final report of the congressional 9/11 Commission.

President Bush justified this action by saying that revealing the contents of the missing pages "would show people how we collect information and on whom we're collecting information, which . . . would be harmful on the war against terror."

Or might it just be harmful to Bush's family and friends? As Julian Borger wrote in *The Guardian,* "The reason pages about the Saudi link to the hijackers (15 out of 19 of whom were Saudi nationals) are blanked out, while Al Qaeda's questionable ties to Iraq and Iran are taken to the UN, is an old but crucial story." The U.S.-Saudi connection "is the mutual dependency of two wealthy junkies dragging each other ever deeper into squalor. The U.S. is addicted to cheap oil, and shows no inclination to wean itself off it. Washington officialdom is hooked on the easy money Riyadh offers in the world of consultancies and think tanks when they retire. The Saudi royal family, meanwhile, has its own addictions. It depends on the U.S. arms industry, of which it is the biggest foreign customer."[16]

So this is how the war on terrorism works: If you're suspected of having ties to an "anti-American" group, you are sent to a cage on Guantánamo Bay, Cuba. But if your patrons bankroll terrorists and your father is collecting millions in fees for meeting with a repressive government that has questionable ties to terror groups, your buddies get a free pass out of the country and you get installed in the Oval Office.

Iraq for Sale

For centuries, pillage by invading armies was a normal part of warfare. . . . Nowadays, at least in more civilized countries, we do not let armies rampage for booty. We leave the pillaging to men in suits, and we don't call it pillaging anymore. We call it economic development.

—BRIAN WHITAKER, *THE GUARDIAN*[17]

IN SEPTEMBER 2003, the looting of Iraq was elevated to official Bush administration policy.

AMERICA PUTS IRAQ UP FOR SALE blared the headline in the British newspaper *The Independent*.

The New York Times gave it the usual government spin: IRAQ OFFERING LAWS TO SPUR INVESTMENT FROM ABROAD.

The articles announced that the United States had decided to privatize and sell off entire sectors of the Iraqi economy, from telecommunications to banking. Foreign corporations could buy 100 percent of Iraqi firms and expatriate all the profits.

This is privatization and globalization on steroids. And who did President Bush appoint to oversee the feeding frenzy? His good friend, banker Tom Foley, a major Republican Party fund-raiser, Connecticut finance chair of Bush 2000, and Bush's former Harvard Business School classmate.

Hovering over all of these deals is the Bush family's savior, James A. Baker III, whom Bush II tapped in December 2003 to renegotiate Iraq's foreign debt but who is widely seen as the de facto secretary of state for Iraq.

Baker is a lawyer-politician who has served as White House chief of staff, treasury secretary, and secretary of state for Bush I. The Bush family calls him in times of political need: He ran the Bush I presidential campaign and was President George W. Bush's point man in Florida during the electoral recount in 2000.

Along with being senior counselor to the Carlyle Group, Baker is a senior partner in the law firm of Baker Botts, which is defending the Saudi government in a lawsuit filed by the families of the victims of the 9/11 attacks. Baker is charged with convincing other governments to forgive Iraq's $120 billion foreign debt— something of great interest to Baker Botts client Saudi Arabia, which is owed $27 billion by Iraq.

With Baker operating out of the White House, self-dealing will be taken to breathtaking new heights. As BBC investigative reporter Greg Palast told *Democracy Now!*, "You have got the lawyer for the creditor being put in charge by a president of a conquering nation to make sure that his friends, the Saudis, and Baker's clients, the Saudis, get their money."[18]

With Iraqi reconstruction estimated to cost between $100 billion and $500 billion (by the time you read this, the numbers will undoubtedly be far higher, but let's not quibble over a couple of billion dollars), the sharks see blood in the water. And they're circling hungrily.

Going in for the kill, the campaign manager for Bush-Cheney 2000 left his job as head of the Federal Emergency Management Agency a few weeks before tanks rolled into Iraq. Joe Allbaugh reappeared as head of a lobbying firm with offices in Baghdad. Allbaugh teamed up with Ed Rogers, a former aide to Bush I, to launch New Bridge Strategies, "a lobbying firm that connects Western businesses with the American and Iraqi power brokers overseeing the reconstruction," as Michael Scherer reported in *Mother Jones* magazine.[19] Said Allbaugh, "It's beneficial to clients that I know who the players are and I know who the decision makers are."

No kidding.

The second phase of the war on Iraq—the crony cash-out—got under way within weeks of the invasion. Lanny Griffith, former assistant secretary of education under Bush I, is a director of New Bridge Strategies. Clayton Yeutter, secretary of agriculture under Bush I, works for the lobbying firm Hogan & Hartson, on the lookout for new agribusiness opportunities in Iraq.

Prominent Democrats are also moseying up to the trough. Former Senator George Mitchell and Clinton's former Secretary of

Defense William Cohen were among those pitching for action.[20] They teamed up with former House Majority Leader Dick Armey to lead an "Iraq Task Force" at the powerful Washington lobbying firm Piper Rudnick.

But what's good for Washington's crony capitalists has not proved very good for Iraq. Take the matter of cellular phone service. For months following the invasion, Iraqis were without working phones. Shortly after the shooting stopped, cellular phone service returned, thanks to some businessmen with Batelco, a Bahrain-based cellular company that figured out how to rig up a cell network compatible with neighboring countries. It seemed just the kind of entrepreneurial problem solving that the Bush administration loves.

The Coalition Provisional Authority promptly shut down the cell network and ordered Batelco to dismantle its cell towers. The crime? These Arab entrepreneurs were providing an important service without enriching any American companies. The aptly named CPA would solve that. A month later, the CPA awarded the estimated $40 million cellular phone contract to MCI, formerly the bankrupt WorldCom. WorldCom is under criminal indictment for committing the largest accounting fraud in history. In August 2003, the General Services Administration suspended MCI from competing for new government contracts.[21] But in lawless Iraq, MCI/WorldCom is right at home.

Within weeks, the only cell phones working in Iraq were the MCI phones belonging to the CPA, and even those didn't work very well.[22] None of which should have been a surprise, since MCI had no experience building cell networks. It is known instead for running the world's largest data network—specifically, the one used by the Pentagon.

The Coalition Provisional Authority soon requested bids for a contract worth up to $200 million to erect cellular towers around the country. The CPA allowed bidders to use wireless technology known as CDMA, which was developed by QUALCOMM, a California company.

The problem is, the rest of the Middle East uses a different technology, known as GSM. But QUALCOMM had a powerful ally in California Republican Representative Darrell Issa, who declared that "any gift of technology to the Iraqis should 'also benefit the American people and the American economy.' "[23]

Issa, a former car alarm salesman, has a distinguished history of buying and selling governments. He spent $1.7 million of his own money to bankroll the California recall vote that bought the California governorship for fellow Republican Arnold Schwarzenegger (who spent $10 million of his own money) in October 2003.

The CPA finally awarded mobile phone contracts in October 2003 to companies whose shareholders included top officials of the Pentagon-backed Iraqi National Congress and a company that included among its shareholders Terry Sullivan, an American official who resigned from the CPA in June to prospect for business.[24]

Eight months after the bombing stopped, millions of dollars had been spent on lavish cell phone deals, but Iraq still had no functioning cell phone network.

And the Winner Is . . .

THE IRAQ INVASION was certainly not the beginning of payback for Washington insiders, Bush supporters, and former administration officials. Like the Carlyle Group, these people were involved in the planning and profiteering long before the first tanks rolled across the Tigris River.

The Defense Policy Board, an internal Pentagon think tank,

provided a chorus of support for the invasion, with its members appearing regularly on television to make the case. And who could blame them? Their members stood to profit handsomely from the war. Members of the Defense Policy Board include Newt Gingrich, Ken Adelman (who promised that the war would be a "cakewalk"), Richard Perle, Dan Quayle, and Bechtel senior vice president General Jack Sheehan. As the Center for Public Integrity reported, nine of the thirty Defense Policy Board members have ties to companies that have won more than $76 billion in defense contracts in 2002.[25]

Don't get me wrong: Doling out the spoils of the war has been difficult. There have just been *so* many large donors to both Republican and Democratic campaigns, it's hard to know who to pay back first (it's a bipartisan plunder—60 percent of the contract-winning companies have ties to Democratic or Republican political officials—although the payback favors companies that have been most generous to Republicans). The Bush administration is doing its best to ensure all its well-connected friends get a juicy slice of the Iraq pie.

The Center for Public Integrity reports that as of October 2003, "more than 70 American companies and individuals have won up to $8 billion in contracts for work in postwar Iraq and Afghanistan over the last two years. . . . Those companies donated more money to the presidential campaigns of George W. Bush—a little over $500,000—than to any other politician over the last dozen years."[26]

Here's a selective list of the companies cashing in on Iraq's misery, highlighting their campaign contributions, past abuses, crony connections, and surging stock value (some of these are privately held companies that do not have stock).[27]

A WINNER!

Science Applications International Corporation (SAIC)

Campaign contributions, 1990–2002: $4.7 million

Total contract value in Iraq and Afghanistan, 2002–2003: $38 million[28]

Stock price: privately held

With $5.9 billion in revenues (2002), SAIC, with 40,000 employees, is the largest employee-owned research and engineering company in the country. Its largest customer is the U.S. government, which accounts for 69 percent of its business.[29]

In 2003, this Top Ten defense contractor, best known for its programs for Special Forces, got the $38 million deal to run the Iraq Media Network (IMN), which was responsible for rebuilding Iraq's mass media. The contract overseen by the Pentagon's psychological operations department is "considered the most ambitious and costly foreign media program ever undertaken by the U.S. government."[30] SAIC hired former Voice of America director Robert Reilly to run the network. Reilly's conservative credentials had been honed in the 1980s when he ran the White House information operation backing the Nicaraguan Contras.

Reilly left after just six months when IMN staffers walked out in protest over lack of funds and the network's irrelevance. Top IMN broadcasters were being paid $120 per month and were given an allowance only for clothing above the waist (i.e., on-camera).[31] SAIC "consultants" on the project were being paid up to $273 per hour.[32]

In 1995, SAIC paid a $2.5 million fine for cheating the Air Force on a contract for fighter jet cockpit displays.

In Venezuela in January 2003, SAIC allegedly participated

in the management strike against President Hugo Chavez that nearly paralyzed the country. According to the Venezuelan energy minister, SAIC declined to provide the Venezuelan government with information needed to keep the oil refineries open as oil company managers participated in an attempt to overthrow the Chavez government.

Crony Connections

- David Kay, the former UN weapons inspector who was hired by the CIA in 2003 to search for weapons of mass destruction in Iraq, was vice president of SAIC until 2002.

- Admiral Bobby Inman, SAIC board member from 1982 to 2003, is a former deputy director of the CIA and a former director of the National Security Agency.

- Christopher "Ryan" Henry was SAIC vice president for strategic assessment and development until February 2003, when he left to become deputy undersecretary of defense for policy.

- General W. A. Downing (U.S. Army, retired), SAIC board member, was a lobbyist for the CIA-backed Iraqi National Congress and its leader, Ahmed Chalabi. Downing was also a board member of the Committee for the Liberation of Iraq, along with Bechtel director and former Secretary of State George Shultz. (For more on CLI, see chapter 15, "Things Get Messy with Sally Jessy.") From October 2001 to July 2002, Downing was deputy assistant director for international counterterrorism initiatives on the National Security Council.

- William Owens, a former SAIC president, serves on Bush's Defense Policy Board.

A WINNER!

Fluor Corporation

Campaign contributions, 1990–2002: $3.6 million

Percentage to Republicans, 1999–2002: 57%

Total contract value in Iraq and Afghanistan, 2002–2003: $500 million

Stock price, pre–Iraq invasion (2/13/03): $27.18

Stock price, post-invasion high (10/14/03): $40.82

Change in stock value: +50%

An international engineering and construction company, Fluor Corporation was one of the lucky half-dozen American contractors invited by the U.S. Agency for International Development to bid for the overall Iraqi reconstruction contract. Fluor has landed three cost-plus Iraq contracts "to rapidly execute design and construction services as needed anywhere" for the U.S. military's Central Command.[33] Each contract could be worth up to $500 million. Fluor is currently repairing the electrical infrastructure in central and southern Iraq.

In 2003, South Africans filed a multibillion-dollar suit against Fluor, charging that it exploited black workers under apartheid.

In May 2001, Fluor paid $8.5 million to settle charges of falsely claiming millions of dollars in costs on defense contracts. In June 1997, Fluor paid $8.4 million to settle a lawsuit that alleged that the company violated the False Claims Act, including an assertion that Fluor "sought government reimbursement for an employee pizza party."[34]

Crony Connections

- Philip J. Carroll Jr., former chairman and CEO of Fluor Corporation and a former Shell Oil Company executive, is overseeing the restructuring of Iraq's oil industry. Carroll receives more than $1 million in retirement benefits and bonuses from Fluor, which are tied to the company's performance, and he owns shares estimated to be worth more than $34 million.[35] Not to worry: Carroll insists, "I will stay so far away from any consideration of the bidding process, evaluation process, or even the administration and arbitration of things associated with any of those companies in which I have a financial interest. . . . I will have absolutely nothing to do with it."[36]

- Admiral Bobby Inman, former deputy director of the CIA, is a Fluor board member. He is also on the boards of SAIC and the oil company Temple-Inland.

- Kenneth Oscar, Fluor's vice president of strategy and government services, was acting assistant secretary of the Army before joining Fluor in April 2002. Oscar directed the Army's $35-billion-a-year procurement budget.[37]

A WINNER!

DynCorp

Campaign contributions, 1990–2002: $1.2 million

   Percentage to Republicans, 1999–2002: 75%

Total contract value in Iraq and Afghanistan, 2002–2003: $50.1 million

Stock price (Computer Sciences Corporation), pre–Iraq invasion (3/13/03): $28.15

Stock price, post-invasion high (9/4/03): $44.95

Change in stock value: +60%

A subsidiary of Computer Sciences Corporation, DynCorp is in the global rent-a-cop—and rent-an-army—business. The company won a $50 million contract to train police and security personnel in Iraq. The contract could ultimately be worth up to half a billion dollars. In 2002, the company spent $1.1 million to lobby government officials on issues related to defense and government privatization.

In 2000, two DynCorp employees ran an underage sex slave ring in Bosnia while there under U.S. contract. The DynCorp employees who exposed this crime were subsequently fired. They later sued; the company paid damages of $200,000 to one whistleblower and settled out of court with another. Though the DynCorp employees involved in the sex ring were fired, none have faced criminal charges.[38] Among numerous fraud claims involving the company, Computer Sciences Corporation paid a $2.1 million fine to settle a 1993 charge of making false and misleading statements and overbilling on a major EPA contract.

Crony Connections

- Van Honeycutt, president/CEO of Computer Sciences Corporation, is chair of President Bush's National Security Telecommunications Advisory Committee (NSTAC), under the Department of Homeland Security.

- Ronald L. Dick, DynCorp's director of information assurance strategic initiatives, was director of the FBI's National Infrastructure Protection Center, part of the agency's counterterrorism division.

- Hayward D. Fisk, vice president, general counsel, and secretary, has served on advisory councils to the Federal Communications Commission.

A WINNER!

Vinnell Corporation

Campaign contributions, 1990–2002: $8.5 million

> Percentage to Republicans (for parent company Northrop Grumman), 1999–2002: 76%

Total contract value in Iraq and Afghanistan, 2002–2003: $48 million

Stock price, pre–Iraq invasion (3/11/03): $79.00

Stock price, post-invasion high (8/21/03): $97.11

Change in stock value: +23%

The Vinnell Corporation, a subsidiary of Northrop Grumman, is another leading global rent-a-cop firm. Vinnell won a $48 million contract to train the new Iraqi army. Among its subcontractors in Iraq are SAIC and Military Professional Resources Incorporated.

Vinnell's best-known client is Saudi Arabia, which since the 1970s has employed the American company to train the Saudi Arabian National Guard. *Jane's Defence Weekly* has described Vinnell as "a kind of Praetorian Guard for the House of Saud, the royal family's defense of last resort against internal opposition."[39] Anger against the Saudi regime has also been directed at Vinnell. An attack on a Vinnell compound in 1995 killed five Americans and two Indians. In May 2003, a triple car bombing in a residential compound used by Vinnell in Saudi Arabia killed thirty-four people, including ten of the company's employees.

You would think that the bombing of a major U.S. corporation would spark a public outcry and calls for revenge. But this was a special case: The corporate media reported little about the fact that it was Vinnell that was attacked. Nor was the company's direct relationship with the CIA and other intelligence agencies mentioned much, or that its contract in Saudi Arabia is run by the U.S. Army.

Vinnell supplied the Saudi regime with some 750 retired U.S. military and intelligence personnel to train the Saudi Arabian National Guard, a 55,000-man military force whose main job is protecting the monarchy from its own people using arms supplied by the United States.[40]

As Bill Hartung wrote in *The Progressive* magazine after the 1995 bombing, "President Clinton tried to paint the bombing as just another senseless act of terrorism perpetrated by armed Islamic extremists. . . . The November bombing was brutal, but it was far from senseless. As a retired American military officer familiar with Vinnell's operations put it, 'I don't think it was an accident that it was that office that got bombed. If you wanted to make a political statement about the Saudi regime you'd single out the national guard, and if you wanted to make a statement about American involvement you'd pick the only American contractor involved in training the guard: Vinnell.'"

On May 14, 2003, the day that Vinnell was attacked again in Saudi Arabia, I was invited on CNN. I was told I would be speaking about the war on terrorism. Once the program began, I immediately raised the issue of the Vinnell bombing:

"I think we see right now in Saudi Arabia how grave the situation is, and I think the U.S. has to be very careful about its policies. I also think we have to look at what happened in Saudi Arabia. [It was a] very grave terrorist attack—a number of Americans and others killed. One of the companies that was targeted was basically a U.S. executive mercenary group called Vinnell Corporation, owned by Northrop Grumman, formerly owned by President Bush Sr.'s Carlyle Group. This is a mercenary organization that trains the Saudi Arabian National Guard that is simply there to shore up the undemocratic Saudi regime. The U.S. should be looking at what U.S. corporations are doing, profiting from war and instability."

The CNN host, Miles O'Brien, cut me off and moved on to his other guest, Cliff May from the right-wing Foundation for the Defense of Democracies, saying, "Let's talk about the war on terrorism here for just a moment."

I'm not sure how O'Brien defines terrorism, but I thought I *was* talking about that. I added, "The fact is there were many more connections between the Saudi government and Al Qaeda than were ever proven between Saddam Hussein and Al Qaeda."

O'Brien had heard enough. "That really wasn't what we really started out to do, to talk about the Saudis here, so let's just leave it at that."

Crony Connections

- Vic Fazio, a former Democratic congressman who was chair of the Democratic Caucus, is on Northrop Grumman's board. Since 1980, he has contributed more than $110,000 to campaigns, mostly to Democratic candidates. Further proof that war profiteering is a bipartisan affair.

- Northrop Grumman board member Philip A. Odeen is a former chair of TRW, and worked in the office of the secretary of defense and on the National Security Council. He is a former vice chairman of the Defense Science Board.

- William Studeman, vice president and deputy general manager for intelligence and information superiority at Northrop Grumman, was the deputy director of the CIA from 1992 to 1995, and is a Bush campaign contributor.

A WINNER!

Bechtel Group

Campaign contributions, 1990–2002: $3.3 million

  Percentage to Republicans: 1999–2002: 59%

Total contract value in Iraq and Afghanistan, 2002–2003: $1 billion

Stock value: privately held

The San Francisco–based engineering group, which had over $13 billion in revenues in 2002, has received more than 2,000 government contracts since 1990, worth $11.7 billion. Just six months after the 2003 invasion of Iraq, Bechtel had surpassed the $1 billion mark in Iraqi contracts—the largest of which allowed no competitive bids. The company scored contracts to rebuild power-generation facilities, electrical grids, water and sewage systems, and airport facilities.[41]

Bechtel was one of twenty-four U.S. companies that supplied Iraq with weapons during the 1980s. In 1976, the U.S. Justice Department sued the company for participating in a boycott of Israeli businesses led by the Arab League. In the 1990s, Bechtel was part of a consortium in Bolivia that privatized the water system. Riots ensued after the company raised water prices, and the consortium pulled out of the project. Bechtel is now attempting to recover $25 million in losses from the Bolivian government.

Crony Connections

Bechtel is umbilically connected to the Republican establishment:

- Reagan-Bush Secretary of State George Shultz was a former Bechtel president and is a current board member.

- Reagan-Bush Secretary of Defense Caspar Weinberger was a former Bechtel general counsel.

- Reagan-Bush Deputy Secretary of Energy W. Kenneth Davis was Bechtel's vice president.

- General Jack Sheehan (USMC, retired) joined Bechtel in 1998 as senior vice president. He is also a member of the Pentagon's Defense Policy Board.

- Andrew Natsios, Bush II's USAID administrator overseeing bids for postwar contracts, was formerly the secretary for administration in Massachusetts, where he oversaw the Boston-area Big Dig tunnel construction project, for which Bechtel was the primary contractor. The Big Dig is currently $1.6 billion over budget.

A WINNER!

The Washington Group International

Campaign contributions, 1990–2002: $1.2 million

Percentage to Republicans, 1999–2002: 67%

Total contract value in Iraq and Afghanistan, 2002–2003: $500 million

Stock price, pre–Iraq invasion (3/5/03): $15.26

Stock price, post-invasion high (12/4/03): $34.33

Change in stock value: +124%

The international engineering and construction firm Washington Group International emerged from bankruptcy to bag a contract for restoring electricity, rebuilding roads, and destroying weapons and weapons infrastructure in Iraq and Afghanistan. The open-ended contract to provide support to U.S. Central Command is worth a minimum of $500,000, and could be worth up to $500 million over time.

In 2000, WGI doubled in size when it purchased Raytheon's engineering and construction division. The Securities and Exchange Commission had been investigating how Raytheon handled its books. After WGI's purchase, the SEC dropped its investigation. The Raytheon purchase drove WGI into bankruptcy, from which it emerged in 2002. In February 2003, Raytheon paid the government $4 million to settle claims of false billing on its jet trainer program.[42]

WGI spent $1.5 million on lobbying on defense and other issues in 2001 and 2002.

Crony Connections

WGI's leadership shows there is a revolving door between top defense contractors, which helps explain why so many of them subcontract with one another. The Center for Public Integrity reports:

- **WGI executive vice president and CFO George H. Juetten was senior vice president and CFO for Dresser Industries, a subsidiary of Halliburton.**

- Senior executive vice president Steve Johnson joined WGI after nearly twenty-seven years with Fluor.

- Gary Baughman, president of Washington Group's Industrial Process business unit, spent fourteen years with Fluor Corporation.[43]

Crony-in-Chief

IN AN ADMINISTRATION that has taken a pledge of allegiance to enrich its billionaire buddies, one crony capitalist trumps them all: Vice President Dick Cheney.

Cheney, secretary of defense under Bush I, spent his years in the wilderness as CEO of Halliburton, one of the world's largest oil services and defense contractors. In September 2003, Cheney boldly declared on *Meet the Press*, "I have no financial interest in Halliburton of any kind and haven't had now for over three years."[44]

Cheney's statement was false. Halliburton is paying Cheney roughly $165,000 per year in deferred compensation through 2005, not to mention his more than $400,000 in stock options. All of which constitutes a clear financial interest, according to the Congressional Research Service.

To Cheney, the $60 million in salary that he drew from Halliburton between 1995 and 2000 was simply fair compensation for his long hours at the office.[45] When vice presidential candidate Joe Lieberman observed during their 2000 debate that Cheney had done well for himself at Halliburton, Cheney replied, "I can tell you, Joe, the government had absolutely nothing to do with it."

Oh, really? As columnist Molly Ivins notes, "Mr. Cheney led Halliburton into the top ranks of corporate welfare hogs, benefiting from almost $2 billion in taxpayer-insured loans from the U.S. Export-Import Bank and the Overseas Private Investment Corp. Mr. Cheney also specialized in getting government contracts for the firm. During his five years as CEO, Halliburton got $2.3 billion in contracts, compared with $1.2 billion in the five years before he took over."[46]

Halliburton, which made campaign contributions of $708,770 between 1999 and 2002—95 percent went to Republicans—has been reaping a handsome return on its investment.[47]

Like Bush's patron, Ken Lay at Enron, Cheney proved better at extracting public money than at accounting for it. Under his watch, Halliburton inflated profits by $234 million over a four-year period, spawning more than a dozen lawsuits for the "accounting irregularity."[48] That's a cheery euphemism for lying and stealing, but if we called it that, you might be shouting for people like Cheney to be put in jail like other thieves.

Maybe I'm just old-fashioned, but I have a problem with lying about $234 million. Remember the Whitewater scandal? That was the one where Republicans spent $60 million investigating a real estate scandal in which the Clintons lost $46,000. The newspapers and right-wing pundits are still flogging that.

Where's the outrage when it comes to Bush's crony-in-chief?

Iraq has been Cheney's own personal piggy bank ever since he led the Pentagon during the Persian Gulf War in 1991. Following that war, Cheney commissioned Brown & Root, a Halliburton subsidiary, to study military outsourcing—the practice of paying private companies to do jobs previously done by the military. The Pentagon subsequently chose Brown & Root to implement its own outsourcing plan. Halliburton later hired—who else?—Dick Cheney to run its affairs and open the spigots for public money to flow its way.

Cheney's outsourcing brainstorm has been a windfall for Halliburton and other private companies. It is estimated that a third of

the $4 billion monthly cost of the Iraq occupation is going to pri-
vate contractors.[49]

Not that the vice president doesn't have his scruples. Just ask
him. Following the 1991 Gulf War, Cheney railed against those
who would profit from dealing with the Iraqi dictator. And he later
told Sam Donaldson, "I had a firm policy that I wouldn't do anything in Iraq."

Alas, that policy was about as firm as an oil slick. Under Cheney,
Halliburton "held stakes in two firms that signed contracts to sell
more than $73 million in oil production equipment and spare
parts to Iraq," *The Washington Post* revealed.[50]

Even with its Iraqi windfall, Halliburton nearly went bankrupt
in 2001 because of its fraudulent accounting practices—and because of Cheney's ill-advised acquisition of Dresser Industries,
which was laden with asbestos liabilities.[51] But as soon as Dick
Cheney got hold of the government purse strings as vice president,
help was on the way. The "war on terror" has been a cash cow for
Halliburton, which quickly became the single biggest government
contractor in Iraq.[52]

Halliburton's whopping tally: more than $5 billion in contracts
from the U.S. government during the war on Iraq, as of January
2004.

And that's only the beginning. Halliburton stands to make
hundreds of millions of dollars in a no-bid contract with the U.S.
Army Corps of Engineers to rehabilitate Iraq's oil wells. In March
2003, Halliburton was awarded a no-bid contract to put out fires at
Iraqi oil wells. Contract value: up to $7 billion.[53]

Two years earlier, Halliburton had secured an unprecedented
ten-year deal from the Pentagon known as the Logistics Civil Aug-
mentation Program (LOGCAP)—a contract that will send Kellogg, Brown & Root anywhere on earth to run military operations
for a profit. Value to date: about $830 million.[54]

Halliburton's bounty has been so big that in August 2003, even the Bechtel Group—itself no slouch at profiteering from the war—withdrew from bidding on $1 billion worth of oil projects in Iraq, complaining that Halliburton had an inside track.[55]

That inside track has dramatically improved Halliburton's fortunes. The company turned a $26 million profit in the second quarter of 2003. This contrasts with a $498 *million loss* in the same period a year earlier. From mid-2002 till mid-2003, while the stock market sank, the value of Halliburton's shares rose by 50 percent.

The Bush administration has ensured that Halliburton and its ilk can plunder Iraq with impunity. In May 2003, President Bush signed an executive order that provides oil industry companies— and *only* oil companies—unprecedented immunity against contractual disputes or lawsuits resulting from discrimination, labor law abuses, environmental disasters, and human rights violations.

"In terms of legal liability," says Tom Devine, legal director of the Government Accountability Project, "the executive order cancels the concept of corporate accountability and abandons the rule of law. It is a blank check for corporate anarchy, potentially robbing Iraqis of both their rights and their resources."[56]

All this wasn't enough for the Texas oil services behemoth. In December 2003, a Pentagon audit revealed that Halliburton subsidiary Kellogg, Brown & Root may have overcharged the Army $61 million for gasoline that it was providing in Iraq. In the same week that it was revealed that Cheney's old company was gouging American taxpayers, President Bush announced that no Iraqi contracts would go to France, Russia, Canada, Germany, or any other country that opposed the invasion of Iraq—ensuring that Bush's political contributors could continue to corner the Iraqi business.

The Cheney Index

- Cheney's 2000 income from Halliburton: $36,086,635

- Number of Halliburton stock options Cheney still owns: 433,333

- Size of his retirement package (not including the stock options): $20 million

- Increase in government contracts while Cheney led Halliburton: 91 percent

- Minimum size of "accounting irregularity" that occurred while Cheney was CEO: $234 million

- Number of the seven official U.S. "state sponsors of terror" that Halliburton contracted with: three out of seven (Iran, Iraq, Libya)

- Pages of Energy Plan documents Cheney refused to give congressional investigators: 13,500

- Amount the energy sector gave to Republican candidates for 2000 elections: $50 million

- Number of energy corporations identified that helped Cheney's Energy Task Force shape national energy policy: 30

Sources: Center for Responsive Politics, Center for Public Integrity, MoveOn.org, U.S. Department of State

Defending his decision to maintain Iraq as an exclusive preserve for U.S.-based multinational corporations, Bush explained why the victor is entitled to the spoils of war. "It's very simple," he said. "Our people risked their lives . . . and therefore the contracting is going to reflect that, and that's what the U.S. taxpayers expect."[57]

3

Drilling and Killing: Chevron and Nigeria's Oil Dictatorship

We're more likely to see other companies as collaborators rather than adversaries. . . . We aren't so much competing with each other as we are competing with the earth. And maybe that's a healthy way to look at it.

—GEORGE KIRKLAND, CHAIRMAN AND MANAGING DIRECTOR, CHEVRON NIGERIA LIMITED

It is very clear that Chevron, like Shell, uses the military to protect its oil activities. They drill and they kill.

—ORONTO DOUGLAS, NIGERIAN HUMAN RIGHTS LAWYER

I'm very proud of my association with Chevron.

—CONDOLEEZZA RICE, NATIONAL SECURITY ADVISOR

ONLY ONE OF GEORGE W. Bush's inner circle can claim the distinction of having had a 136,000-ton oil tanker named after her: National Security Advisor Condoleezza Rice. A member of Chevron's board of directors from 1991 until 2001, Rice was paid a $35,000 annual retainer by the oil company, plus meeting fees.[1] As of 2000, she held Chevron stock worth a quarter of a million dollars.[2] She was in charge of the board's public policy committee for the last two years of her tenure, when the board fought off shareholder resolutions demanding that Chevron improve its human rights and environmental record in its Nigerian oil operation.[3]

In 1998, I had a chance to witness Chevron's foreign policy firsthand. I traveled with my colleague Jeremy Scahill to Nigeria, Africa's most populous country and largest oil producer, to investigate Chevron's practices in the oil-rich Niger Delta.

The Niger Delta is on fire. Leaky gas pipelines frequently explode; in one of many such disasters, an explosion in October 2000 killed more than 700 people. Now another fire burns in the delta: the rage of millions of people kept in desperate poverty, who provide oil to the most powerful countries in the world while being kept powerless themselves.

The oil companies continually say that they're working with the Nigerian government. It's true: The oil companies work to shore up dictatorships, which in turn keep the oil flowing and the people pacified. A U.S.-backed dictatorship is an oil corporation's best friend. Renowned Nigerian writer Ken Saro-Wiwa traveled the world exposing the nexus between multinational corporations and the military junta in his country. In 1994, Saro-Wiwa came to the United States, where I interviewed him on WBAI with my colleague Bernard White. He told us at that time that he was a marked man.

I'm ashamed to say that I had never heard of Ken Saro-Wiwa when he walked unannounced into WBAI's studios. Our morning show was already overbooked, but since he'd come from Nigeria, we told him we could do a brief interview. Our plans changed the moment he began to talk on air; we knew immediately that an extraordinary person was in our midst. As he spoke of the plight of his people, we were captivated and canceled one guest after another.

Saro-Wiwa described for us the landscape in Ogoniland, his home in the Niger Delta region. Nigeria earns 90 percent of its foreign exchange from oil sales, but it comes at a high human cost.[4] Pipelines crisscross the land, he said, and flares the size of apartment buildings light up the sky around the clock. Children never know a dark night, living in the shadow of the flame. They breathe in the pollution from these flares, a cheap method of burning off methane waste rarely allowed in the United States. The people don't have oil or gas for themselves.

Upon Saro-Wiwa's return to Nigeria, the military regime arrested him and eight other environmental and human rights activists. Shell representatives monitored the kangaroo court proceedings. According to Ken's brother, Dr. Owens Wiwa, the head of Shell's Nigerian operations, Brian Anderson, promised "to get Ken and the others freed if we stopped the protest campaign abroad." Wiwa continued, "Even if I had wanted to, I didn't have the power to control the international environmental protests."[5]

In Nigeria, it was Shell that had the power. Ken Saro-Wiwa and his eight compatriots refused to stop speaking out. They were hanged on November 10, 1995.

After hearing Ken speak, I promised myself that one day I would go to Nigeria to see what he was describing.

In August 1998, I finally took that journey. Although the feared dictator General Sani Abacha had just died of a heart attack, the brutality and paranoia of the military junta endured. A new military man, Major General Abdulsalami Abubaker, had taken control of the country. Meanwhile, the democratically elected president of Nigeria, Chief Moshood Abiola, had also just died—as a prisoner. Many Nigerians, including Abiola's immediate family, believe he was poisoned. Just after sipping a glass of tea, Abiola died in the lap of President Clinton's envoy, Thomas Pickering, who together with Susan Rice, undersecretary of state for African affairs, had come to pressure him to renounce his presidency as a condition for his release.[6] Four months before, when Abiola and the dictator Abacha were still alive, Clinton made a trip to Africa and said he would not object if General Abacha ran for president.

Clinton was committed to preserving the status quo in Nigeria—keeping the oil and money flowing, no matter how brutal the means. The Nigerians were grateful for such patronage. Two years earlier, former Illinois Senator and 2004 presidential candidate Carol Moseley Braun came back from a visit with Sani Abacha with a letter in which the dictator wished Clinton "a successful campaign and a resounding victory at the polls."[7] In 1998, Abacha announced he would be the sole candidate in the elections.

Jeremy and I knew that getting into Nigeria would not be easy. Foreign journalists and human rights groups had long had great difficulty getting visas. We were advised by Nigerian friends that sneaking into the country was not a wise option, so we decided to say we were tourists.

We spent days reading up on wildlife parks and culture in Nigeria before heading to the consulate in New York, where we were to be "interviewed" as a requirement for getting visas. After an hour of questioning by the junta's men, some of whom wore dark sunglasses inside the building, we were given tourist visas. "Make sure you visit the north," said our chief interrogator. "It's the most beautiful part of my country." The comment gave us chills, knowing that Abacha was from the north, the epicenter of power that had brutally repressed the oil-rich south of the country for so long.

Within weeks, we were headed to a country ruled by one of Africa's most vicious regimes. Air France stopped in Paris, where we prepared for the next leg of the trip: arriving in Lagos. At JFK and Charles de Gaulle airports, we saw the sign posted in so many airports around the world warning passengers of the dangers of flying into Murtallah Mohammed Airport in Lagos. As we sat on the plane, we copied dozens of pages of documents by hand into tiny notebooks. Some were human rights reports; others were contacts we would soon need to meet. As the plane neared Nigerian airspace, Jeremy and I took turns going into the plane's bathroom, tearing up the original documents and flushing them down the toilet.

We exited the plane and realized that with the exception of a few Nigerians, the passengers consisted of the two of us and foreign oilmen. The military presence was everywhere in the airport. After passing through customs with little hassle, we saw that we were the only people in the airport without a security detail waiting to escort us.

Before leaving the United States, we had established contact with a number of groups and people that had offered to help us in our investigation in Nigeria. Now we were operating on faith. Minutes rolled by with no sign of anyone to meet us. Soldiers began approaching us and offering to "help." We decided that the best move was simply to walk out of the airport confidently and head for the nearest taxi as though we had done it a million times before, even though neither of us had ever been to Nigeria.

As we neared the exit, a mob of police, soldiers, and others was staring at us, the last two arriving passengers. We stepped out of the airport and noticed a one-eyed man discreetly holding a cardboard sign reading "Amee Godman and Jermy Shill." Olu would later get us out of many binds.

Our first priority after leaving the airport was to ditch anyone from the military who might be following us. We had given as our Lagos address the posh Sheraton Hotel, the favorite hangout of the regime's thugs and visiting oilmen. Of course we didn't go anywhere near the Sheraton that night. Instead, we checked in at a small, shabby hotel where we thought we could lie low for a while before heading to the Niger Delta. Ironically, there was a local conference on media in progress at the hotel. Cameras were everywhere and they all wanted a shot of the visiting foreigners. As much as we tried to avoid the cameras, pleading with the journalists not to film us, we ended up on the nightly news—covering our faces.

That first night we were followed by men wearing leather trench coats. We never found out who they were; at the time we didn't want to know. We barricaded ourselves in our room and waited for Olu to appear the next morning. In the middle of the night, we heard a knock on the door. Through the peephole, we could see Olu and another man. We removed the furniture and opened the door. In walked Oronto Douglas, a man who would teach us a great deal about his country.

A human rights lawyer who had served on Ken Saro-Wiwa's defense team, Oronto had spent his share of time in prison. When we met him, he had just started an organization called Chicoco, a pan-delta resistance movement that sought to call the attention of the world to the plight of the people of the Niger Delta. That night, we coordinated with Oronto our plan to head south.

The highways to the Niger Delta are dotted with military checkpoints. The soldiers at the checkpoints serve two purposes: They steal as much money as possible, and they attempt to prevent unwelcome visitors. The situation at any one of these stops can quickly escalate out of control, presenting mortal danger, especially to Nigerians. Accompanying unwanted foreigners like us only made it worse for them. Oronto and Olu, along with their colleagues, took major risks in assisting us in our investigations in Nigeria. But they repeatedly told us the risks were greater if word didn't get out.

As we traveled through the south, we came upon a Shell oil flare blazing near a small village. We exited our car and began taking pictures. As we set out on the road back to Port Harcourt, we saw a checkpoint in the distance that had not been there a short while earlier when we had entered the area. We considered turning around and trying to find another way out, but one of our guides, a Nigerian journalist named Rex, told us they might shoot if we turned around. So we proceeded slowly up the road. Oronto's deputy Felix was sitting in the front seat of the car next to the driver. "It's the Kill 'n' Go," he said, referring to the feared Nigerian mobile police.

When we arrived at the checkpoint, one of the soldiers spit in Felix's face and ordered us out of the car. They began asking us why we were taking pictures, what we were doing on private property. As they became more and more aggressive, we feared that they would kill the Nigerians with us. One of the soldiers held a leather whip and was screaming at our driver.

But Rex noticed a Mercedes-Benz coming up the road. He flagged the car down and managed to shame the senior officer inside, asking, "How will this look to America to treat its citizens like this?" Rex knew that the new dictator of the country was at that moment trying to solidify his relationship with Washington. As the officer pondered this, we seized the moment to drive away. Our Nigerian colleagues refused to believe we were safe until we reached Port Harcourt.

From there, we traveled by speedboat and canoe to Ilajeland to investigate a case of corporate involvement in the killing of the Niger Delta's indigenous people. The incident involved the U.S. oil giant Chevron. The corporation facilitated an attack by the feared Nigerian navy and notorious mobile police on a group of people from Ilajeland who had occupied one of Chevron's offshore drilling facilities. Among the people's demands: clean drinking water, electricity, environmental reparations, employment, and scholarships for young people.

In May 1998, a group of about a hundred villagers traveled by boat to Chevron's offshore drilling rig and said they would not leave until they could negotiate with the top man at Chevron. They knew the Americans were ultimately in control. They wanted to talk with George Kirkland, the head of Chevron Nigeria Ltd., which is a wholly owned subsidiary of Chevron in California. Chevron flew a Nigerian spokesperson out to negotiate. Community elders met with him while others stayed on the oil rig. The protesters waited to learn if there would be compensation for the oil spills and jobs for the local youth. They wanted to know if the communities would finally get something back from these corporations that were draining the wealth from their country.

On May 28, after occupying the facility for three days, villagers thought they were about to receive Chevron's final response to their demands when helicopters swooped down. "We were looking at these helicopters thinking . . . people inside these helicopters might have been Chevron's reps who are actually coming to dialogue," one of the activists, known as Parrere, told us. "They were about to land when we heard the shooting of tear gas and guns." Instead of company negotiators, Nigerian police and soldiers jumped out of the Chevron helicopters. The Nigerian troops shot to death two protesters, Jola Ogungbeje and Aroleka Irowaninu; critically wounded a third man, Larry Bowato; and injured as many as thirty others. Bowato told us, "When they shot these guys, I was rushing there to rescue [them] . . . it is then they shot me."

We spent several days interviewing survivors and witnesses of the attack, visiting with the elders, and traveling around the river community. The area is truly beautiful—until you see the huge oil tankers, the devastated ecosystem, and the dead fish and animals lining the shores.

After hearing the stories of the Ilaje, we headed back to Lagos to the Chevron compound. Here in the middle of Nigeria we found what looked like an American suburb. There were lush green lawns with swimming pools in a picture-perfect gated community. The only hint that the company might not be so welcome there was that the entire compound was surrounded by a moat and security guards.

Once we negotiated our way in, we asked Chevron spokesperson Sola Omole about the killings in Ilajeland. Specifically, who flew in the Nigerian military?

Omole replied, "We did. We did. Chevron did. We took them there."

How were they transported? we continued.

"Helicopters," replied Omole. "Yes, we took them in."

And who authorized the call for the military to come in?

"That's Chevron's management," said Omole.

We later requested further comment from Chevron's headquarters in San Francisco. Michael Libbey, the company's manager of media relations, wrote us a letter stating that Sola Omole's comments "fully represent the views of both our Nigerian business unit and of Chevron."

Chevron's acting head of security in Nigeria, James Neku, admitted he flew in with the military the day of the attack. He further revealed that the naval attack force included members of the mobile police—the notorious Kill 'n' Go. As Oronto Douglas, who had exposed the brutal record of the Kill 'n' Go in Ogoniland, described them, "The Kill 'n' Go shoot without question, they kill, they maim, they rape, they destroy."

Chevron spokesperson Omole conceded that the villagers were unarmed. "I cannot say they came armed," he told us. "There was talk of local charms and all that, but that's neither here nor there." When we pushed further about whether the protesters came on board the oil rig with weapons, his answer was no.

Chevron contends that when the helicopters landed on a barge at the facility, the soldiers got out and issued a warning. Villagers say there was no warning; the soldiers simply started shooting. After the shooting incident, eleven activists were held in a barge shipping container for hours and then jailed for three weeks. Bola Oyinbo says that during his imprisonment he was handcuffed and hung for hours from a ceiling-fan hook for refusing to sign a statement written by Nigerian authorities that stated the protesters had destroyed a helicopter.

For the people of the Niger Delta, it is a fact of life that the Nigerian military serves as a hired gun for the transnational oil companies. But most oil companies do not want to admit this. When asked who paid the military, Chevron spokesperson Omole said, "Those [soldiers] were working for the contractor; I guess you have to ask the contractor that." But Bill Spencer, area manager of ETPM, the company that leased the barge to Chevron, told us this was not true. "[The security forces] were not ours. They were paid. They were supplied by Chevron, all of them. Everybody that was out there."

Soon after our visit, Oronto Douglas filed a lawsuit in the United States against Chevron on behalf of the victims of the attack. "It is very clear that Chevron, like Shell, uses the military to protect its oil activities," he says. "They drill and they kill."

The United States buys nearly half of all Nigeria's oil and has its own corporate-government alliance. As Steve Lauterbach, then the spokesperson for the U.S. embassy in Nigeria, told us, "It is the policy of the embassy to support American companies and their operations abroad."

Upon our return to the United States, Jeremy and I produced

a radio documentary, *Drilling and Killing: Chevron and Nigeria's Oil Dictatorship*. In response, Chevron threatened to sue us. They banned Pacifica reporters from attending their press conferences. But it wasn't just Chevron that was paying attention. Several congressional representatives got involved and questioned Chevron officials about the killings.

In April 1999, I managed to attend a Chevron shareholders meeting in California. I don't make a practice of wearing habits, but I did use the proxy of the Ursuline Sisters of Tildonk, an order of Belgian nuns. I felt it was important to question the top Chevron officials. I got up during the question-and-answer period when shareholders are allowed to address the well-protected top executive. I asked Chevron CEO Kenneth Derr if he would stop Chevron's practice of allowing the Nigerian military to kill protesters on company sites.

"No, that's a ridiculous question," he replied. And he moved on.

For the people of the Niger Delta, it is a question of life or death. In January 1999, eight months after the Ilajeland killings, the Nigerian military used a Chevron helicopter and Chevron boats to attack two villages in the delta. At least four people were killed, scores are missing, and the villages were burned to the ground.[8]

Condoleezza Rice was on Chevron's board of directors during these killings. She left in January 2001—not in protest of her company's abysmal human rights record, but to become President Bush's national security advisor. "I'm very proud of my association with Chevron," Rice told FOX News, "and I think we should be very proud of the job that American oil companies are doing in exploration abroad, in exploration at home, and in making certain that we have a safe energy supply."[9]

Oronto Douglas' lawsuit against Chevron for the killings in Ilajeland is slowly moving through the courts in California. Years after the Chevron-backed murders, he hopes that justice will finally be done.

Chevron removed Condoleezza Rice's name from its oil tanker "to eliminate any unnecessary attention" after she became national security advisor.[10] In late 2003, President Bush put her at the helm of the Iraq reconstruction efforts. Armed with Bush's May 2003 executive order that legally immunizes oil companies doing business in Iraq from any consequences for abusing human rights or polluting the environment, Rice doesn't have to worry about any similar lawsuits against her corporate friends operating there.

The Iraqi people, on the other hand, have a great deal to worry about.

4

Crackdown

*First they came for the communists, but I was not a
communist so I did not speak out. Then they came for the
socialists and the trade unionists, but I was neither, so I did
not speak out. Then they came for the Jews, but I was not a
Jew, so I did not speak out. And when they came for me,
there was no one left to speak out for me.*

—MARTIN NIEMÖLLER (1892–1984), PROTESTANT PASTOR IN NAZI
GERMANY

THE YOUNG MAN SAT off to the side of the communal toilet
and kept his distance from the other inmates at the immigration
detention center in Denver. He looked out of place. Confused.
Scared.

In short, he looked like a lot of foreign-born people in the
United States caught in the crossfire of the new war on immigrants.

The young man's name is Yashar Zendehdel. The Iranian-born
student was a junior at the University of Colorado at Boulder. In the
spring of 2002, he decided to change his major from computer science to economics. His academic adviser suggested that he drop a
tough course in computer science, temporarily reducing his course

load from fourteen credits to ten credits. To me, it sounded like routine college course juggling.

But to Attorney General Ashcroft, it bore all the hallmarks of international terrorism. Zendehdel was promptly locked up.

Take a quiz on what landed Yashar in jail:

(A) robbery

(B) rape

(C) murder

(D) not enough college credits

The correct answer? D.

Yashar Zendehdel was one of at least six Middle Eastern college students studying in Colorado who were jailed that fall for failing to take twelve hours of college credit. Because he was an Iranian on a student visa, Yashar was required to register with the Immigration and Naturalization Service (INS) in December 2002, as part of a special registration that the U.S. government was demanding of citizens from twenty-five different countries.

He never could have imagined what would happen next. "I decided to change my major after talking to many career counselors and advisers," Yashar told *Democracy Now!* "My adviser suggested I drop one very tough computer course. The international office told me that there is a law that I must get permission from school to go under twelve credit hours. So I did that. The day I went for special INS registration in Denver, the agent didn't know about this law, and he took me into custody and set bond at $5,000. Then he took me to jail."

Yashar asked the INS official to call his school, since he had approval for dropping the course in the spring but he didn't have the written permission with him at that moment. Yashar had already resumed a twelve-credit load by the time he was speaking to the agent, but the official was still objecting to his class schedule from the previous spring.

"I even told [the INS agent] I'd leave my credit card, my ID, my passport—anything he needed—and go get it." No dice. And no phone calls were permitted to university officials who could corroborate Yashar's story.

Instead of cramming for exams, Yashar spent a night in jail before three of his friends bailed him out. It was a lesson Yashar hadn't counted on learning in America. "Even if this wasn't a law, they shouldn't have sent me to jail for taking two credits less than what you are supposed to."

In the twisted and paranoid post-9/11 climate, Yashar Zendehdel was one of the lucky ones. He had friends on the outside and a prestigious university to come to his defense. Other immigrants, lacking such allies, have simply been terrorized and abused during the witch hunt Bush and Ashcroft have unleashed. Civil liberties advocates calculate that more than 5,000 foreign nationals have been subject to preventive detentions since the 9/11 attacks. But according to David Cole, a Georgetown University law professor and author of *Enemy Aliens*, only three of these detainees were charged with a terrorism-related crime: Two of those were acquitted on the terrorism charges, and the case of the lone man convicted of supporting terrorists is on appeal.[1] "Thousands were detained in this blind search for terrorists without any real evidence of terrorism, and ultimately without netting virtually any terrorists of any kind," Cole charged.[2] And as civil liberties advocates point out, abusing immigrants' rights is often just a warm-up for an all-out assault on the rights of Americans.

Just forty-five days after 9/11, with virtually no debate, George

W. Bush rammed the USA PATRIOT Act through a panicked Congress. The law—its name is an acronym for Uniting and Strengthening America by Providing Appropriate Tools Required to Intercept and Obstruct Terrorism—was supposed to facilitate the crackdown on terror in the aftermath of 9/11. No discussion or amendments were permitted on the bill before senators were forced to vote on it. As Nat Hentoff says, it was the dawn of the "You're with us or you're with the terrorists" era. The Senate vote for the USA PATRIOT Act was 96–1. Only Wisconsin Senator Russ Feingold was with the terrorists that day.

With the nation reeling from the terror attacks and anthrax letters, the Bush administration suggested that members who questioned the USA PATRIOT Act would be blamed for any further attacks.[3] Ashcroft warned the Senate Judiciary Committee on December 6, 2001: "To those who scare peace-loving people with phantoms of lost liberty, my message is this: Your tactics only aid terrorists, for they erode our national unity and diminish our resolve. They give ammunition to America's enemies, and pause to America's friends."

With cowed politicians afraid to speak out, the Bush administration embarked on a nationwide scorched-earth antiterror campaign. Tactics include preventive detention, coercive interrogation, and secret deportation hearings.

There is no end to the USA PATRIOT Act's startling provisions. As the American Civil Liberties Union explains, the USA PATRIOT Act

- Expands terrorism laws to include "domestic terrorism," which could subject political organizations to surveillance, wiretapping, harassment, and criminal action for political advocacy.

- Expands the ability of law enforcement to conduct secret searches, gives them wide powers of phone and Internet surveillance, and access to highly personal medical, financial, mental health, and student records with minimal judicial oversight.

- Allows FBI agents to investigate American citizens for criminal matters without probable cause of crime if they say it is for "intelligence purposes."

- Permits non-citizens to be jailed based on mere suspicion and to be denied re-admission to the U.S. for engaging in free speech. Suspects convicted of no crime may be detained indefinitely in six-month increments without meaningful judicial review.[4]

The assault on civil liberties doesn't end with the USA PATRIOT Act. President Bush decided that he can declare an American citizen an "enemy combatant" who can be locked up, denied counsel, and tried before a military tribunal instead of a regular court. The United States can send these prisoners into a legal netherworld on Guantánamo Bay in Cuba.

Whose warped vision of America is this?

Asked to explain how the "enemy combatant" clause works, a concerned federal prosecutor confided recently to my brother: "This means that when we don't have the goods on someone, we can just export them to a kind of Constitution-free zone. Then we can do what we like with them. It makes a mockery of our entire legal system."

Michael Ratner, head of the Center for Constitutional Rights and an attorney for Guantánamo detainees, observes, "It is as if Guantánamo is on another planet, a permanent United States penal colony floating in another world."

Jailbait

JUST WHEN CROSS-CULTURAL understanding is at a premium, the Bush administration has singled out academics as prime targets for investigation and harassment. Students and scholars are receiving far more scrutiny than tourists. No matter that a terrorist would have a far easier time entering the country pretending to be on holiday than doing what Yashar Zendehdel did, majoring in economics at the University of Colorado. And only one of the 9/11 hijackers was in the United States on a student visa, and he never showed up for class (but the INS did issue student visas to two of the other hijackers—six months after they died crashing planes into the World Trade Center).[5]

The crackdown has dramatically slowed the rate of growth in foreign student admissions, bringing it to the lowest rate since 1995. In 2002–2003, more than 586,000 foreign students were studying in the United States.[6] Many of them could be snared in the same net that caught Yashar Zendehdel. Schools are now required by law to enter extensive information about each international student in a computer database called the Student and Exchange Visitor Information System. SEVIS is run by the U.S. Department of Homeland Security, and its data is accessed by U.S. immigration officials at all ports of entry and by consular officials overseas.

Colleges must enter into SEVIS the minutiae of students' lives: what they are doing, what they're studying, where they live, and what they're majoring in. If there is an error—even so much as a typo—it could result in a student being deported or denied entry to the United States. University officials have been meeting with administrators and professors, warning them not to make any mistakes. The university is being forced to play the role of a cop, and they want to avoid triggering any false arrests.

But even if professors don't make mistakes, SEVIS will. The system "is now notorious for its inefficiencies and mistakes," wrote Catharine Stimpson, dean of the Graduate School of Arts and Science at New York University, in the *Los Angeles Times*.[7]

But the campus snooping doesn't end there, and the consequences are grave—for the entire country. "We believe that as a result of such tactics," Stimpson wrote, "visas for more of our students have been denied this year than ever before. Our international students are at the heart of our nation's scientific and technological future. Forty-one percent of engineering graduates are international, as are 39% of the mathematics and computer science graduates. Two-thirds of our international science- and engineering-degree recipients stay in the United States, where they make educational, economic, and intellectual contributions. One-third of all U.S. Nobel laureates were not born here."

Stimpson told *Democracy Now!* that students who have been admitted to her school are "being told by a consular official when they go for their visa that they're too dumb to come to New York University."

Experience at Johns Hopkins University shows the chilling effect that this multifaceted attack is having on the academic community, particularly on those who are interested in public health. International students, typically from those countries deemed "suspicious," are either denied entry visas for study or denied re-entry after visiting home. The Johns Hopkins Bloomberg School of Public Health, the largest and oldest public health school in the world and a magnet for international students, has seen its top recruits denied visas. Even American researchers studying ways to reduce HIV transmission have been notified that their proposals and studies are being subject to special scrutiny by the National Institutes of Health and by Congress. The entire discipline of epidemiology—the study of the cause and spread of disease—has been put on a State Department watch list for visiting students and scientists.

In an era where diseases such as SARS, AIDS, and the West Nile virus readily cross international boundaries, the Bush administration is trying to restrict the movement and inquiry of physicians and public health experts who are trying to slow that spread. International scholars coming for meetings or to monitor studies in their home countries have been detained at airports and shipped back. Recently, a "no cause" investigation of the university was conducted by the departments of commerce and defense, ostensibly interested in Johns Hopkins' "exports."

What was the "export" that drew the government interest? Students.

The result of these heavy-handed government procedures is that talented foreign students are fleeing the United States for Canada and Europe. They go in search of a better education, rather than the midnight arrests and deportations that now hang over their heads here. And the contributions they might have made to the United States—including the $12 billion they contribute to the economy in tuition and living expenses—will be made to a country that respects their rights.[8]

"No Laws Apply"

DOING A DAILY news show, I often encounter people who are in the middle of a crisis. Such was the case when Eugene Angelopoulos came to the *Democracy Now!* studio. The distinguished professor from the National Technical University of Athens had been brought to us by a Greek friend of his. He had been invited by New York University to address a philosophy conference in February 2003.

His colleagues consider him a scholar. The FBI considers him a potential terrorist.

Angelopoulos knows what fascism is like. He is from Greece, where a brutal military junta ruled from 1967 to 1974. He just didn't expect such a strong whiff of it when he got off the plane in New York.

At the airport, Angelopoulos expected to be met by an NYU welcoming committee. Far from it. "When I arrived, they told me to follow a man to his office." The professor was then handcuffed and spent five hours in a dingy room being interrogated. "I said, 'If I am going to be cuffed, I want to know the charges against me.' They said, 'It's just the rules. Do not take it personally.' I said, 'I will not cooperate with you. I will not resist, but I will not help you.' So they put on the cuffs by force. They told me I was not in U.S. territory officially, so no laws apply."

He said the agent then began the questioning.

"Are you against the war?"

"Is that why you have handcuffed me?" Angelopoulos asked, incredulous.

"Answer the question. Are you antiwar?"

"Yes, I am."

"Are you anti-American?"

"What?" the astonished professor shot back. "What do you mean? I am against the war, as many people are. Is this anti-American? It's against America's own interest to do the war on Iraq."

He said the agent then wrote down, "He is against war on Iraq."

The agent asked Angelopoulos about his involvement with an alleged Greek terrorist group. He was aware of the group, and he had known one of its members in his youth, some forty years earlier. Angelopoulos was among a handful of people who wrote letters to the editor of a Greek newspaper protesting the presumption of guilt in the man's case. He had not seen the man in many years, but as an eminent academic, Angelopoulos had been asked to testify as a character witness at the man's upcoming trial.

"Why should they treat me like a terrorist, although I am not a terrorist?" he asked. "I am confident that reason will prevail in the FBI and the other services."

The nutty professor. He must have been thinking of another America, from another time.

Professor Angelopoulos was finally released from JFK Airport after agreeing to the FBI's request for a second interview. He insisted that the interview take place at New York University, feeling it would at least be neutral ground. But when he returned to his hotel after leaving our studio, he received a phone message from the FBI. The message said that the agents wouldn't go to NYU. They instructed him to come to their office for an "uninterrupted conversation."

At that point, Professor Angelopoulos called the Greek consulate in New York. They contacted the FBI to inform them that Angelopoulos would not be coming to the interview. He immediately checked out of his hotel.

The professor went to his conference, but rewrote his speech to reflect the disturbing event he had just experienced. On Sunday he called to tell me he was cutting his trip short and would be leaving under the protection of the Greek consul general. I headed up to the consulate, rang the bell, and asked if the professor was there. Probably concerned that I was with the government, the official wouldn't answer.

Then Professor Angelopoulos pulled up to the curb. A car with dark-tinted windows was waiting to bring him to the airport. I asked him for a final comment before he left.

"I still think America is a big democratic country and the

hopes of all the world rely on the American people's actions." Reflecting on the previous day, February 15, when millions marched around the world in support of peace, Angelopoulos said, "There were demonstrations all over the world yesterday. I think we can all live in peace, and I think democracy will prevail in the end."

The Greek consul general motioned for Professor Eugene Angelopoulos to get into the diplomatic car. He was on the last plane to Paris before a blizzard shut down JFK Airport.

Round-up

IN DECEMBER 2002, I went to Long Beach, California, for a meeting of the Muslim Public Affairs Council (MPAC). More than 1,500 Muslims were there. It was December 21, the day after the second special registration of immigrants in the United States. The special registration was originally going to cover just five countries, but each month the INS added another set of countries to the list. Between November 2002 and April 2003, all male noncitizens over the age of 16 from twenty-five different countries—almost all of them predominantly Muslim or Arab nations—were required to register and be "interviewed" by the INS.* The previous day the special registration had ended for men from Iran, Iraq, Libya,

---

*The Department of Homeland Security, which inherited the program from the INS, ended the special registration program in January 2004. But the damage had already been done: Of the 83,519 males from the twenty-five countries who voluntarily registered, nearly one in six—about 17 percent—were placed in deportation proceedings. The government said that 2,870 people were detained during the special registrations. Of these, eleven individuals had "suspected terrorist ties," although a Homeland Security spokesman had no information on their cases (*Los Angeles Times*, December 2, 2003). Laura W. Murphy, director of the ACLU Washington legislative office, cautioned, "These changes . . . leave untouched the other provisions that still unfairly target immigrants for detention and deportation because of their religion, ethnicity or national origin" (*Pittsburgh Post-Gazette*, December 3, 2003).

the Sudan, and Syria. Earlier in the week, thousands of Iranian-Americans had staged protests.

What the government touted as a harmless bureaucratic exercise turned out to be a setup. At the immigration registration in Los Angeles, police arrested so many people that they ran out of plastic handcuffs.[9] Hundreds of people were detained for routine visa infractions. Within twenty-four hours, the men were shipped to detention locations in four different states. Terrified families searched, often in vain, to find out where their loved ones were.

Hearing the stories that people told me that day drove home the different worlds that we live in. What is going on in the immigrant community, especially among the Muslims, Muslim-Americans, Arabs, Arab-Americans, and people from South Asian countries, is a nightmare. They are being hit doubly hard by a government crackdown and a spike in hate crimes.

Joseph Zogby, a Justice Department lawyer at the MPAC meeting, urged Muslims to report any such crimes. But one man in the audience asked him, Isn't it true that if we call the civil rights division to report a hate crime, our name could be handed over to the INS, which could then begin an investigation of us?

Yes, came the reply.

So much for civil rights.

Connie Rice, the second cousin of Bush's national security advisor Condoleezza Rice, was also at the meeting. She is an impassioned civil rights attorney and had come to show her solidarity with those present. She compared their struggle with the civil rights struggle of African-Americans. "I know what you are going through," she told them, visibly angered by the arrests that had taken place.

Banafsheh Akhlaghi, an Iranian-American attorney for detained immigrants, spoke forcefully at the meeting of her experience trying to represent people being rounded up. She said her clients had been shuttled around the country and been denied legal counsel.

"They were placed on a plane and sent to Arizona, then sent to Kentucky, then sent to Chicago, then back to Arizona, back to Oakland, and Bakersfield. Sometime around four a.m. this morning they made their way to INS in San Diego. We don't even have access to these guys. I am representing twelve of them and I hadn't spoken to my clients until just a few hours ago because they were finally able to be in a location where they could speak to their counsel.

"What happened to the Sixth Amendment? What happened to due process?" Akhlaghi asked.

She continued, "It's not a Muslim thing. It's not an Iranian thing. It's not an Arab thing. It's a human thing . . . Today it's men over the age of sixteen from these countries. Tomorrow it will be women over the age of sixteen from these countries. Then we will go to permanent residents. . . . It's a wake-up call."

Immigrants, many of whom have spent their entire adult lives in this country working long hours for low wages to feed their families, have been faced with an impossible dilemma: register, and risk arrest and deportation for unknown offenses. Or don't register, and risk arrest and deportation for not registering.

Just ask the people in Little Pakistan. This Brooklyn community, home to 120,000 Pakistani immigrants prior to the crackdown, has seen a mass exodus since it became the focus of a siege by FBI and INS agents. Some 15,000 have left in panicked escapes to Canada, Europe, or Pakistan.[10] Many others have been deported in secret airlifts.

Immigrants are terrified: Pakistani residents come home to discover the business card of an FBI or INS agent stuck in the door, with a chilling note instructing them to call in. By now every Pakistani in Brooklyn knows someone who has made that call to a federal agent—and then vanished.

Families in Little Pakistan have yanked their children out of school and spirited them away in the middle of the night to avoid being "disappeared." For some, however, there was no escape: Canadian officials began turning back Pakistanis at the border throughout the winter in 2003. Hundreds were locked up after they were forced to reenter the United States. Throughout Little Pakistan, homes, jobs, families, and lives were hastily abandoned in fear of a U.S. government out of control.

This is the America of Bush and Ashcroft.

The Justice Department has arrested thousands of people in the course of this campaign. But Attorney General Ashcroft has refused to reveal the names of these detainees, he insists, "out of respect for their privacy, and concern for saving lives."[11] When immigrants are arrested, some don't get to call an attorney. Many are held in immigration cells and deported to places like Pakistan, which receives secret airlifts every few months.

Democracy Now! and other media outlets began reporting these stories shortly after 9/11, but it took until June 2003 for the Justice Department to acknowledge that illegal abuses were occurring. The inspector general of the Justice Department revealed that people who had been arrested after 9/11 on suspicion of terrorism or for routine immigration violations—anything from failure to renew a visa to moving without notifying authorities to having a neighbor who suspected you were a terrorist—were held for an average of eighty days, instead of being released immediately on bond. Detainees were abused, beaten, shackled hand and foot, and held in cells illuminated twenty-four hours a day. Their families were often lied to about their whereabouts. Even when judges would order the release of a detainee, the government would simply ignore the order and keep the men locked up.

"They were treated as terrorists, even though they were not," said Michael Ratner of the Center for Constitutional Rights.

Attorney General Ashcroft offered no apologies.

Hero or Terrorist?

THESE INCIDENTS LAY bare the operating assumption of the war on terror: guilty until proven innocent. Basic constitutional principles are thrown aside, replaced by racial profiling and guilt by association.

That's what the family of Mohammed Salman Hamdani learned on September 11, 2001. Hamdani was a New York City police cadet and emergency medical technician who raced to the World Trade Center when he heard about the plane crash. He was never heard from again.

Talaat and Mohammed Hamdani launched an anguished search for their 23-year-old son, plastering his picture throughout the community. For three weeks, they searched morgues and waited for word of what happened to him. In October, they traveled to Mecca to pray for their son.

On October 12, 2001, while the Hamdanis were away, they were shocked to learn of a story that came out in the *New York Post*. MISSING—OR HIDING? MYSTERY OF NYPD CADET FROM PAKISTAN, screeched the *Post* headline. "Hamdani was last seen, Koran in hand, leaving his Bayside, Queens home for his job as a research assistant at Rockefeller University," the *Post* reported in sinister tones, "but he never made it to work."

Overnight, Mohammed Salman Hamdani went from hero to villain. Federal agents laid siege to the Hamdani home in the following weeks, and reporters quizzed them about their son, the suspected terrorist.

Hamdani's DNA was later found at Ground Zero. Officials were forced to apologize. His funeral at a local mosque was attended by the mayor of New York and the police commissioner. President Bush singled him out for praise, and he was cited in the USA PATRIOT Act as a hero. But irreparable damage had been done to his family and community.

I interviewed Talaat Hamdani and her husband on the eve of the second anniversary of 9/11 as they joined hundreds in a quiet procession through the streets of New York to Ground Zero. Talaat said that when her family went, like so many others, to register Salman's name as one of the missing, they were afraid to say his first name was Mohammed, instead calling him Sal. Her nieces and nephews, in second and third grade when the planes hit the World Trade Center, shared similar fears.

"Armeen became Amy," Talaat told *Democracy Now!* on September 10, 2003, "and one became Mickey and the other one became Mikey and the fourth one became Adam. We asked them, 'Why you change your names?' And they said, 'Because, you know, we don't want to be called terrorists in the school.'"

The nieces and nephews learned this not only from what happened to their uncle Salman, but also from classroom discussions. Talaat herself is a teacher. In class she asked her students to define what a terrorist is. "The first word everybody echoed was *Muslim*," Talaat said. "The second brainstorm topic was to define Islam. And the first word that they came up with was *bin Laden*.

"And that is where I find myself," Talaat said with a sad sigh. "Defending myself, my faith, my people, my community, my fellow Americans who are Muslims."[12]

"Don't Take My Father!"

NADINE YOUNG-ULVIE WAS in the shower in her Brooklyn apartment at 6:30 a.m. on November 8, 2002, when she heard a crash at her door. Her 7-year-old daughter Brittany went to see what was happening. She was greeted by men who demanded to be let in. They had broken down the front door to the apartment building. Nadine shouted to her daughter not to let them in, but the frightened girl screamed that it was the police. Nadine leaped out of the shower and attempted to close the bathroom door while she put on clothes. The men had already stormed inside, and ordered her to keep the bathroom door open while she dressed. They shouted for Nadine's three young children to go into the bedroom. Then they ordered Nadine's husband Faisal, a salesman in a clothing store, to get out of bed.

Faisal Ulvie is a Pakistani tae kwon do expert who traveled to the United States in 1996 for a martial arts competition and then applied for political asylum. He failed to show up for his last asylum appointment that year and was ordered deported, but Ulvie remained in the country. Like so many others, the undocumented immigrant scratched out a living. In April 2001, he married Nadine Young, a U.S. citizen. He helped raise Nadine's two children from a previous relationship, Devon and Brittany. In 2001, they had a child of their own named Shaheen.

Faisal had never had trouble with the law. But now he was caught in the antiterror dragnet, and so was his terrified family.

"They told my husband to get out of the bed and to go into the living room," Nadine told me on *Democracy Now!* "I asked, 'What is the situation? What's going on?'

"The officer replied, 'We only address questions to him. And you need to mind your business.' And I'm, like, 'But you need to provide me with a search warrant or a warrant for his arrest.' They told me no. That was their answer." It set the tone for what was about to come.

"They asked [Faisal] to put up his fingerprints to place against a piece of paper. After they asked him some questions, they told him, 'Get dressed. We're taking you. You've got to go with us.'

"My son said to the officer, 'Don't take my father!' And I just gave [Faisal] a hug and a kiss good-bye. And I told him, 'Don't worry. I will fight this.'"

On Sunday evening, November 17, nine days after being detained, Faisal called Nadine. "They posted a handwritten letter next to my picture for me to pack up my stuff and get dressed," he told her. He feared, correctly, that he was going to be deported. Nadine immediately contacted Ahsanullah (Bobby) Khan, director of the Coney Island Avenue Project, a group that advocates for the rights of Pakistani immigrants, who called attorney Elizabeth OuYang.

Bobby had no time to drop his wife and 2-year-old daughter off, so he picked up OuYang and they all rushed to Faisal's jail. On the way, Nadine called Bobby's cell phone to say she was coming. OuYang said there was no guarantee Nadine would see Faisal.

Nadine replied, "I don't care. He's my husband. I need to be there."

It was pouring rain when they reached the jail. "When I went in there," OuYang said, "Faisal was in shackles and plainclothes. And he was scared."

Faisal told her, "I don't know what's going on. They ordered us to put our civilian clothes on and to pack up. There are twenty-two of us back there that were ordered to do this. They won't tell us where we're going or what they're doing." Despite the shackles on his ankles, he kept pacing back and forth.

She told Faisal, "Stay calm and we'll try to do everything that we can." As OuYang came out, Nadine arrived at the jail. She was not allowed to speak to her husband.

OuYang wanted to ensure that the INS knew that Faisal was married to an American citizen and was in the process of getting legal residency in the country. But she had another concern: "I have been told, I have heard stories, I have received e-mails, that mass deportations are going on."

The rumors came to life at 3:30 a.m., when a white bus pulled up to the detention center. IMMIGRATION AND NATURALIZATION SERVICE was emblazoned on the side of the bus in large green letters.

OuYang ran back inside and demanded, "I want to talk to Immigration. I want to know where they're taking Faisal."

In the tense encounter that followed, a prison guard came out to warn OuYang, "[INS] won't talk to you. They've got orders to take him." She said he added a threat: "If any of you follow that bus, you will be arrested."

Outside in the rain, OuYang calmed Nadine down as much as she could. Nadine wanted to follow the bus. OuYang reasoned with her. "If you get arrested, how will you help him?"

So they each went home to work the phones. Nadine called the Pakistani consulate, her Congressmember Nydia Velázquez, and Senator Hillary Clinton. At 5:00 a.m., OuYang reached an emergency deportation officer. She explained what had just transpired. "I don't know where they're taking him. I need information—please," the attorney begged. At 7:00 a.m., a different deportation officer called back. This officer was taking Faisal to the airport. He said, "All I can tell you is he's on a flight at eleven-thirty this morning." OuYang said if she was able to get the stay, how could she reach him? That's when OuYang got a crucial piece of information: the officer's cell phone number.

Only one option remained. OuYang rushed to the courthouse in New Jersey. As Bobby was driving her, she called ahead to the court clerk to alert her that an emergency stay of the deportation order was coming. Just as they were about to enter the Holland Tunnel, the New Jersey court clerk told her that Faisal's file was in Manhattan. They turned the car around and headed to 26 Federal Plaza in lower Manhattan. The original judge on Faisal's case was no longer there, so the case had to be reassigned to another immigration judge.

Meanwhile, the clock kept ticking. At 10:15 a.m., Judge Patricia Rohan approved the request for an emergency stay of deportation, agreeing to hold a hearing for Faisal at a later date. "Judge Rohan breathed life into our Constitution's principle of due process," said OuYang. "By the grace of God, we were able to get the judge to sign the emergency stay."

But the drama wasn't over. After Judge Rohan signed the stay, OuYang announced, "Your Honor, I have nowhere to fax the order to, they're already at the airport. He's boarding." OuYang pleaded with the judge to call the deportation officer's cell phone. Meanwhile she had to run downstairs to pay the $110 fee for the legal motion. When OuYang returned, the court clerk said she wasn't able to reach the deportation officer on his phone.

OuYang went outside the courtroom to call the officer. It was busy. OuYang then realized it was probably Nadine pleading for a final time with the officer to release her husband. OuYang reached Nadine and told her to get off the phone. Then Bobby Khan's phone rang. It was the deportation officer, asking who was trying to reach him. OuYang grabbed the phone and started running to the courtroom. A court officer came out of nowhere and yelled, "No cell phones in the courtroom!" OuYang just kept running, shouting, "It's for the judge!" The officer followed in hot pursuit. OuYang burst into the courtroom. The judge had already begun a new hearing. Upon seeing OuYang, she came off the bench and grabbed the phone. "This is Judge Rohan. Immigration judge, New York. I'm ordering you to take Faisal Ulvie off the plane."

Just before the plane doors slammed shut, agents took Faisal away. Dozens of other men were deported to Pakistan that day.

Faisal Ulvie was reunited with his family. He is now going through the normal immigration process to become a permanent resident of the United States.

Nadine's son Devon, a fourth grader, is still shaken by having seen Faisal, the man he calls Pappy, vanish with armed men.

He says, "I'm just scared."

5

Smackdown

We can bomb the world to pieces. But we can't bomb it into peace.

—MICHAEL FRANTI, HIP-HOP ARTIST

ON THE MORNING OF April 9, 2002, Lynne Stewart was in her apartment when she heard a commotion at the front door. She looked out the window and saw four or five unfamiliar people. She immediately assumed they were police. The veteran civil liberties attorney figured they were coming to hassle her husband, a well-known activist. He was outside talking heatedly with the visitors.

"Calm down, calm down, we'll take care of this," Stewart told her husband as she came out to intervene. It was a familiar role to Stewart.

An FBI agent looked at the rumpled attorney and said, "We're not here for him. We're here for you." With that, they put her in handcuffs and whisked her away to FBI headquarters in Manhattan.

It had finally come to this: The Bush-Ashcroft juggernaut was now locking up the lawyers. And who better than Lynne Stewart, the attorney for the imprisoned blind sheikh Omar Abdel Rahman, who is serving a life sentence for conspiring to blow up several New York landmarks and to assassinate Egyptian president Hosni Mubarak. She was accused of passing messages between the sheikh and an Egyptian terrorist organization.

An outspoken civil liberties attorney with a long history of defending dissidents and activists, Stewart was a prize catch for the Bush regime. More important, the arrest of this prominent radical lawyer was intended to send a message: Not only are immigrants and dissidents under serious attack, but if you dare represent them, you, too, will go down.

That night, Attorney General Ashcroft went on the *Late Show with David Letterman* and explained to the comic how the feds just arrested a terrorist lawyer. "We simply aren't going to allow people who are convicted of terrorism to continue . . . directing the activity from their prison," he told Letterman.

How clever of the attorney general. Avoid tough questions at a news conference and carry your message to late-night TV, where most Americans get their news. Letterman did not, of course, challenge Ashcroft. No tough questions about the erosion of civil rights. No questions about whether Stewart was really guilty. Instead, the late-night comic went deadpan. "God bless America," Letterman responded, and applauded. The audience followed suit.

Lynne Stewart came on *Democracy Now!* the next day. The 62-year-old lawyer with seven grandchildren was rattled but resolute. "I would like David Letterman to let me come on his show . . . because I think that our message of freedom and justice is just as compelling a message as Ashcroft's message of 'We will hunt them down wherever they are.'"

As the Detroit *MetroTimes* editorialized, Ashcroft "took on the wrong grandma."[1] Stewart is nothing if not a fighter. "If John

Ashcroft wants to make me a poster child," she declared on our show, "I'm happy to accept that responsibility."

Far from intimidating other attorneys, Stewart's case has instead galvanized many. Every time Stewart appears in court for her case, the room is packed with supporters, lawyers among them. "This case was, from the beginning, an attempt to chill the exercise of vigorous advocacies," said Stewart's attorney Michael Tigar.

Stewart adds, "The case is really about two things: The first is that this could happen to you, too, because basically I did nothing that any good defense lawyer would not do. And the second thing is that if it does happen to you, there won't be a lawyer to call."[2]

In July 2003, the main terrorism charges against Stewart— that she conspired to support a terrorist organization—were thrown out of federal court. The judge ruled that the charges were unconstitutionally vague and "reveal a lack of prosecutorial standards."

Ashcroft refused to give up. In November 2003, the Justice Department filed a "reframed indictment," advancing a new theory about why Stewart should be charged with terrorism. The government replaced the dismissed terrorism charges with new charges that she supported terrorists by, among other offenses, providing "covering noises" while her jailed client held discussions with his translator. She warned the sheikh that he could get a heart attack from eating too much chocolate. The government accused Stewart of having used code words with her client.

"This type of re-indictment on 'new' charges based on the same facts was almost unheard of in the pre-Ashcroft days," wrote Elaine Cassel. "No prosecutor can match John Ashcroft for persistence and vindictiveness . . . Whoever beats Ashcroft better leave the country."[3]

While Letterman was applauding the attorney general, Jay Leno recently had a take on things rarely heard on late-night talk shows—including his own. "I hear the Iraqis need a new constitution," Leno quipped on *The Tonight Show.* "Why not take ours? We're not using it!"

Patriot Games

IN THE SPRING of 2003, Jason Halperin learned the hard way what immigrants have known all along: The U.S. Constitution is a shredded fig leaf in the face of the USA PATRIOT Act. Halperin, who worked at the time for an international humanitarian relief organization, had gone out to dinner in midtown Manhattan when he unexpectedly came face-to-face with the sharp end of Bush's judicial system. He told his story on *Democracy Now!* and described it in an article for the *Los Angeles Times* and AlterNet:[4]

> [On] March 20th, my roommate Asher and I were on our way to see the Broadway show *Rent.* We had an hour to spare before curtain time so we stopped into an Indian restaurant just off of Times Square in the heart of midtown. . . .
>
> We helped ourselves to the buffet and then sat down to begin eating our dinner. I was just about to tell Asher how I'd eaten there before and how delicious the vegetable curry was, but I never got a chance. All of a sudden, there was a terrible commotion and five NYPD in bulletproof vests stormed down the stairs. They had their guns drawn and were pointing them indiscriminately at the restaurant staff and at us.
>
> "Go to the back, go to the back of the restaurant," they yelled.

I hesitated, lost in my own panic.

"Did you not hear me? Go to the back and sit down," they demanded.

I complied and looked around at the other patrons. There were eight men including the waiter, all of South Asian descent and ranging in age from late teens to senior citizen. One of the policemen pointed his gun point-blank in the face of the waiter and shouted: "Is there anyone else in the restaurant?" The waiter, terrified, gestured to the kitchen.

The police placed their fingers on the triggers of their guns and kicked open the kitchen doors. Shouts emanated from the kitchen and a few seconds later five Hispanic men were made to crawl out on their hands and knees, guns pointed at them.

. . . Two [agents] walked over to our table and identified themselves as officers of the INS and Homeland Security Department.

I explained that we were just eating dinner and asked why we were being held. We were told by the INS agent that we would be released once they had confirmation that we had no outstanding warrants and our immigration status was okayed.

In pre-9/11 America, the legality of this would have been questionable. After all, the Fourth Amendment to the Constitution states: "The right of the people to be secure in their persons, houses, papers and effects, against unreasonable searches and seizures, shall not be violated; and no warrants shall issue, but upon probable cause, supported by oath or affirmation, and particularly describing the place to be searched and the persons or things to be seized."

"You have no right to hold us," Asher insisted.

"Yes, we have every right," responded one of the agents. "You are being held under the PATRIOT Act following suspicion under an internal Homeland Security investigation."

. . . When I asked to speak to a lawyer, the INS official informed me that I do have the right to a lawyer but I would have to be brought down to the station and await security clearance before being granted one. When I asked how long that would take, he replied with a coy smile: "Maybe a day, maybe a week, maybe a month."

We insisted that we had every right to leave and were going to do so. One of the policemen walked over with his hand on his gun and taunted: "Go ahead and leave, just go ahead."

We remained seated. Our IDs were taken and brought to the officers with laptops. I was questioned over the fact that my license was out of state and asked if I had "something to hide." The police continued to hassle the kitchen workers, demanding licenses and dates of birth. One of the kitchen workers was shaking hysterically and kept providing the day's date, March 20, 2003, over and over.

As I continued to press for legal counsel, a female officer who had been busy typing on her laptop in the front of the restaurant walked over and put her finger in my face. "We are at war, we are at war, and this is for your safety," she exclaimed. As she walked away from the table, she continued to repeat it to herself: "We are at war, we are at war. How can they not understand this?"

. . . After an hour and a half the INS agent walked back over and handed Asher and me our licenses. A policeman took us by the arm and escorted us out of the building. Before stepping out to the street, the INS agent apologized. He explained, in a low voice, that they did not think the two of us were in the restaurant. Several of the other patrons, though of South Asian descent, were in fact U.S. citizens. There were four taxi drivers, two students, one newspaper salesman—unwitting customers, just like Asher and me. I doubt, though, they received any apologies from the INS or the Department of Homeland Security.

Every American citizen, whether they support the current war or not, should be alarmed by the speed and facility with which these changes to our fundamental rights are taking place. And all of those who thought that these laws would never affect them, who thought that the PATRIOT Act only applied to the guilty, should heed this story as a wake-up call. Please learn from my experience. We are all vulnerable, so speak out and organize; our Fourth Amendment rights depend upon it.

A Voice of Conscience

IN 1941, MILITARY authorities declared Americans of Japanese descent subversive and part of an enemy race. Over 110,000 people of Japanese origin had their property confiscated and were held in detention camps during World War II.

A 22-year-old Japanese-American, Fred Korematsu, refused the internment orders and appealed to the U.S. Supreme Court to stop the roundups. In an infamous ruling, the court upheld the internments, deferring to military authorities in time of war. Years later, Korematsu's conviction for defying the government was thrown out, and he was awarded the Presidential Medal of Freedom. And in 1988, in recognition of the massive violation of civil rights that had occurred, Congress approved payments of $20,000 to each surviving internee.

In 2003, a frail and aged Fred Korematsu reemerged to fight again—this time on behalf of detainees being held without charge and without access to attorneys, notably over 600 prisoners on Guantánamo Bay, Cuba. Korematsu filed a friend-of-the-court brief in support of the Guantánamo detainees, who are being held indefinitely and without charge at the whim of the U.S. government. His brief is also in support of Yaser Esam Hamdi, a U.S. citizen who has been designated an enemy combatant by President Bush and denied the protection of the Bill of Rights. Hamdi has been held in isolation in a brig in Virginia and denied access to a lawyer. Under the enemy combatant laws, Hamdi can be held indefinitely.

Why no lawyer? Because, the government contends, it would disturb his isolation and interrogation and thus hinder the government's effort to pry information out of him. In December 2003, after the Supreme Court began considering a request to review Hamdi's case, the Pentagon finally allowed him to meet with an attorney, saying it was finished interrogating him. Critics say this may just be a ruse to moot Hamdi's Supreme Court appeal, which takes place in 2004.

Korematsu has said of his experience defending civil liberties, "In order for things like this to never happen, we have to protest . . . So don't be afraid to speak up."[5]

Librarians as Freedom Fighters

SOME UNLIKELY HEROES have stepped forward to defend our civil liberties: librarians. In George Bush's war on terror, libraries have become a battlefront.

According to Section 215 of the USA PATRIOT Act, an FBI agent can enter a library or bookstore and demand records of the books patrons read and what Internet sites they visit. If an agent makes such a request, librarians are forbidden to tell anyone about the visit. They can't tell fellow librarians, they can't tell journalists, and they certainly can't tell the patron. They can only raise it with a coworker if that person has the information the FBI is requesting. If a librarian does talk about a request from the FBI, she or he can be prosecuted.

"Bookstores are subject to the same provision as libraries and Internet service providers," said Leigh Estabrook, director of the School of Library and Information Science at the University of Illinois, on *Democracy Now!* "They can walk into any business that maintains any kind of record in any kind of form or in any medium, and demand it, if they obtain one of these warrants from the Foreign Intelligence Surveillance Act [FISA] Court."

A survey of 1,029 libraries in 2002 revealed that 83 libraries had already been asked by federal or local law enforcement officers for information about their patrons. Some 118 libraries said that their staff is now more restrictive regarding patron use of the Internet.[6] This contradicted a claim made by Ashcroft in August 2003 that no libraries had been visited.

The number of libraries that are being snooped on may be far greater than anyone realizes. "There's a high possibility we are just simply not hearing about these kinds of searches because they're constrained by law from talking about it. So it's very frustrating to find out exactly what's going on out there," said Estabrook.

And when the feds do show up at your local library, librarians have little control over what records the authorities take. One community media center director told me that the FBI came to his center one day, allegedly to search for information about a particular individual. But before they knew what was happening, the FBI had copied all of the center's computer files.

Because of how libraries have been targeted, librarians are now debating whether to post signs, as some have already, alerting patrons that government agents may monitor their library use. But there is a delicate balance between warning people and scaring them away from one of this country's precious resources. Sadly, the people hardest hit by library surveillance will be those who are too poor to have a computer and cannot afford to shop at Barnes & Noble.

The American Library Association has found a clever way to fight back and protect the privacy of their patrons. The ALA has been encouraging libraries not to keep any unnecessary paper trails, and to use circulation software that automatically erases any record of a patron's book use—provided the book is returned and all the fines are paid. It's a great idea for a national library ad campaign: Get your library book back on time . . . or else.

Libraries in Boulder, Colorado, and Santa Cruz, California, now destroy book-borrowing records several times per week. It's just another chore for the corner librarian: Take out the trash, sweep the halls, and delete patron information each day to keep the attorney general away.

Ashcroft didn't see it that way. He was enraged by the cheeky librarians. On September 15, 2003, he lashed out, slamming librarians and the American Library Association as "hysterics" and calling them "ridiculous." A Justice Department spokesman later added that the ALA, the world's largest library association, was "deluded."[7]

The librarians relished the denunciation. "If he's coming after us so specifically," said Emily Sheketoff, executive director of the ALA's Washington office, "we must be having an impact."

Revised Patriot Act Will Make It Illegal to Read Patriot Act

WASHINGTON, DC—President Bush spoke out Monday in support of a revised version of the 2001 USA Patriot Act that would make it illegal to read the USA Patriot Act. "Under current federal law, there are unreasonable obstacles to investigating and prosecuting acts of terrorism, including the public's access to information about how the federal police will investigate and prosecute acts of terrorism," Bush said at a press conference Monday. "For the sake of the American people, I call on Congress to pass this important law prohibiting access to itself." Bush also proposed extending the rights of states to impose the death penalty "in the wake of Sept. 11 and stuff."

—from the satirical newsmagazine *The Onion*, September 17, 2003

Total Information Awareness

IT'S NOT ONLY librarians and progressives in this country who are concerned about these issues. By attacking our civil liberties, George W. Bush has united an unprecedented cross section of society . . . against him.

First came the Ashcroft-inspired Operation TIPS, the Terrorism Information and Prevention System, which encouraged everyone from the UPS driver to the meter reader to next-door neighbors to spy on one another. Under TIPS, the government had a goal of recruiting 10 million Americans to "sneak a peek" at their neighbors and to report anything suspicious that they saw.

Then came Total Information Awareness. One of the strongest

critiques of TIA came from a seemingly unlikely source: *New York Times* columnist William Safire. In November 2002, he wrote a chilling column entitled, "You Are a Suspect":

> If the Homeland Security Act is not amended before passage, here is what will happen to you:
>
> Every purchase you make with a credit card, every magazine subscription you buy and medical prescription you fill, every Web site you visit and e-mail you send or receive, every academic grade you receive, every bank deposit you make, every trip you book and every event you attend—all these transactions and communications will go into what the Defense Department describes as "a virtual, centralized grand database."
>
> To this computerized dossier on your private life from commercial sources, add every piece of information that government has about you—passport application, driver's license and bridge toll records, judicial and divorce records, complaints from nosy neighbors to the FBI, your lifetime paper trail plus the latest hidden camera surveillance—and you have the supersnoop's dream: a "Total Information Awareness" about every U.S. citizen.[8]

Yes, that's the former Nixon speechwriter sounding the alarm over the Bush administration's war on privacy. But Safire knows a thing or two about surveillance—Henry Kissinger had his phone bugged when they both worked at the Nixon White House. Safire wasn't alone among conservatives, many of whom joined the attack on Total Information Awareness.

"[TIA] goes against our very character as a nation to accept that anybody is guilty until proven innocent in America," said Lori Waters, executive director of the Eagle Forum, the conservative group founded by Phyllis Schlafly. The Eagle Forum was joined by a unique left-right coalition that included the National Rifle Association, the American Conservative Union, the American Civil Liberties Union, People for the American Way, and Americans for Tax Reform.[9]

The outcry forced the Pentagon to respin the program. The man who fathered these programs, John Poindexter, had himself been resuscitated. After his 1990 felony conviction for conspiracy, lying to Congress, defrauding the government, and destroying evidence in the Iran-Contra scandal, one might have assumed Poindexter's public life was finished.* But Poindexter had a few more covert tricks up his sleeve.

First, the Pentagon tried changing the name of the program: Total Information Awareness became Terror Information Awareness. As in so many aspects of American post-9/11 life, the Pentagon tried to play on people's fears in renaming the program. It was clever, but not clever enough. Ultimately, the Information Awareness Office at the Pentagon was defunded and closed in September 2003.

And, there was one more program that came to an end in September 2003: the Policy Analysis Market, also known as the Terrorism Betting Parlor or Terror Futures. This was an $8 million scheme that would have allowed people to bet on the likelihood of terrorist attacks, assassinations, and coups. Examples given on the Information Awareness website included betting on the assassination of Yasser Arafat or the overthrow of the Jordanian monarchy. Congress refused to fund it, and Poindexter was officially forced out of his job in August 2003.

---

*Poindexter was convicted in 1990 of lying to Congress, but an appeals court overturned his five felony convictions the following year on a technicality. The appeals court ruled 2–1 that Poindexter's testimony to Congress, which was used against him by the prosecution, had been given under a grant of immunity.

But the official end of these programs is certainly not the end of the spying. The government has set up a Terrorist Index—a massive computerized list that will contain over 100,000 names of individuals the government claims are known and suspected terrorists. Attorney General John Ashcroft has praised the list, saying it will "provide one-stop shopping so that every federal antiterrorist screener is working off the same page—whether it's an airport screener, an embassy official issuing visas overseas, or an FBI agent on the street."[10]

Michael Ratner, head of the Center for Constitutional Rights, retorts, "Everybody on that list is innocent. The question is, Why is there a list at all, other than to basically say people are guilty until proven innocent."[11]

If that doesn't grab you, maybe this will: the Computer Assisted Passenger Profiling System, or CAPPS II, a database of 100 million airline passengers, categorized according to your perceived dangerousness or your risk score. In keeping with Homeland Security Secretary Tom Ridge's love of color-coding schemes, you'll be labeled green, yellow, or red—like a stoplight:

Green: You should make it on the plane without much hassle.

Yellow: You could be in for some delays and searches.

Red: Find a hotel—or a lawyer. Red won't fly.

Under the program, simply checking in at the airport will trigger an assessment of your criminal record, your credit history, and potentially your religion and ethnicity. This in turn will be entered into some mysterious mathematical formula that will spit out your potential risk factor. It gives new meaning to the idea of carry-on baggage.

The Four Rs: Reading, 'Riting, 'Rithmetic, and Recruiting?

THE PRIVACY RIGHTS of high school kids are also under attack. My brother David wrote a piece in *Mother Jones* entitled "No Child Unrecruited: Should the Military Be Given the Names of Every High School Student in America?"

> Sharon Shea-Keneally, principal of Mount Anthony Union High School in Bennington, Vermont, was shocked when she received a letter in May 2002 from military recruiters demanding a list of all her students, including names, addresses, and phone numbers. The school invites recruiters to participate in career days and job fairs, but like most school districts, it keeps student information strictly confidential. "We don't give out a list of our kids to anybody," says Shea-Keneally, "not to colleges, churches, employers—nobody."
> But when Shea-Keneally insisted on an explanation, she got another surprise. The recruiters cited the No Child Left Behind Act, President Bush's sweeping education law passed in 2002. There, deep within the law's 670 pages, is a provision requiring public secondary schools to provide military recruiters not only with access to facilities but also with contact information for every student—or face a cutoff of federal aid. . . . The military complained that up to 15 percent of the nation's high schools are "problem schools."[12]

Now, I used to think problem schools were where kids weren't reading or writing. But for the recruiters, "problem school" has a different meaning. In 1999, the Pentagon says recruiters were denied access to schools on nearly 20,000 occasions. So Republican Congressman David Vitter from Louisiana added this little-known section into the No Child Left Behind Act.

Students can opt out of having their names sent to the military—*if* they know their rights. When schools do inform families of this opt-out clause, students use it. In Bennington, Vermont, the high school principal sent home a letter explaining the new military recruitment provision, and included a simple opt-out checkoff form for parents and students to sign and return. The result: One-sixth of the student body opted out. A school in Fairport, New York, sent home a letter with a similar opt-out checkoff form. The result was that out of 1,200 juniors and seniors, only 43 families chose to let their names go to recruiters.[13]

Schools are now being turned into extensions of military recruitment offices. For unwitting students whose names go to the military, they are in for a hard sell. As the *Mother Jones* article concludes: "Recruiters are up-front about their plans to use school lists to aggressively pursue students through mailings, phone calls, and personal visits—even if parents object. Said Major Johannes Paraan, head U.S. Army recruiter for Vermont and northeastern New York, 'The only thing that will get us to stop contacting the family is if they call their congressman. Or maybe if the kid died, we'll take them off our list.'"

A Crackdown Sampler

Former White House spokesman Ari Fleischer warned on September 26, 2001, that Americans "need to watch what they say, watch what they do."[14] *Democracy Now!* regularly reports on cases that prove the Bush administration was serious. Here's a post-9/11 sampler of how civil liberties are under daily assault:

Protester with Sign Charged with Threatening the President's Safety

Brett Bursey, the executive director of the South Carolina Progressive Network, was arrested for holding a sign that read "No War for Oil" outside a venue where President Bush was giving a speech in October 2002 and charged with threatening the president's safety. Bursey, who was nowhere near the president, said the police told him he should move to a free speech zone. He refused, saying, "I thought the whole country was a free speech zone" (*Democracy Now!*, June 24, 2003).

Class Comments Lead to Interrogation

In a class discussion at Oakland High School about politics and President Bush, two boys made comments that their teacher claimed were a threat against the president. Secret Service agents showed up at the high school the next day to interrogate the 16-year-old boys without the knowledge or consent of their parents. One of the boys said the police "asked questions like 'was I a good sniper.' I was very scared," said the boy. "I was crying because of what they said to us" (*In These Times*, September 19, 2003).

Ashcroft Bans Gay Pride

In June 2003, the man in charge of enforcing the nation's civil rights, Attorney General John Ashcroft, banned a gay pride event organized by some 200 Justice Department employees. Agency workers have held pride events for years—including in 2002, when John Ashcroft's number two official, Deputy Attorney General Larry Thompson, spoke to about 150 employees (*Democracy Now!*, June 10, 2003).

Working Out with Big Brother

As Barry Reingold was working out at his local gym in San Francisco, he talked about "Bush, bin Laden, and the politics of oil." When he returned home, he found two FBI men at his door waiting to question him about his views. The utility company retiree learned his lesson: Working out and speaking out don't mix. "Before, I was much, much more open about talking to anyone and everyone," he said. "Now I'll be much more selective" (*Democracy Now!*, December 24, 2001).

Feds Discover Hip-Hop

A day after hip-hop artist Michael Franti's band Spearhead performed at an antiwar rally, the mother of one of his bandmates got a visit from some unlikely fans: plainclothes investigators from the military. The bandmate's brother was in the armed forces in the Persian Gulf. The agents interrogated the bandmate's mother, showing her the bank and travel records of her musician son, as well as pictures of him performing the previous day. Franti said: "They . . . basically were intimidating, told her which members of the press she could talk to and which members of the press she should not speak to" (*Democracy Now!*, March 27, 2003).

Cop Hunts Pacifist Teacher

Barre, Vermont, police officer John Mott went into Spaulding High School at 1:30 a.m. to take photographs of the classroom of Tom

Treece, a pacifist history teacher. The photographs, which were not part of any official report, appeared within days on the website of archconservative talk show host and admitted drug abuser Rush Limbaugh (*Democracy Now!*, May 9, 2003).

FBI Seizes Reporters' Mail

In September 2002, a reporter with the Associated Press in the Philippines sent a FedEx package to an AP colleague in Washington containing unclassified FBI documents being used for a story. The package never arrived. FedEx claimed it fell off their truck. AP soon learned it had been seized and confiscated by the FBI. Unnamed FBI officials told *The New York Times* the documents were too sensitive for public consumption (*Democracy Now!*, April 25, 2003).

Police Spy On Antiwar Activists

San Francisco police conducted unauthorized undercover surveillance on antiwar activists, videotaping protests in October 2002 and in January and February 2003. Police officials claimed the tapes were needed for criminal investigations, but the city's Office of Civilian Complaints and the police commissioner both called for a full investigation and the destruction of the videotapes (*Democracy Now!*, March 14, 2003).

Busted for Peace T-shirt

On March 3, 2003, a father and son went shopping at a mall outside of Albany, New York. The two had bought T-shirts at the mall and promptly put them on. Stephen Downs' shirt read "Give Peace a Chance" and "Peace on Earth." His son, Roger, had a shirt that read "Let Inspections Work" and "No War With Iraq." A mall security guard requested that both men take off the T-shirts. When Stephen Downs refused, the mall called the police. Soon Downs, a retired attorney with the New York State Commission on Judicial Conduct, was in handcuffs, arrested on trespassing charges. Two days later, 150 supporters wearing peace T-shirts protested at the mall, forcing the mall to drop the charges against Downs (*Democracy Now!*, March 6, 2003).

High-Flying Spying

Beginning in February 2003, the FBI secretly flew a high-tech spy plane to monitor residents around Bloomington, Indiana. FBI agents told the Associated Press they were not aware of any threat to the region, but confirmed the FBI was watching many international students who might have connections to terrorists (*Democracy Now!*, March 5, 2003).

Cuffing the NYPD

New York police have long been restricted from monitoring political activity. In early 2003, a court granted an NYPD request to lift restrictions in order to fight terrorism. But the court reimposed the restrictions after the NYPD broke its own rules by holding political interrogations of antiwar protesters detained during the mass antiwar rally on February 15, 2003 (*Democracy Now!*, October 2, 2003).

Antiwar Actor Banned

Following actor Danny Glover's public criticism in November 2001 of the use of military tribunals, the Modesto, California, city council attempted to disinvite Glover as the featured speaker for the of-

ficial celebration of Martin Luther King Day 2002. Glover wondered if King, who called the United States "the greatest purveyor
of violence in the world today," would have been invited to his own
birthday celebration if he were still alive (*Democracy Now!*, January 15, 2002).

Peace Advocate Forced to Resign from U.S. Institute of Peace

Barbara Wien, longtime peace educator and activist, resigned from
the U.S. Institute of Peace under severe pressure, after stating publicly that she hoped that the United States didn't retaliate for 9/11
quickly and without thinking (*Democracy Now!*, January 9, 2002).

High School Suspends Student for Antiwar T-shirt

Katie Sierra, a 15-year-old high school student from Charleston,
West Virginia, wore a T-shirt to school with a handwritten message: "When I saw the dead and dying Afghani children on TV, I
felt a newly recovered sense of national security. God Bless America." The school suspended her. Sierra and her mother sued the
school, arguing that her free speech rights were violated. But a
West Virginia judge ruled in favor of the school, saying that the
disruption she caused at school overrode her right to free speech.
Sierra's mother pulled her out of school after she endured physical
threats, and even accusations of treason from school board members
when she went before them to protest her suspension (*Democracy
Now!*, December 11, 2001).

Academic Blacklist

The conservative American Council of Trustees and Alumni com-
piled a list of 117 "anti-American" statements made by professors

and students on college campuses since September 11. Joel Beinin, a professor of Middle Eastern history at Stanford University and president of the Middle East Studies Association, earned a place in the Council's report for saying the United States should bring Osama bin Laden before an international tribunal if he is found guilty, instead of bombing Afghanistan (*Democracy Now!*, November 26, 2001).

Free Speech Locked Up

Sherman Austin, a 20-year-old webmaster of an anarchist website called raisethefist.com, began a year-long prison term in September 2003, following which he will be banned from associating with anyone who wants to "change the government in any way." Austin was convicted of running a server on which someone posted information on how to build Molotov cocktails (*Democracy Now!*, September 3, 2003).

Could It Happen Here?

CHILEAN AUTHOR ARIEL Dorfman narrowly escaped death on September 11, 1973, when a last-minute change kept him from his work at the Presidential Palace in Santiago, where he was a cultural adviser to Chilean President Salvador Allende. Allende died that day when Chilean troops stormed the palace, and Dorfman was forced into exile. On the second anniversary of the September 11 attacks in the United States, he wrote an essay, "Lessons of a Catastrophe," from which this is excerpted:

> It can't happen here.
> Thirty years ago that is what we chanted, that is what we sang, on the streets of Santiago de Chile.

It can't happen here. There can never be a dictatorship
in this country, we proclaimed to the winds of history
that were about to furiously descend on us; our democracy is too solid, our armed forces too committed to popular sovereignty, our people too much in love with
freedom.

But it did happen.

The bombing by the air force of the Presidential Palace
on [September 11, 1973] started a dictatorship that was
to last seventeen years and that, today, even after we have
recovered democracy, continues to haunt and corrode my
country.

. . . In the coming years, could something similar
befall those nations with apparently stable democracies?
Could the erosion of freedom that so many in Chile
accepted as necessary find a perverse recurrence in the
United States or India or Brazil, in France or Spain or
Britain?

What has transpired thus far, in the two years since
the disastrous attacks on New York and Washington, is
far from encouraging . . .

We also thought, we also shouted, we also assured the
planet:

It cannot happen here.

We also thought, on those not-so-remote streets of
Santiago, that we could shut our eyes to the terrors that
were awaiting us tomorrow.[15]

6

Lockdown

Imagine living, eating, sleeping, relieving oneself,
day-dreaming, weeping—but mostly waiting, in a room
about the size of your bathroom. Now imagine doing all
those things—but mostly waiting, for the rest of your life.
Imagine waiting—waiting—to die.

—MUMIA ABU-JAMAL[1]

IN 1997, *DEMOCRACY NOW!* made a decision that resulted in the program getting thrown off of twelve radio stations in one fell swoop. It knocked us completely off the air in the entire state of Pennsylvania.

Our crime was airing the commentaries of a death row prisoner named Mumia Abu-Jamal.

A former journalist and activist in Philadelphia, Abu-Jamal has been on death row in Pennsylvania since being convicted of the 1981 murder of a police officer. Abu-Jamal maintains he is innocent of the charges, and an international solidarity movement has grown up around his case. Among those supporting his cause are Nelson Mandela and the European Parliament. Amnesty International says Abu-Jamal never received a fair trial.

Mumia Abu-Jamal has been an outspoken voice for the thousands of people on death rows around this country. He has written articles for the *Yale Law Review*. His popular book, *Live from Death Row,* is a collection of his commentaries.

Abu-Jamal's essays touch on a broad range of issues. None of them were about his own case. He speaks of capital punishment being punishment for those without capital. And he talks about father hunger—the idea that so many young black men in prisons do not have fathers. Abu-Jamal reflected on the irony of being a father figure to those prisoners, despite the fact that he can't be a father to his own children or grandchildren. He writes in *Death Blossoms*:

> Here, in this restrictive place of fathers without their
> children and men who were fatherless, one senses and
> sees the social costs of that loss. Those unloved find it
> virtually impossible to love, and those who were
> fatherless find themselves alienated and at war with their
> own communities and families.

In October 1996, the San Francisco–based Prison Radio Project taped thirteen essays with Abu-Jamal, and *Democracy Now!* began airing the pieces in early February 1997. (The Philadelphia Fraternal Order of Police declined our invitation to comment on air.) But minutes before the first broadcast, the twelve stations in Pennsylvania owned by Temple University that aired *Democracy Now!* pulled our show entirely and ended their contract with the Pacifica Network. They said it was "inappropriate" to air the commentaries of Mumia Abu-Jamal; his voice should not be heard on the public airwaves.

Temple is a public university, so for us it was not only an issue of freedom of the press but also an issue of academic freedom and free speech at a publicly funded institution. The Temple stations replaced *Democracy Now!* with jazz.

A tremendous outcry followed. The president of Temple received more than a thousand calls, e-mails, letters, and faxes from academic associations and activists all over the country. *The Washington Post* and *The New York Times* both framed the incident as a free speech issue. Hundreds of students turned out for a forum against censorship at Temple University Law School.

One reason Abu-Jamal's commentaries were groundbreaking is because it is rare to hear voices from jail—journalists are increasingly being barred from prisons. Virginia, California, Pennsylvania, Indiana, and Illinois are among the states that heavily restrict journalists' access to jails. California bans all face-to-face interviews. The state senate in Virginia killed a bill that would have ensured that reporters could interview prisoners. And just days after Abu-Jamal recorded his prison commentaries, the Pennsylvania Department of Corrections barred one-on-one media interviews with inmates.[2]

Abu-Jamal has faced multiple obstacles as he has tried to have his voice heard. On August 12, 1999, Mumia Abu-Jamal called in to *Democracy Now!* to comment on the release of sixteen Puerto Rican political prisoners. As Abu-Jamal began to speak, a prison guard yanked the phone out of the wall. Abu-Jamal called back a month later and recounted that "another guard appeared at the cell door hollering at the top of his lungs, 'This call is terminated.' I immediately called to the sergeant standing by and looking on and said 'Sergeant, where did this order come from?' He shrugged his shoulders and answered, 'I don't know. We just got a phone call to cut you off.'"[3]

These rules are not typically made by legislatures; they are edicts handed down by various prison authorities. As journalists, we must ensure that prisons are accountable to the public. These are public institutions, not the fiefdom of some prison boss. And as prisons become increasingly privatized, we have to ensure that the civil liberties of prisoners are respected.

The Society of Professional Journalists understood how threatening Temple's action was. "I am outraged that administrators at Temple University decided to silence an alternative voice," said then SPJ president Steve Geimann to *The Washington Post.* "SPJ, like Pacifica Radio, isn't taking a stand on Abu-Jamal's guilt or innocence. This issue today is all about allowing him—and other prisoners—the right to be heard."[4]

The Prison-Industrial Complex

WE NEED TO know what is happening inside prisons because the prison population is exploding at an unprecedented rate. In 2002, the number of prisoners in the United States exceeded 2 million for the first time in history—up from 200,000 in 1970.[5] The rate of incarceration in the United States—701 inmates per 100,000 population (in 2002)—is the highest reported rate in the world.[6]

Racial disparities in prison are startling. Forty-five percent of prisoners in 2002 were black; 18 percent were Hispanic. According to the Department of Justice, black males have about a one in three chance of landing in prison at some point in their lives. Draconian drug laws have taken a particularly high toll: 57 percent of federal prisoners are incarcerated for drug-related offenses; a fifth of state prisoners are there for drug-related charges.

All this has helped the booming prison industry. Corrections is now a $50-billion-a-year business. Due partially to immigrant lockups and harsh drug laws, prisons, like weapons manufacturing, are a growth industry. From 1994 to 2002, the number of people in state prisons increased by 30 percent. During the same period, the number held in federal BCIS (Bureau of Customs and Immigration Services) and ICE (Immigration and Customs Enforcement) custody increased by 275 percent. The explosion in immigrant prisoners follows the special registrations for immigrants from twenty-five countries that started in November 2002 and ran to January 2004. The federal government's 2003 budget for locking up immigrants was $672 million.

Nobody is cashing in on the immigrant lockdown like the private for-profit corporations that run prisons. The $3-billion-a-year private prison industry profits handsomely when immigrants end up in their cells. The federal government pays county jails $35 a day for murderers, rapists, and white-collar thieves, but the jails get from $75 to $100 a day for immigrant detainees.[7] And it's certainly not because the immigrant prisoners are getting more services.

"It is clear that since September 11, there's a heightened focus on detention, [and] more people are gonna get caught," Steve Logan, the chairman of Cornell Corrections, a private corrections company, cheerfully informed his shareholders. "So I would say that's positive. The federal business is the best business for us, and September 11 is increasing that business."[8]

America's death rows have also been busy places. The United States has executed over 885 people since 1976. Over 3,500 men and women are currently on death row.[9]

Death row is a monument to racial injustice. As a U.S. General Accounting Office study confirms, "The single most reliable predictor of whether someone will be sentenced to death is the race of the victim."[10] Over 80 percent of people executed were convicted of killing whites, even though half the homicide victims in this country are people of color. And a Justice Department study revealed that "80 percent of the cases submitted by federal prosecutors for death penalty review in the past five years have involved racial minorities as defendants. In more than half of those cases, the defendant was African-American."[11]

In Oklahoma and North Carolina, killers of white victims are four times more likely to get the death penalty than are killers of black victims. In Mississippi, they are five times more likely; in Maryland, seven times. Forty percent of the people on death row are black—yet African-Americans make up just 12 percent of the population. In Pennsylvania alone, more than two-thirds of the people on death row are African-American.

The most disturbing fact may be this: Since 1977, 140 death row prisoners (as of January 2004) have been exonerated.[12] Were it not for the relentless work of families, activists, attorneys, and reporters who cared, these innocent people would have been executed.

Condemned to Silence

TEMPLE UNIVERSITY INSISTED that the idea to banish Mumia Abu-Jamal from the airwaves didn't originate with them: They were merely following the lead of National Public Radio. "We share the view of NPR on Abu-Jamal's commentaries," said Temple spokesman George Ingram.[13]

Temple was referring to the fact that in 1994, NPR commissioned Mumia Abu-Jamal to do a series of commentaries unrelated to his case. When the NPR editor left the prison, she claimed that these were some of the finest commentaries she had ever heard.[14] They were scheduled to air, and NPR heavily promoted the series.

"We read his material and evaluated its content," said Ellen Weiss, executive producer of NPR's *All Things Considered*. "He is a good writer and brings a unique perspective to the air."[15] She added that the commentaries were a way for public radio to broaden its coverage of crime and punishment.

NPR knew these segments might be controversial, and they were. The day before the commentaries were to begin on NPR, leaders of the Philadelphia Fraternal Order of Police were attending a national event in Washington, D.C. The police put tremendous pressure on NPR not to air the commentaries. Senator Bob Dole denounced the radio network on the floor of the Senate.

NPR could not take the heat. Within a couple of days, it pulled the commentaries, abruptly changing its tune about them. "There is a different standard for a convicted murderer," said Bruce Drake, NPR's managing editor. "In the end, I didn't feel that what he had to say was compelling enough to overcome our misgivings."[16]

NPR then put the tapes in a vault and refused to return them to Mumia Abu-Jamal—even now, a decade later. But the commentaries finally did appear—in Abu-Jamal's book *Live from Death Row*.

NPR's cowardice had a ripple effect. They set a precedent by caving to pressure from the police, and then they dressed it up as principle. Then smaller networks such as Temple University Public Radio cited NPR as the example of why they wouldn't air a controversial voice.

In April 1997, NPR called poet Martin Espada and asked him to write a poem to commemorate National Poetry Month. The poem would air on *All Things Considered*. Espada, an acclaimed poet and a professor of English at the University of Massachusetts at Amherst, was pleased to take the assignment. While traveling in Philadelphia, he read an article about a development in Abu-Jamal's case: an "unnamed prostitute" had come forward with important new information. Espada was intrigued. So he wrote

"Another Nameless Prostitute Says the Man Is Innocent," a poem about Abu-Jamal's case, then faxed it in to NPR.

Suddenly Espada was poet non grata. NPR would not return his calls.

Espada could not understand what happened. He had read poems on *All Things Considered* before. NPR had pursued him to get this poem and he felt he had sent them a very good one. It was done the way NPR wanted it: as poetry, but also addressing news of the day. Finally he reached an NPR editor and asked what was going on.

We won't be airing it, came the reply.

"But you asked me for a poem," Espada protested.

Yes, but we can't do this poem, the editor replied, because it deals with Mumia Abu-Jamal.

Espada quickly figured out what was happening. "NPR is refusing to air this poem because of its political content?"

Yes, was the reply from *All Things Considered* producer Diantha Parker. According to Dennis Bernstein of Pacifica's KPFA, Parker said Espada should have known better.

Kathy Scott, NPR's communications director, told *The Boston Globe,* "NPR has already been criticized for not running the commentaries. Obviously, Mr. Espada thinks Mumia is innocent. In our way of thinking, this was a way to throw that back in our face."[17]

NPR was now attempting to muzzle both Mumia Abu-Jamal and Martin Espada. Both refused to be silenced. Espada came on *Democracy Now!* to talk about his case. *The Progressive* magazine published his poem, and it circulated widely on the Internet.

"If I didn't speak out, then I would be governed by the same fear that governs NPR, and that would be wrong," said Espada. "All a writer wants is to be judged on the merit of his work. They censored my piece for political reasons."[18]

Journalists are not entertainers. We are reporters. We go to places that are unpopular. We broadcast voices that are controversial. We are not here to win popularity contests. We are here to cover the issues critical to a democratic society. We have to pressure the media, to shame the media into going into these forgotten places where so many are sent to waste away in silence.

Here is the poem that NPR didn't want you to hear:

ANOTHER NAMELESS PROSTITUTE SAYS THE MAN IS INNOCENT[19]

—for Mumia Abu-Jamal, Philadelphia, Pa./Camden, N.J., April 1997

By Martin Espada

The board-blinded windows knew what happened;
the pavement sleepers of Philadelphia, groaning
in their ghost-infested sleep, knew what happened;
every black man blessed
with the gashed eyebrow of nightsticks
knew what happened;
even Walt Whitman knew what happened,
poet a century dead, keeping vigil
from the tomb on the other side of the bridge.

More than fifteen years ago,
The cataract stare of the cruiser's headlights,
the impossible angle of the bullet,
the tributaries and lakes of blood,
Officer Faulkner dead, suspect Mumia shot in the chest,
the witnesses who saw a gunman
running away, his heart and feet thudding.

The nameless prostitutes know,
hunched at the curb, their bare legs chilled,
Their faces squinted to see that night,
rouged with fading bruises. Now the faces fade.
Perhaps an eyewitness putrefies eyes open in a bed of soil,
or floats in the warm gulf stream of her addiction,
or hides from the fanged whispers of the police
in the tomb of Walt Whitman,
where the granite door is open
and fugitive slaves may rest.

Mumia: the Panther beret, the thinking dreadlocks,
dissident words that swarmed the microphone like a hive,
sharing meals with people named Africa,
calling out their names even after the police bombardment
that charred their black bodies.
So the governor has signed the death warrant.
The executioner's needle would flush the poison
down into Mumia's writing hand
so the fingers curl like a burned spider;
his calm questioning mouth would grow numb,
and everywhere radios sputter to silence, in his memory.

The veiled prostitutes are gone, gone to the segregated
    balcony of whores.
But the newspaper reports that another nameless prostitute
says the man is innocent, that she will testify at the next
    hearing.
Beyond the courthouse, a multitude of witnesses chants,
    prays,
shouts for his prison to collapse, a shack in a hurricane.

Mumia, if the last nameless prostitute
becomes an unraveling turban of steam,
if the judges' robes become clouds of ink
swirling like octopus deception,
if the shroud becomes your Amish quilt,
if your dreadlocks are snipped during autopsy,
then drift above the ruined RCA factory
that once birthed radios
to the tomb of Walt Whitman,
where the granite door is open
and fugitive slaves may rest.

7

Lies of Our *Times*

From a marketing point of view, you don't introduce new products in August.

—Andrew H. Card, White House chief of staff, speaking about the Iraq War P.R. campaign, September 6, 2002[1]

IN THE MIDST OF the buildup to war, a major scandal was unfolding at *The New York Times*—the paper that sets the news agenda for other media. The *Times* admitted that for several years a 27-year-old reporter named Jayson Blair had been conning his editors and falsifying stories. He had pretended to be places he hadn't been, fabricated quotes, and just plain lied in order to tell a sensational tale. For this, Blair was fired. But the *Times* went further: It ran a 7,000-word, five-page exposé on the young reporter, laying bare his personal and professional escapades.

The *Times* said it had reached a low point in its 152-year history. I agreed. But not because of the Jayson Blair affair. It was the *Times* coverage of the Bush-Blair affair.

When George W. Bush and Tony Blair made their fraudulent

case to attack Iraq, the *Times,* along with most corporate media outlets in the United States, became cheerleaders for the war. And while Jayson Blair was being crucified for his journalistic sins, veteran *Times* national security correspondent and best-selling author Judith Miller was filling the *Times'* front pages with unchallenged government propaganda. Unlike Blair's deceptions, Miller's lies provided the pretext for war. Her lies cost lives.

If only *The New York Times* had done the same kind of investigation of Miller's reports as it had with Jayson Blair.

THE WHITE HOUSE PROPAGANDA blitz was launched on September 7, 2002, at a Camp David press conference. British Prime Minister Tony Blair stood side by side with his co-conspirator, President George W. Bush. Together, they declared that evidence from a report published by the UN International Atomic Energy Agency (IAEA) showed that Iraq was "six months away" from building nuclear weapons.

"I don't know what more evidence we need," crowed Bush.

Actually, *any* evidence would help—there was no such IAEA report. But at the time, few mainstream American journalists questioned the leaders' outright lies. Instead, the following day, "evidence" popped up in the Sunday *New York Times* under the twin byline of Michael Gordon and Judith Miller. "More than a decade after Saddam Hussein agreed to give up weapons of mass destruction," they stated with authority, "Iraq has stepped up its quest for nuclear weapons and has embarked on a worldwide hunt for materials to make an atomic bomb, Bush administration officials said today."[2]

In a revealing example of how the story amplified administration spin, the authors included the phrase soon to repeated by President Bush and all his top officials: "The first sign of a 'smoking gun,' [administration officials] argue, may be a mushroom cloud."

Harper's publisher John R. MacArthur, author of *Second Front: Censorship and Propaganda in the Gulf War*, knew what to make of this front-page bombshell. "In a disgraceful piece of stenography," he wrote, Gordon and Miller "inflated an administration leak into something resembling imminent Armageddon."

The Bush administration knew just what to do with the story they had fed to Gordon and Miller. The day the *Times* story ran, Vice President Dick Cheney made the rounds on the Sunday talk shows to advance the administration's bogus claims. On NBC's *Meet the Press*, Cheney declared that Iraq had purchased aluminum tubes to make enriched uranium. It didn't matter that the IAEA refuted the charge both before and after it was made. But Cheney didn't want viewers just to take his word for it. "There's a story in *The New York Times* this morning," he said smugly. "And I want to attribute the *Times*."[3]

This was the classic disinformation two-step: the White House leaks a lie to the *Times*, the newspaper publishes it as a startling exposé, and then the White House conveniently masquerades behind the credibility of the *Times*.

"What mattered," wrote MacArthur, "was the unencumbered rollout of a commercial for war."[4]

Judith Miller was just getting warmed up. Reporting for America's most influential newspaper, Miller continued to trumpet administration leaks and other bogus sources as the basis for eye-popping stories that backed the administration's false premises for war. "If reporters who live by their sources were obliged to die by their sources," Jack Shafer wrote later in *Slate*, "Miller would be stinking up her family tomb right now."

After the war, Shafer pointed out, "None of the sensational allegations about chemical, biological, or nuclear weapons given to

Miller have panned out, despite the furious crisscrossing of Iraq by U.S. weapons hunters."[5]

Did *The New York Times* publish corrections? Clarifications? Did heads roll? Not a chance: Judith Miller's "scoops" continued to be proudly run on the front pages.

Here are just some of the corrections the *Times* should have run after the year-long campaign of front-page false claims by one of its premier reporters, Judith Miller.

From *The New York Times* Department of Corrections

Scoop: "U.S. Says Hussein Intensifies Quest for A-Bomb Parts," by Judith Miller and Michael R. Gordon, September 8, 2002. The authors quote Ahmed al-Shemri (a pseudonym), who contends that he worked in Iraq's chemical weapons program before defecting in 2000. "'All of Iraq is one large storage facility,' said Mr. Shemri, who claimed to have worked for many years at the Muthanna State Enterprise, once Iraq's chemical weapons plant." The authors quote Shemri as stating that Iraq is stockpiling "12,500 gallons of anthrax, 2,500 gallons of gas gangrene, 1,250 gallons of aflatoxin, and 2,000 gallons of botulinum throughout the country."

Oops: As UN weapons inspectors had earlier stated—and U.S. weapons inspectors confirmed in September 2003—none of these claims were true. The unnamed source is one of many Iraqi defectors who made sensational false claims that were championed by Miller and the *Times*.

Scoop: "White House Lists Iraq Steps to Build Banned Weapons," by Judith Miller and Michael Gordon, September 13, 2002. The article quotes the White House contention that Iraq was trying to purchase aluminum pipes to assist its nuclear weapons program.

Oops: Rather than run a major story on how the United States had falsely cited the UN to back its claim that Iraq was expanding its nuclear weapons program, Miller and Gordon repeated and embellished the lie.

Contrast this with the lead paragraph of a story that ran in the British daily *The Guardian* on September 9: "The International Atomic Energy Agency has no evidence that Iraq is developing nuclear weapons at a former site previously destroyed by UN inspectors, despite claims made over the weekend by Tony Blair, western diplomatic sources told *The Guardian* yesterday." The story goes on to say that the IAEA "issued a statement insisting it had 'no new information' on Iraq's nuclear program since December 1998 when its inspectors left Iraq."[6]

Miller's trumped-up story contributed to the climate of the time and the *Times*. A month later, numerous congressional representatives cited the nuclear threat as a reason for voting to authorize war.

Scoop: "U.S. Faulted Over Its Efforts to Unite Iraqi Dissidents," by Judith Miller, October 2, 2002. Quoting Ahmed Chalabi and Defense Department adviser Richard Perle, this story stated: "The INC [Iraqi National Congress] has been without question the single most important source of intelligence about Saddam Hussein."

Miller airs the INC's chief complaint: "Iraqi dissidents and administration officials complain that [the State Department and CIA] have also tried to cast doubt on information provided by defectors Mr. Chalabi's organization has brought out of Iraq."

Oops: Miller championed the cause of Chalabi, the Iraqi exile leader who had been lobbying Washington for over a decade to support the overthrow of Saddam Hussein's regime. As *The Washington Post* revealed, Miller wrote to *Times* veteran foreign correspondent John Burns, who was working in Baghdad at the time, that Chalabi "has provided most of the front page exclusives on WMD [weapons of mass destruction] to our paper."[7]

Times readers might be interested to learn the details of how Ahmed Chalabi was bought and paid for by the CIA. Chalabi heads the INC, an organization of Iraqi exiles created by the CIA in 1992 with the help of the Rendon Group, a powerful public relations firm that has worked extensively for the two Bush administrations. Between 1992 and 1996, the CIA covertly funneled $12 million to Chalabi's INC.[8] In 1998, the Clinton administration gave Chalabi control of another $98 million of U.S. taxpayer money. Chalabi's credibility has always been questionable: He was convicted in absentia in Jordan of stealing some $500 million from a bank he established, leaving shareholders high and dry. He has been accused by Iraqi exiles of pocketing at least $4 million of CIA funds.[9]

In the lead-up to war, the CIA dismissed Chalabi as unreliable. But he was the darling of Pentagon hawks, putting an Iraqi face on their warmongering. So the Pentagon established a new entity, the Office of Special Plans, to champion the views of discredited INC defectors who helped make its case for war.

As Howard Kurtz later asked in *The Washington Post*: "Could Chalabi have been using the *Times* to build a drumbeat that Iraq was hiding weapons of mass destruction?"[10]

Scoop: "C.I.A. Hunts Iraq Tie to Soviet Smallpox," by Judith Miller, December 3, 2002. The story claims that "Iraq obtained a particularly virulent strain of smallpox from a Russian scientist." The story adds later: "The information came to the American government from an informant whose identity has not been disclosed."

Smallpox was cited by President Bush as one of the "weapons of mass destruction" possessed by Iraq that justified a dangerous national inoculation program—and an invasion.

Oops: After a three-month search of Iraq, "'Team Pox' turned up only signs to the contrary: disabled equipment that had been rendered harmless by UN inspectors, Iraqi scientists deemed credible who gave no indication they had worked with smallpox, and a laboratory thought to be back in use that was covered in cobwebs," reported the Associated Press in September 2003.[11]

Scoop: "Illicit Arms Kept Till Eve of War, an Iraqi Scientist Is Said to Assert," by Judith Miller, April 21, 2003. In this front-page article, Miller quotes an American military officer who passes on the assertions of "a man who said he was an Iraqi scientist" in U.S. custody. The "scientist" claims that Iraq destroyed its WMD stockpile days before the war began, that the regime had transferred banned weapons to Syria, and that Saddam Hussein was working closely with Al Qaeda.

Who is the messenger for this bombshell? Miller tells us only that she "was permitted to see him from a distance at the sites where he said that material from the arms program was buried. Clad in nondescript clothes and a baseball cap, he pointed to several spots in the sand where he said chemical precursors and other weapons material were buried."

And then there were the terms of this disclosure: "This reporter was not permitted to interview the scientist or visit his home. Nor was she permitted to write about the discovery of the scientist for three days, and the copy was then submitted for a check by military officials. Those officials asked that details of what chemicals were uncovered be deleted."

No proof. No names. No chemicals. Only a baseball cap—and the credibility of Miller and the *Times*—to vouch for a "scientist" who conveniently backs up key claims of the Bush administration.

Miller, who was embedded with MET Alpha, a military unit

searching for WMDs, pumped up her sensational assertions the next day on PBS's *NewsHour with Jim Lehrer*:

> **Q**. Has the unit you've been traveling with found any proof of weapons of mass destruction in Iraq?
>
> **JUDITH MILLER**: Well, I think they found something more than a smoking gun. What they've found . . . is a silver bullet in the form of a person, an Iraqi individual, a scientist, as we've called him, who really worked on the programs, who knows them firsthand.
>
> **Q**: Does this confirm in a way the insistence coming from the U.S. government that after the war, various Iraqi tongues would loosen, and there might be people who would be willing to help?
>
> **JUDITH MILLER**: Yes, it clearly does. . . . That's what the Bush administration has finally done. They have changed the political environment, and they've enabled people like the scientists that MET Alpha has found to come forth.[12]

Oops: The silver bullet got more tarnished as it was examined. Three months later, Miller acknowledged that the scientist was merely "a senior Iraqi military intelligence official." His explosive claims vaporized.

A final note from the Department of Corrections: The *Times* deeply regrets any wars or loss of life that these errors may have contributed to.

Up in Smoke

TOM WOLFE ONCE wrote about a war-happy *Times* correspondent in Vietnam (same idea, different war): The administration was "playing [the reporter] of *The New York Times* like an ocarina, as if they were blowing smoke up his pipe and the finger work was just right and the song was coming forth better than they could have played it themselves."[13]

But who was playing whom? *The Washington Post* reported that while Miller was embedded with MET Alpha, her role in the unit's operations became so central that it became known as the "Judith Miller team." In one instance, she disagreed with a decision to relocate the unit to another area and threatened to file a critical report in the *Times* about the action. When she took her protest to a two-star general, the decision was reversed. One Army officer told the *Post*, "Judith was always issuing threats of either going to *The New York Times* or to the secretary of defense. There was nothing veiled about that threat."[14]

Later, she played a starring role in a ceremony in which MET Alpha's leader was promoted. Other officers were surprised to watch as Miller pinned a new rank on the uniform of Chief Warrant Officer Richard Gonzales. He thanked her for her "contributions" to the unit.[15] In April 2003, MET Alpha traveled to the compound of Iraqi National Congress leader Ahmed Chalabi "at Judy's direction," where they interrogated and took custody of an Iraqi man who was on the Pentagon's wanted list—despite the fact that MET Alpha's only role was to search for WMDs. As one officer told the *Post*, "It's impossible to exaggerate the impact she had on the mission of this unit, and not for the better."

After a year of bogus scoops from Miller, the paper gave itself a bit of cover. Not corrections—just cover. On September 28, 2003, *Times* reporter Douglas Jehl surprisingly kicked the legs out from under Miller's sources. In his story headlined AGENCY BELITTLES INFORMATION GIVEN BY IRAQ DEFECTORS, Jehl revealed:

An internal assessment by the Defense Intelligence Agency has concluded that most of the information provided by Iraqi defectors who were made available by the Iraqi National Congress was of little or no value, according to federal officials briefed on the arrangement.

In addition, several Iraqi defectors introduced to American intelligence agents by the exile organization and its leader, Ahmed Chalabi, invented or exaggerated their credentials as people with direct knowledge of the Iraqi government and its suspected unconventional weapons program, the officials said.

The Iraqi National Congress had made some of these defectors available to . . . *The New York Times*, which reported their allegations about prisoners and the country's weapons program.

Poof. Up in smoke went thousands of words of what can only be called rank propaganda.

This *Times* confession was too little, too late. After an unnecessary war, during a brutal occupation, and several thousand lives later, the *Times* obliquely acknowledged that it had been recycling disinformation. Miller's reports played an invaluable role in the administration's propaganda war. They gave public legitimacy to outright lies, providing what appeared to be independent confirmation of wild speculation and false accusations. "What Miller has done over time seriously violates several *Times'* policies under their code of conduct for news and editorial departments," wrote William E. Jackson in *Editor & Publisher*. "Jayson Blair was only a fluke deviation. . . . Miller strikes right at the core of the regular functioning news machine."[16]

More than that, Miller's false reporting was key to justifying a war.

And the *Times'* unabashed servitude to the administration's war agenda did not end with Iraq.

On September 16, 2003, the *Times* ran a story headlined SENIOR U.S. OFFICIAL TO LEVEL WEAPONS CHARGES AGAINST SYRIA. The stunningly uncritical article was virtually an excerpt of the testimony about to be given that day by outspoken hawk John R. Bolton, undersecretary of state for arms control. The article included this curious caveat: The testimony "was provided to *The New York Times* by individuals who feel that the accusations against Syria have received insufficient attention." The article certainly solved that problem.

The author? Judith Miller—preparing for the next battlefront.

Protesters? What Protesters?

ON OCTOBER 26, 2002, the *Democracy Now!* crew headed to Washington, D.C., to cover a major protest against an attack on Iraq. Although the police in Washington, D.C., no longer issue official estimates of crowd size, they told us unofficially that there were between 150,000 and 200,000 people.

The next day, *The New York Times* reported that "fewer people had attended than organizers had hoped for . . . even though the sun came out." NPR reported "fewer than 10,000" showed up.

It was clear to all of us who were actually *there* (more on this in a moment), including the police, that the size of the crowd was significant. In addition to our broadcast on Pacifica, C-SPAN was carrying the protest live. Anyone watching from home could clearly see the masses of people. And not all media outlets misreported the event. *The Washington Post* headline was ANTIWAR PROTEST LARGEST SINCE '60s; ORGANIZERS SAY 100,000 TURNED OUT.

The *Times* had gotten it so wrong that we had to ask: Was the reporter even there?

Democracy Now! producer Mike Burke got on the case. He recognized the people quoted in the *Times* article: They had spoken at a press conference a few days earlier. So he tracked down each person quoted in the story. There was an MIT professor, a student from the University of North Carolina, and Eli Pariser, a staff person with the organization MoveOn.org.

Pariser confirmed that the *Times* reporter had interviewed him a few days earlier. The MIT professor told Mike the same thing.

The UNC student said, "She did interview me at the rally—on my cell phone. I asked her why she wasn't here. She said she was working on another story." It turns out that the *Times* reporter covering the rally was pulled away to work on the Washington sniper story that day.

Now, we all know that the *Times* has an army of reporters it could deploy to cover any story, but it's a matter of what they care about and where they decide to put their resources.

Three days later, *The New York Times* ran another story on the same protest. The headline declared that the rally "is said to invigorate antiwar movement."

"The turnout startled even organizers, who had taken out permits for 20,000 marchers," stated this new, improved *Times* report. "They expected 30 buses, and were surprised by about 650, coming from as far as Nebraska and Florida." The article continued, "The demonstration on Saturday in Washington drew 100,000 by police estimates and 200,000 by organizers'." An accompanying photo caption noted that the rally was "the biggest antiwar protest since the Vietnam War era."

Who do you believe: *The New York Times* . . . or *The New York Times?*

Democracy Now! attempted to question the reporter and her

editors at the *Times* about their coverage, but the *Times* declined to comment. Finally, after we did our show on the misreporting, the reporter called us and confirmed that she had left the protest before it had even started. She had seen only the early crowds trickling in, not the actual demonstration. When she realized that the rally was much bigger, she called in a correction to her editors, but they didn't change the numbers.

Numerous people who attended or watched the rallies called both NPR and the *Times* to complain. On October 30, NPR ran an on-air correction. Host Robert Siegel stated: "We erroneously reported on *All Things Considered* that the size of the crowd was fewer than 10,000. While Park Service employees gave no official estimate, it is clear that the crowd was substantially larger than that. . . . We apologize for the error."

After *Democracy Now!* ran a story on the rally article discrepancies, producer Kris Abrams asked a *Times* editor, "Why didn't you print a correction stating that your first article was wrong?"

Because we didn't make a mistake, he replied.

"Well, what do you call it, then?" she asked.

A matter of emphasis, he answered.

8

State Media, American Style

Good morning, Baghdad!
—Dan Rather, *CBS Evening News* anchor, describing the message being sent by President Bush with the first bombs on Baghdad, March 19, 2003

George Bush is the president. . . . Wherever he wants me to line up, just tell me where and he'll make the call.
—Dan Rather on *Late Night with David Letterman*, September 17, 2001

One of the things that we don't want to do . . . is to destroy the infrastructure of Iraq because in a few days we're going to own that country.
—Tom Brokaw, *NBC Nightly News*, March 19, 2003

JUST BEFORE THE WAR on Iraq got under way, each of the TV networks had a critical journalistic decision to make: What catchy name should they choose for their special coverage?

The Pentagon had the answer, and MSNBC, NBC, and FOX looked no further: Operation Iraqi Freedom. True, it wasn't the

Pentagon's first choice. It was rumored DoD spinsters originally had another name for the invasion: Operation Iraqi Liberation. But they were concerned about the acronym—OIL.[1]

As if literally adopting the Pentagon's propaganda slogan for their coverage wasn't enough, the networks bombarded viewers with an unending parade of generals and colonels paid to offer on-air analysis. It gave new meaning to the term *general news*.

Once the bombs started falling, the diversity of programming went something like this: live Pentagon press briefing, followed by a White House briefing, followed by the State Department, then overseas for an update from the British Defense Ministry, then to some commercials, then back to the studio for some analysis from the retired generals, then over to CENTCOM, then to reporters embedded with the troops.

The network generals were paid to say—well, pretty much what you would expect them to say. Take Vice Admiral McGinn on MSNBC: "We're coming, and you can't do anything about it."

Then there's the range of questions asked. Take this exchange between Greta Van Susteren and Lieutenant General Thomas McInerney from *On the Record with Greta Van Susteren* on FOX:

> VAN SUSTEREN: General McInerney, to the Apache helicopter today—two POWs. Why were they using an Apache helicop-ter in that battle? Why not use a fighter plane?
>
> MCINERNEY: That's a very good question. . . . [2]

What about whether either of these weapons should be used? And when do they get to the part where they discuss how many Iraqi children died from these amazing weapons exploding in their neighborhoods?

It's basically *This Old House* goes to war: a talk show featuring our lethal hardware and the men who admire it most.

That's the twisted state of affairs that Michael Moore was reacting to shortly after winning an Academy Award for his movie *Bowling for Columbine*: "I would like to call for the immediate removal of all U.S. troops—from CBS, ABC, NBC, FOX, and CNN!"

Add to this slurry of war talk the gung-ho embrace of the practice of embedding reporters in the military; the freezing out of almost all antiwar voices on network news; the attacks on journalists who expressed skepticism about the war (more on that later), and you have to ask the question: If we had state media in the United States, how would it be any different?

Why does the corporate media cheerlead for war? One answer lies in the corporations themselves—the ones that own the major news outlets. At the time of the first Persian Gulf War, CBS was owned by Westinghouse and NBC by General Electric. Two of the major nuclear weapons manufacturers owned two of the major networks. Westinghouse and GE made most of the parts for many of the weapons in the Persian Gulf War. It was no surprise, then, that much of the coverage on those networks looked like a military hardware show. We see reporters in the cockpits of war planes, interviewing pilots about how it feels to be at the controls. We almost never see journalists at the target end, asking people huddled in their homes what it feels like not to know what the next moment will bring.

The media have a responsibility to show the true face of war. It is bloody. It is brutal. Real people die. Women and children are killed. Families are wiped out; villages are razed.

"The coverage of war by the press has one consistent and pernicious theme—the worship of our weapons and our military might," writes Chris Hedges, a veteran war correspondent for *The*

New York Times and the author of *What Every Person Should Know About War.* "Retired officers, breathless reporters, somber news anchors, can barely hold back their excitement, which is perverse and—frankly, to those who do not delight in watching us obliterate other human beings—disgusting. We are folding in on ourselves, losing touch with the outside world, shredding our own humanity and turning war into entertainment and a way to empower ourselves as a nation and individuals.

"None of us are untainted," adds Hedges. "It is the dirty thrill people used to get from watching a public execution. We are hangmen. And the excitement we feel is in direct proportion to the rage and anger we generate around the globe. We will pay for every bomb we drop on Iraq."[3]

Since the first Gulf War, the media have become even more homogenized—and the news more uniform and gung ho. Six huge corporations now control the major U.S. media: Rupert Murdoch's News Corporation (FOX, HarperCollins, *New York Post*, DirecTV, and 34 TV stations), General Electric (NBC, CNBC, MSNBC, Telemundo, Bravo, and 13 TV stations), Time Warner (AOL, CNN, Warner Bros., *Time*, and its 130 magazines), Disney (ABC, Disney Channel, ESPN, 10 TV and 29 radio stations, and Hyperion, our publisher), Viacom (CBS, MTV, Nickelodeon, Paramount Pictures, Simon & Schuster, and 185 U.S. radio stations), and Bertelsmann (Random House and its more than 100 imprints, and Gruner + Jahr and its 80 magazines).

The lack of diversity *behind* the news helps explain the lack of diversity *in* the news. In 2001, the media watchers Fairness and Accuracy in Reporting (FAIR) looked at who appeared on the evening news on ABC, CBS, and NBC. Ninety-two percent of all U.S. sources interviewed were white, 85 percent were male, and where party affiliation was identifiable, 75 percent were Republican.[4]

On radio, it's even worse. In most towns and cities in the

United States, there are many radio stations, but only one right-wing viewpoint. Take the case of Albany, Georgia. Cumulus Media owns 8 of the 15 radio stations in the city; it owns 260 stations nationwide.[5] During the invasion, you couldn't hear the Dixie Chicks on most stations in Albany because Cumulus Media banned the group from its airwaves after lead singer Natalie Maines told a London audience that she was ashamed President George W. Bush was from her home state of Texas. Cumulus even sponsored an event in Louisiana in which a 33,000-pound tractor obliterated a collection of Dixie Chicks CDs, tapes, and other fan memorabilia.

It was just like a good ol'-fashioned book burning.

Then there's radio behemoth Clear Channel Communications. The company went from one radio station in San Antonio, Texas, in 1972 to owning 1,200 radio stations, 36 television stations, and 776,000 advertising displays in 66 countries. The company's explosive expansion occurred in the wake of the Telecommunications Act of 1996, a Clinton/Gore–sponsored giveaway of our airwaves that removed long-standing restrictions on how many stations a single company could own in one listening area.

Clear Channel is hardwired into the Bush political machine. The company co-chair is Tom Hicks, who purchased the Texas Rangers from George W. Bush in 1998, a deal that made Bush a multimillionaire.[6] During the war on Iraq, Clear Channel stations sponsored prowar Rallies for America around the country. After promoting these contrived events, stations reported on them on their news shows as if they were somehow a spontaneous outpouring of support for George W. Bush. One Clear Channel talk show host, who had been named South Carolina Broadcaster of the Year, was forced to attend a prowar rally. She was subsequently fired when she made antiwar statements on the air (see Chapter 10, "Killing the Messenger").

Shortly after 9/11, filmmaker Michael Moore wrote about an e-mail he had received from a radio station manager in Michigan. The manager forwarded Moore a confidential memo from the radio conglomerate that owns his station: Clear Channel. "The company," Moore wrote, "has ordered its stations not to play a list of 150 songs during this 'national emergency.' The list, incredibly, includes 'Bridge Over Troubled Water,' 'Peace Train,' and John Lennon's 'Imagine.'

"Rah-rah war songs, though, are OK," Moore continued. "And then there was this troubling instruction: 'No songs by Rage Against the Machine should be aired.' The entire works of a band are banned? Is this the freedom we fight for? Or does this sound like one of those repressive dictatorships we are told is our new enemy?"[7]

Even that was not enough for the media moguls. They wanted more control. As General Colin Powell led the war on Iraq, his son Michael Powell, chair of the Federal Communications Commission (FCC), led the war on diversity of voices at home. In the spring of 2003, Michael Powell tried to hand over the airwaves and newspapers to fewer and fewer tycoons by further loosening restrictions on how many media outlets a single company could own.

This would enable Rupert Murdoch, the man who brings us the flag-waving FOX News Channel, to control the airwaves of entire cities. That would be fine with Bush and the Powells, since Murdoch is one of their biggest boosters.

Murdoch declared in February 2003, "The greatest thing to come of this [the war] to the world economy, if you could put it that way, would be $US20 a barrel for oil. That's bigger than any tax cut in any country."

Murdoch added that President George W. Bush "will either go down in history as a very great president or he'll crash and burn. I'm optimistic it will be the former by a ratio of two to one."[8]

Murdoch leaves nothing to chance: His FOX News Channel is doing all it can to help.

Former FOX News Channel (FNC) producer Charlie Reina recently revealed that every morning, the staff of the FOX newsroom gets their marching orders. It comes in the form of an executive memo. "The Memo is the Bible. If, on any given day, you notice that the Fox anchors seem to be trying to drive a particular point home, you can bet The Memo is behind it," wrote Reina in a damning letter to the journalism website Poynter Online.

"The Memo was born with the Bush administration, early in 2001, and, intentionally or not, has ensured that the administration's point of view consistently comes across on FNC. This year, of course, the war in Iraq became a constant subject of The Memo." Reina explained, "One day this past spring, just after the U.S. invaded Iraq, The Memo warned us that antiwar protesters would be 'whining' about U.S. bombs killing Iraqi civilians, and suggested they could tell that to the families of American soldiers dying there. Editing copy that morning, I was not surprised when an eager young producer killed a correspondent's report on the day's fighting—simply because it included a brief shot of children in an Iraqi hospital."[9]

Reina says that during the buildup to the invasion, an "eager-to-please newsroom chief ordered the removal of a graphic quoting UN weapons inspector Hans Blix as saying his team had not yet found WMDs in Iraq. Fortunately, the electronic equipment was quicker on the uptake (and less susceptible to office politics) than the toady and displayed the graphic before his order could be obeyed."

Reina notes, "Virtually no one of authority in the newsroom makes a move unmeasured against management's politics, actual or perceived. At the Fair and Balanced network, everyone knows management's point of view, and in case they're not sure how to get it on air, The Memo is there to remind them."

But it's not just the newsroom that gets FOX's executive memos. In the days following 9/11, FOX news chief Roger Ailes wrote a secret letter to President Bush's senior political adviser Karl Rove, saying of the decision to go to war, "The American public would tolerate waiting and would be patient, but only as long as they were convinced that Bush was using the harshest measures possible. Support would dissipate if the public did not see Bush acting harshly."[10]

Ailes is used to doling out advice to the Bushes—he was the chief media consultant for Bush I. He also worked for Ronald Reagan and Richard Nixon. As Reina put it, "Everyone [at FOX] understands that FNC is, to a large extent, 'Roger's Revenge'—against what he considers a liberal, pro-Democrat media establishment that has shunned him for decades."

Expecting FOX News to report real news is about as silly as waiting for George Bush and Dick Cheney to tell the truth. But at least there's public broadcasting, right? The people's media, supported by public money, always looking out for the public interest? Sorry, but . . .

When actors Tyne Daly and John Valentine decided in spring 2003 to record a radio adaptation of John Hersey's *Hiroshima,* they naturally approached National Public Radio. Daly and Valentine had assembled a star-studded cast of actors to record this Pulitzer Prize–winning author's book, which told the story of the first atomic bombing through the eyes of six Hiroshima survivors. The actors wanted to introduce this classic to a new generation.

NPR turned them down. NPR spokeswoman Jenny Lawhorn told *The Washington Post*: "It was NPR's sense that this was a pitch

"One for the People, Zero for the Knuckleheads!"

On March 19, 2003, the night that the bombing of Iraq began, musician Ani DiFranco asked me to come speak at her concert at the New Jersey Performing Arts Center. The beginning of the war was a somber moment, but the show had to go on: 3,000 people were packed into the concert hall in Newark, New Jersey, to see Ani, a wonderful artist, perform.

Ani asked me to introduce her, to explain the importance of independent media in a time of war, and to let people know where they could get alternative information. There were also going to be tables in the lobby offering political information.

As usual, I was running late. As I raced over to the concert hall, I called Ani's cell phone. I was surprised when she answered—I thought she was getting ready to go on stage. "What are you doing answering this phone?" I asked.

She said, "I don't know if the concert's going to go on. They'll probably close down the concert if you go on the stage. They are telling us that no political speech is allowed."

Ani didn't miss a beat. "We are willing to risk it."

It turns out Ani's New Jersey Performing Arts Center event was booked by Clear Channel Communications. While Clear Channel hadn't issued any edicts about Ani's show, the managers of the concert hall took it upon themselves to try to muzzle us.

Ani is no stranger to politics or censorship. She is part of a great tradition of performers whose songs are a mix of poetry and social commentary. She sings what she sees, and that has gotten her into trouble. In July 2001, CBS's *Late Show with David Letterman* canceled her appearance after she refused to substitute a

that clearly represented a reaction to looming events [the Iraqi war], and from a news perspective it was premature."[11]

Premature? The book was published in 1946! I could only think how appropriate it was to be turned down on the hundredth more "upbeat" song for "Subdivision," a song about white fear and racism.

As we were heading into the New Jersey Performing Arts Center, security people searched us and our bags. We thought they were looking for weapons; I guess they found them. In a backpack, we had hundreds of flyers announcing *Democracy Now!*'s special coverage of the imminent invasion of Iraq. They said we couldn't bring the flyers in. I asked if they were going through everyone's bags, reading their literature. We ditched the backpack but not before we had stuffed hundreds of flyers into our pockets.

I was rushed backstage by one of Ani's people, along with *Democracy Now!* correspondent Jeremy Scahill, who had just flown in from Baghdad, and antiwar activist Miles Solay. Ani's staff warned Miles to zip up his sweatshirt to cover the subversive logo of his organization, Not in Our Name, which was printed across his T-shirt.

The woman then quickly instructed us, "Take the microphone and make your statement about media in a time of war. If they close the mike, which we expect them to do, there will be another mike right behind you. That's Ani's mike. Reach back, pick it up, and just keep on talking. If they close down the show . . ." She just shrugged. Ani would rather be kicked out than censored.

The house lights dimmed, and we got up and gave our speeches. Jeremy threw some of the banned flyers out into the audience. The mikes kept working. We introduced Ani, the crowd gave a warm round of applause, and Ani came out.

"That's one for the people," she shouted, "and zero for the knuckleheads!" The crowd roared their approval, and the show went on.

anniversary of the birth of George Orwell. He was the author of *1984*, a novel about an all-controlling society in which all old works are burned and "newspeak" replaces history.

And so the actors turned to Pacifica Radio, the only independent media network broadcasting in the United States, where their voices could be heard. On August 6, 2003, the fifty-eighth anniversary of the atomic bombing of Hiroshima, listeners throughout the country heard a vivid reading of this wartime classic.

Maybe NPR was right to be concerned about the impact this reading would have on listeners. It captured exactly what war is. As Shigeko Sasamori, a Hiroshima survivor who observed the recording of the program, told *Democracy Now!*, "When I listened to that program my heart is so calm. Yet from my eyes, tears came down like hot water. . . . My memory came back. I thought of all the people that died. . . . [It was] the most horrible war weapon that Japan had ever heard. Never, never should we use them [nuclear weapons] again."

She implored, "Everybody, not just presidents and congressmen, need to be educated about how war is a horrible thing. But time passes, and they forget. . . . I have a mission to tell people how terrible it was so that people can recognize that war is nothing good. . . . I have to help people understand—not just understand, take action so that there is no more war. No more Hiroshima."

When the voices of victims—be they in Japan, Iraq, Afghanistan, the West Bank—are heard in the media, their lives begin to be valued in the same way as those of the people who died in the World Trade Center. We've heard a lot about the victims of 9/11, as we should. But the lives taken in retaliation for theirs are blank spaces in our collective consciousness. The more the lives of victims are valued, the less killing there will be. Because people rise up and object when they know that someone innocent has died. They don't ask about a person's political party or religious persuasion.

Americans care, but it's tough to care when you don't know

what's going on. That ignorance is what the warmakers count on—and what the corporate media delivers.

Look Who's Talking

TELEVISION PUNDITS AND "experts" are often identified benignly as simply former government officials or analysts. Their credibility is boosted by their seeming impartiality.

What you aren't told is their current affiliation, in which they may be profiting from the policy they are advocating. Thanks to the revolving door that spins between government and private business, public officials morph seamlessly into company directors and private consultants with a financial stake in the very issues they hold forth on. Their real expertise is in enriching themselves.

On March 20, 2002, *Democracy Now!* featured two guests to speak about whether the United States should invade Iraq. One was former U.S. Attorney General Ramsey Clark, who is founder of the International Action Center. The other was James Woolsey, a former director of the CIA and a partner at the Washington, D.C., law firm of Shea & Gardner. As CIA director, Woolsey was paymaster to the Iraqi National Congress; now his law firm represents the CIA-funded group. But you never heard about these connections during Woolsey's numerous television appearances.

Here is my conversation with Clark and Woolsey. Decide for yourself whether it matters who's paying someone to talk:

AMY GOODMAN: James Woolsey, what about the involvement of the Iraqi National Congress, the Iraqi opposition that has been funded to the tune of, I think, something like just under $100 million by the U.S. government? What role do you think that should play in what you've laid out as the scenario that would topple Saddam Hussein?

JAMES WOOLSEY: I look on the INC somewhat like Solidarity in Poland in the early 1980s. It's a loose collection of organizations, all of which are working in one way or another toward a free Iraq. . . .

GOODMAN: James Woolsey, you have been very much pushing forward the Iraqi National Congress, but your firm itself, Shea & Gardner . . . is a paid foreign agent for the Iraqi National Congress, is that right?

WOOLSEY: Everybody but me. The INC came to me two or three years ago and asked if I would represent them in Washington. . . . I declined my—I sealed myself off on this representation from my firm, both financially and substantively. So I say what I want to on Iraq. But the firm does represent the INC.

GOODMAN: So it profits from the [group,] and you're a partner who profit-shares with the firm.

WOOLSEY: No, no, no, I said I sealed myself off financially from it. I take no fees from the INC.

GOODMAN: Though your firm does represent them. Do you see that as an issue on—

WOOLSEY: No. Not by anybody who's fair-minded. Not by anybody who's fair-minded.

RAMSEY CLARK: Sure, it's a clear conflict of interest. I mean, money's fungible, you know? If a million dollars comes into the firm, the firm is a million dollars better off and it can pay Mr. Woolsey . . .

WOOLSEY: Mr. Clark . . .

CLARK: . . . any part of that that they want to . . .

WOOLSEY: [talking over Ramsey Clark] Mr. Clark has no idea how our firm's compensation is worked and I'm telling you . . .

CLARK: I know how money works, and I know it's a clear conflict of interest. I know Shea & Gardner is not involved in this type of business. [The INC is] there for one reason, and that's because you're there.

WOOLSEY: That's not true.

CLARK: That's the only reason they came there. They'd have gone to other firms otherwise, and that's obvious.

WOOLSEY: That's nonsense.

Educating Charlie Rose

ON MARCH 12, 2003, I was a guest on *The Charlie Rose Show* on PBS. It was a week before Bush invaded Iraq, and Charlie wanted to bring in someone who could explain what the millions of antiwar protesters around the world were so concerned about.

Things went fine until I began to draw the links between who owns the media corporations and what the media says:

AMY GOODMAN: NBC, CBS, and ABC—they have provided a very serious disservice to the people of this country when it comes to a true debate around war. Most people are opposed to war, yet the vast majority of guests across the board on the networks are for war. They're a parade of retired generals and—

CHARLIE ROSE: It's not dictated by whoever the corporate ownership is. I promise you that—they are not dictating. They are not saying we want you to have more generals who are in favor of the war than you have generals who are in opposition to the war. That's just not the way it works.

GOODMAN: They don't have to *say* that. They hire the people who will do just that.

ROSE: The argument I have, with respect, is Peter Jennings, Tom Brokaw, and Dan Rather—a whole range of people—are journalists who have paid their dues, and they are very competent journalists who are reporting for newsmagazines and those broadcasts—

GOODMAN: It's not about just one person.

ROSE: You are suggesting that because they choose the people—

GOODMAN: Let me quote Dan Rather himself on BBC: He says he thinks he would be necklaced. He thinks that he cannot simply speak out and ask the kinds of questions that should be asked. That's quoting Dan Rather.

ROSE: I'm surprised to hear that. Don't doubt that he said—or don't know that he said it—but I'm not quarreling with your source. I'm surprised since he and I are colleagues at *60 Minutes II* that he doesn't . . . I just don't believe that that is his . . . that that is his opinion that he can't ask anything he wants to. I think he felt like he could ask anything of Saddam Hussein he wanted to [during his February 2003 interview with the Iraqi president] and he said to me [he] chose the questions he wanted to ask. Not dictated by anybody in New York.

GOODMAN: Well, I would just challenge the mainstream media to open up the ranks to provide a forum for the full diversity of voices that represent this country and people around the world.

ROSE: That's a perfectly good idea. I don't have any argument with that idea. I mean, I do have an argument with it sort of—with what you have said about who they listen to in terms of their reporting because I have such respect for the people going to the battlefields and reporting from New York in terms of their own integrity. It's wrong to impugn their integrity.

GOODMAN: I was just quoting Dan Rather.

Let's let Dan speak for himself. On BBC *Newsnight* on May 16, 2002, Rather talked candidly about how he and other journalists censor themselves. "There was a time in South Africa that people would put flaming tires around people's necks if they dissented," he said. "And in some ways the fear is that you will be necklaced here, you will have a flaming tire of lack of patriotism put around your neck. Now it is that fear that keeps journalists from asking the toughest of the tough questions, and to continue to bore in on the tough questions so often. And again, I am humbled to say, I do not except myself from this criticism."

Rather went on to talk about how the self-censorship of journalists occurs. "It starts with a feeling of patriotism within oneself. . . . And one finds oneself saying: 'I know the right question, but you know what? This is not exactly the right time to ask it.'"

I gained some more insight into how censorship works from Al Hunt. Hunt is a cohost on CNN's *Capital Gang,* a weekly show that features four journalists debating the issues of the week, often joined by a politician who has been in the news. When it came to issues of war and peace, the chatty quartet largely echoed the Democrats and Republicans: They support war (actually, the biggest skeptic about the war on *Capital Gang* was its most conservative flack, Robert Novak). So it's not really much of a debate.

Capital Gang was coming to New York and Hunt—the executive Washington editor of *The Wall Street Journal* and one of the more liberal *Gang* members—came on *Democracy Now!* in March 2002. I asked him why *Capital Gang* didn't include some of the great intellectual scholar-activists of our time, such as Howard Zinn, Cornel West, and Noam Chomsky. These people are virtually excluded from the mainstream networks.

Hunt replied, "During the Persian Gulf War, one of the great doves was Pat Buchanan. Now, was Pat Buchanan an antiwar activist then? He was every bit as much against the war as Cornel West and Howard Zinn or Noam Chomsky."

I replied, "There is a vast array of other people outside of right-wing extremists, and they can be interviewed as well on the networks."

"I agree with you," said Hunt. But he insisted that those decisions aren't up to him. I pressed him: "Who decides who gets on the networks?"

"Walter Isaacson makes the ultimate decision," he answered.

I then raised an October 2001 memo from Isaacson, then chairman and CEO of CNN, that had been leaked to *The New York Times* and *The Washington Post* (Hunt said he had not seen it). Isaacson said when showing disturbing images of civilian casualties and destruction of villages in Afghanistan, reporters should "make sure we do not seem to be simply reporting from their vantage or perspective." Another memo written by CNN executive Rick Davis said if correspondents cannot "make the points clearly," the anchors could make the points with the following sample statements:

> We must keep in mind, after seeing reports like this from Taliban-controlled areas, that these U.S. military actions are in response to a terrorist attack that killed close to 5,000 innocent people in the U.S.
>
> *or*

We must keep in mind, after seeing reports like this, that
the Taliban regime in Afghanistan continues to harbor
terrorists who have praised the September 11 attacks that
killed close to 5,000 innocent people in the U.S.

or

The Pentagon has repeatedly stressed that it is trying to
minimize civilian casualties in Afghanistan, even as the
Taliban regime continues to harbor terrorists who are
connected to the September 11 attacks that claimed
thousands of innocent lives in the U.S.[12]

Isaacson told *The Washington Post* that it "seems perverse to
focus too much on the casualties or hardship in Afghanistan."

Quick—what do dead women and children in Afghanistan
have to do with 9/11? Absolutely nothing, except that the Bush administration wants you to believe that somehow killing a poor family in Asia or the Middle East makes us safer against attacks from
Saudi terrorists.

Isaacson added, "I want to make sure we're not used as a propaganda platform."

I'm a little confused: Was he concerned about being used by
the Pentagon or the Taliban?

Flacking for the Pentagon

The major evening news shows (ABC, CBS, NBC, CNN, FOX, and PBS) during the first three weeks of the Iraq war:

Sources who were prowar	64%
Sources who were antiwar	10%
U.S. sources who were prowar	71%
U.S. sources who were antiwar	3%
U.S. sources who were military	47%
Sources who were current or former government employees	63%
Sources from academia, think tanks, and nongovernmental organizations	4%
U.S. government sources from the military	68%
Number of current or former government officials on TV	840
Number of those who were antiwar	4
Sources on FOX News who were prowar	81%

Source: "Amplifying Officials, Squelching Dissent," by Steve Rendall and Tara Broughel, *Extra!*, May/June 2003.

9

In Bed with the Military

Without censorship, things can get terribly confused in the public mind.

—GENERAL WILLIAM C. WESTMORELAND, U.S. MILITARY COMMANDER IN VIETNAM

IT WAS BOUND TO happen. People start sleeping together, and the next thing you know, they're talking commitment.

That was the basic theme underlying most of the embedded reporting during the invasion of Iraq. As reporters rode shotgun on tanks and Humvees and slept alongside soldiers in Iraq, what journalistic distance there ever was vanished into the sands of the desert.

Don't take it from me. Take it from Gordon Dillow of *The Orange County Register*, who wrote: "The biggest problem I faced as an embed with the Marine grunts was that I found myself doing what journalists are warned from J-school not to do: I found myself falling in love with my subject. I fell in love with 'my' Marines."[1]

And CBS's Jim Axelrod, who was embedded with—I would

say in bed with—the 3rd Infantry Division, echoed: "This will sound like I've drunk the Kool-Aid, but I found embedding to be an extremely positive experience. . . . We got great stories and they got very positive coverage."[2]

From the Pentagon's point of view, this one-sided reporting worked like a charm. "Americans and people around the world are seeing firsthand the wonderful dedication and discipline of the coalition forces," declared Pentagon spokeswoman Victoria Clarke.[3]

For Clarke, a former top executive with Hill & Knowlton, the world's largest public relations firm, nothing was left to chance. "We put the same planning and preparation into this [embed program] as military planners put into the war effort," she said.[4]

The embed program for the invasion of Iraq was the culmination of years of effort and experimentation by the Pentagon to control the media during war. In World War II and Vietnam, many reporters were in the field alongside soldiers. But as the Southeast Asian quagmire deepened, the Pentagon became exasperated with journalists who reported the increasingly grim realities that they saw: dispirited troops, futile efforts by the United States to win the "hearts and minds" of the Vietnamese through carpet bombing, and even occasional dispatches about war crimes. It became an article of faith that "the media lost Vietnam"—as if the American public would otherwise have gladly accepted the staggering toll of 58,000 Americans killed, 300,000 wounded, and at least 2 million Vietnamese killed in a pointless war.

For the 1983 invasion of Grenada, the military tried a different approach. There would be no journalists at all. No photos of civilian casualties, no pictures of dead or wounded Americans, at least in the short term. Reporters who tried to reach the Caribbean island by boat were turned back at gunpoint.

When U.S. troops invaded Panama in 1989, the military

promised greater access, but on terms of its choosing. During the initial bloody assault, hundreds of frustrated reporters were left to wait on planes in Costa Rica and Miami. Reporters were not allowed in during the first day or two, when 23 American soldiers died and 265 were wounded.

"About one hundred fifty reporters were held in Miami," said *Democracy Now!* cohost Juan Gonzalez, who was one of the reporters held hostage by the U.S. military. "After much protest, we were flown to Panama, where we were held at Howard Air Force Base. They wouldn't let us off the base. But after we protested, they agreed to send reporters at our own risk. At that point, El Chorillo had been destroyed." El Chorillo was the poor neighborhood in Panama City that the U.S. military bombed and burned to the ground, killing hundreds of Panamanians and leaving thousands homeless.

In the 1991 Persian Gulf War, the Pentagon took media control to new levels. During the initial assault, a news blackout was declared. On one aircraft carrier, reporters were actually rounded up and detained in a special room at the start of the fighting.[5] The Pentagon permitted only pool coverage, with a handful of reporters allowed onto the battlefield. Frontline dispatches were subject to censorship and delays. Reporters who defied Pentagon restrictions and ventured out on their own to report on the war were subject to arrest. Nearly fifty reporters were detained and some arrested for attempting to report on the war independently.[6]

The media bargained politely with the Pentagon over media restrictions prior to the Persian Gulf War, but the big newspapers were more concerned with ensuring that their correspondents got the precious few coveted pool assignments to cover the war. It was left to a group of alternative news outlets to play hardball. On January 10, 1991, Pacifica Radio, *The Nation, Harper's, The Village Voice, LA Weekly,* and others sued the Pentagon, charging that the media restrictions were unconstitutional. None of the big television networks or the major dailies joined the suit or contributed friend-of-the-court briefs. Getting them even to cover it was futile. After the war, a judge ruled that restricting the press from the battlefield was subject to judicial review even in wartime, but with the war over, he threw out the lawsuit, calling it moot.

As the invasion of Iraq showed, it was hardly moot.

The large corporate media did complain loudly about their treatment in the 1991 war—after the war was over. By and large, they acquiesced to the heavy-handed Pentagon restrictions prior to the first shot being fired.[7] During the Gulf War, the Pentagon managed not only to protect itself, but also its friend Saudi Arabia, telling media outlets they had to apply to the Saudi government for approval to cover U.S. troops there.

And a lot of good it did to go along to get along. As former *New York Times* executive editor Howell Raines said of the press after the war, "We lost. They managed us completely. If it were an athletic contest, the score would be 100 to 1."[8]

A committee of representatives of some of the largest U.S. news organizations came to the same conclusion in a 1991 review of Gulf War coverage: "In the end, the combination of security review and the use of the pool system as a form of censorship made the Gulf War the most undercovered major conflict in modern American history. In a free society, there is simply no place for such overwhelming control by the government. . . . Television, print, and radio alike start with one sobering realization: There was virtually no coverage of the Gulf ground war until it was over."[9]

The program of embedded reporting was the logical next step for the Pentagon. The idea was for the Pentagon to give the appearance of access during the invasion of Iraq, but to maintain total control. The wild card was the press. The Pentagon was counting on reporters to be awed and compliant. The generals were not disappointed.

Not surprisingly, most of the "in-beds" were simply a megaphone for the views of the military who were keeping them alive. The fawning reports became a grand display of the Stockholm syndrome, where hostages come to identify and sympathize with their captors. "These journalists do not have access to their own transportation," noted *New York Times* war correspondent Chris Hedges. "They depend on the military for everything, from food to a place to sleep. They look to the soldiers around them for protection. When they feel the fear of hostile fire, they identify and seek to protect those who protect them. They become part of the team. It is a natural reaction. I have felt it."[10]

The embeds were supposedly there to offer frontline coverage. But what can you cover from the turret of a tank? You can cover what it feels like to shoot people. Then you can get the gunner's response and the commander's spin. That is one narrow slice of the war experience.

What about the victims? Shouldn't reporters be embedded in Iraqi communities and hospitals? Shouldn't there be reporters embedded in the peace movement to give us an intimate understanding of what catalyzed the largest coordinated international protest in history, when 30 million people around the globe marched against war on February 15, 2003?

A few reporters were honest about what was going on—off-camera, overseas, in private, and talking and writing among colleagues. That's where journalists told the real story of how embedding worked.

Like Dan Rather. He understood the Pentagon program for what it was: spin control. In an unusually candid interview about the "war on terror" with the BBC, he said, "There has never been an American war, small or large, in which access has been so limited as this one. Limiting access, limiting information to cover the backsides of those who are in charge of the war, is extremely dangerous and cannot and should not be accepted." Unfortunately, he added, "it has been accepted by the American people. And the current administration revels in that, they relish that, and they take refuge in that."[11]

Rather leaves out a key participant as he doles out blame here: the media themselves. Networks and newspapers didn't just go along passively with the Pentagon's rules of journalistic engagement. They actively helped to limit our perspective on what was happening in Iraq.

John Donvan, who worked the Iraq invasion as a unilateral—unembedded—reporter for ABC, told a classic story. "Our car was literally looted in Safwan the first day. The very first day, I reported that it was unstable in the place where just yesterday people were cheering. And our editors in New York were saying, 'Well, John, could you get us some of those pictures of people cheering?'"[12]

Jonathan Foreman, an embed for the *New York Post,* also found himself being discouraged from telling the truth—even about the soldiers he was with. "On more than one occasion," he said, "I'd be writing stories about how exhausted and pissed off the troops were." But when the paper came out, "I'd find they were topped by a headline like TROOPS CAN'T WAIT TO GET THEIR HANDS ON THE REPUBLICAN GUARD."[13]

Journalism *was* a respectable profession. Journalists are supposed to expand our understanding, taking risks to provide an independent view of the world. We trust reporters to speak truth to power, to ask the uncomfortable questions. In war, journalists should offer a nuanced mosaic, telling stories of everybody from the troops to civilians to victims to families back home. You form your opinions based on the full range of views that you hear. But you've got to hear from all sides, and that was what was so deeply compromised by what happened with the embedding of reporters during the invasion of Iraq.

Point-and-Shoot Journalism: "I Went Over to the Dark Side"

WITH SOME EMBEDDED reporters, the line between journalist and soldier vanished as soon as the troops started moving toward Baghdad. The most startling case in point was Jules Crittenden, a reporter for the *Boston Herald* embedded with the 3rd Infantry Division. Crittenden posted a diary on Poynter Online, a journalism website, where he described what happened as "his" division entered Baghdad:[14]

> It was here I went over to the dark side. I spotted the silhouettes of several Iraqi soldiers looking at us from the shadows twenty feet to our left. I shouted, "There's three of the f——right there."
>
> "Where are the f——?" Howison said, spinning around in his hatch.
>
> "The f——are right there," I said, pointing.
>
> "There?" he said, opening up with the 50. I saw one man's body splatter as the large-caliber bullets ripped it up. The man behind him appeared to be rising, and was cut down by repeated bursts.
>
> "There's another f——over there," I told Howison. The two soldiers in the crew hatch with me started firing their rifles, but I think Howison was the one who got him, firing through the metal plate the soldier was hiding behind.

If this sounds like an anguished confession of a reporter's culpability, Crittenden certainly didn't mean it that way. "Now that I have assisted in the deaths of three human beings in the war I was sent to cover, I'm sure there are some people who will question my ethics, my objectivity, etc.," he wrote. "I'll keep the argument short. Screw them, they weren't there. But they are welcome to join me next time if they care to test their professionalism."

Pillow Talk: What the In-Beds Tell Each Other, but Don't Tell You

The Baghdad fight was a close enough thing that at one point a marine gave me a hand grenade to throw if the enemy started to overwhelm us. It had been more than thirty years since I'd held a grenade (I'd been an Army sergeant in Vietnam), and I knew that my having it violated written and unwritten rules. Still, it felt comforting in my hand.

—Gordon Dillow, columnist for *The Orange County Register,* embedded with the U.S. Marines

It was difficult. We were dressing like them and we were eating and sleeping with them and we became a part of them.

—Rick Leventhal, embedded correspondent, FOX News Channel

This project is flat-out cool. It's *Band of Brothers* in real time . . . Through my long contact with the Marines (I have been a speaker at their media training seminars for ten years), I have been embedded with that noble service. . . . I came away with a dim view of many so-called international journalists, who so often report with their convictions rather than their eyes.

—Chuck Stevenson, producer for CBS News' *48 Hours Investigates,* embedded with the U.S. Marines

Finding fault with Crittenden is easy. As F. Marshall Maher wrote for the media watch group FAIR: "War correspondents are civilians, afforded specific protection under the Fourth Geneva Convention. By picking up a weapon or assisting in the fighting, they not only strip themselves of that protection, they also put every other journalist covering the war in jeopardy by blurring the line separating reporters from combatants."[15]

The embedding process is the best single move the American military has ever made in its relations with the press.

—Bob Arnot, correspondent for MSNBC and NBC News, embedded with the U.S. Marines

During my travels with the Marines, I couldn't shake the sense that we were cheerleaders on the team bus. . . . Much of the Marine command that I met saw us not as neutral journalists who had a job to do, but as instruments to reflect the accomplishments and glory of the United States Marine Corps. A press officer leaned back in the chow hall one day and scanned a color spread in *Time* on Marines preparing for battle. "Money can't buy this kind of recruitment campaign," he said.

—John Burnett, correspondent for NPR, embedded with the U.S. Marines[16]

I was a noncombatant, but I told them I'd be willing to pick up a gun if I had to. They're pretty easy to use. It's point and shoot.

—Chantal Escoto, *The Leaf-Chronicle,* Clarksville, Tennessee[17]

At least Crittenden was being honest. The prowar propaganda that appeared on the networks and in bigger publications resulted in the deaths of far more than three people.

Unfortunately, Crittenden couldn't stop conflating the role of a journalist with that of a conqueror. In April 2003, he was caught bringing into the United States a large painting taken from one of Saddam's palaces. He defended his actions, stating it was "the time-honored tradition among soldiers of bringing home reminders of some of the most intense experiences of their lives."[18]

Yes, pillaging certainly is time-honored—among marauding soldiers, not journalists. But Crittenden had long since forgotten which helmet he was wearing. And the *Herald*'s publisher, Patrick J. Purcell, remained upbeat about his embed. "I am very proud of the job Jules Crittenden has done covering the front lines of the war," he said after Crittenden's pillaging had been exposed.[19] No criminal charges were filed against Crittenden, and U.S. Customs eventually returned the confiscated items.

Crittenden took a parting swipe at his colleagues. Complaining about their coverage of his war booty escapade, he sniffed, "I will only say that it was not of high caliber."

I'm confused—was he referring to their weapons or their words? With embedded reporters, you never know.

The Old Postmortem

A FEW MONTHS after President George W. Bush prematurely declared the war on Iraq over, it was safe for corporate journalists to begin the time-honored ritual of postmortem introspection.

"We never show you how horrible it really is," admitted John Donvan of ABC News. "And we talk all the time about that:

Should we break that taboo? And if we did, that would have huge impact. Huge."[20]

Unfortunately, Donvan's useful insights about the reality of war had no impact. He was speaking in July 2003 to a conference of other journalists. And most of the guilty morning-after confessions took place in journalism trade magazines.

The impact of Iraq coverage *was* huge—for all the wrong reasons. On September 10, 2003, CNN's top war correspondent, Christiane Amanpour, discussed why on CNBC's *Topic A With Tina Brown*: "I think the press was muzzled, and I think the press self-muzzled. I'm sorry to say, but certainly television and, perhaps, to a certain extent, my station was intimidated by the administration and its foot soldiers at FOX News. And it did, in fact, put a climate of fear and self-censorship, in my view, in terms of the kind of broadcast work we did."[21]

Amanpour, who appeared on the show with former Pentagon spinmistress Victoria Clarke and author Al Franken, was asked if there were stories that she didn't report. "It's not a question of couldn't do it, it's a question of tone," she said. "It's a question of being rigorous. It's really a question of really asking the questions. All of the entire body politic in my view, whether it's the administration, the intelligence, the journalists, whoever, did not ask enough questions, for instance, about weapons of mass destruction. I mean, it looks like this was disinformation at the highest levels."

Victoria Clarke sputtered, "It's just—it's—it's categorically untrue."

FOX spokeswoman Irena Briganti said later, "Given the choice, it's better to be viewed as a foot soldier for Bush than a spokeswoman for Al Qaeda."[22]

"You're with us or you're against us" is a false choice. This

FOX-hole mentality is lethal for journalism, and it endangers a democratic society.

In May 1999, I asked Amanpour about CNN's prowar bias—which certainly didn't begin with the invasion of Iraq. Our exchange took place at the Newseum in New York; it was part of the ceremonies for the George Polk Award, which *Democracy Now!* won for our *Drilling and Killing* documentary.

I asked about CNN's use of retired military officers and its exclusion of voices of the antiwar movement. Wouldn't this always slant the news toward supporting war? And why not include voices of the antiwar movement in their analyses?

Amanpour's disembodied image was videoconferenced in from Bosnia into this auditorium of journalists. She responded flippantly, "I suggest they [peace activists] offer their services to CNN and the other organizations. I suggest that most people who want to offer their services do."

Amanpour's tone then changed to exasperation. "Look, this is way above what I do. I have no control over what the organization does. They feel that it adds to their content. I agree with you. Perhaps we should have a range of people with different views."

Perhaps? Isn't this a basic tenet of journalism? CNN's chief international correspondent left little hope that she would advocate such a crazy idea.

10

Killing the Messenger

There is no flag large enough to cover the shame of killing innocent people.

—HOWARD ZINN

TROUBLE CAME EARLY ON April 8, 2003. At 7:45 a.m., Tareq Ayyoub, chief Baghdad correspondent for the Arab news service Al-Jazeera, was standing on the roof of the network's Baghdad bureau, intently narrating a pitched battle between Iraqi troops and two American tanks that had earlier appeared on the nearby Al-Jumhuriya Bridge. Ayyoub's cameraman, an Iraqi named Zuheir, was panning back and forth from the battle to the reporter for the accompanying shots.

Suddenly, the sound of gunfire was drowned out. An American fighter jet came swooping in low across the city. Ayyoub and Zuheir instinctively looked up and saw the jet bank its wing and head straight for where they were standing. "The plane was flying so low that those of us downstairs thought it would land on the roof—that's how close it was," recounted Ayyoub's colleague, Maher Abdullah, to Robert Fisk of the London *Independent*.[1]

Inside the bureau, Ayyoub's other colleagues could hear the rocket launch from the plane. There was a high-pitched whine, followed by the thunderous roar of an explosion. "It was a direct hit—the missile actually exploded against our electrical generator," Abdullah recalled. Colleagues frantically scooped up the shattered body of 35-year-old Ayyoub and carried him out in a blanket to an ambulance. But it was too late. "Tareq died almost at once," said Abdullah. The cameraman was injured, but survived.

Moments later and less than a mile away, the journalists and staff of Abu Dhabi Television—which is written in large blue letters on the roof of their building—took cover in their offices. They had just heard that the United States had bombed Al-Jazeera. Twenty-five staff members huddled in the basement, phoning and pleading over the air for someone to help save them. Again, their pleas fell on deaf ears. U.S. soldiers battered their offices with artillery. Miraculously, there were no serious injuries.

Just before noon, it was the turn of the international press corps. At the Palestine Hotel, where a hundred unembedded reporters were staying, many watched in horror as a U.S. tank positioned on the Al-Jumhuriya Bridge slowly rotated its gun in their direction. A French television crew filmed the armored behemoth as it took aim and suddenly, with no warning, unleashed a round into the side of the towering hotel. The bomb struck the fifteenth floor, making a direct hit on the room serving as a bureau for Reuters, the international news agency. A veteran Ukrainian cameraman for Reuters, Taras Protsyuk, 35, was killed instantly. Jose Couso, 37, a cameraman for Telecinco Spanish television, who was filming one floor below, was also killed. Three other international journalists were seriously injured.[2]

That afternoon, as the news began to buzz across international datelines, spokesmen at U.S. Central Command headquarters in Qatar offered justifications. They claimed the tank had been responding to "significant enemy fire from the Palestine Hotel in Baghdad."[3] A parade of military spokespeople repeated this claim, saying it was the fault of Iraqi forces that had been attacking from civilian locations such as the Palestine.

American networks chimed right in. Speaking on *Larry King Live* that night, CNN military commentator General Wesley Clark assured viewers, "It's a case of a very unfortunate accident of war. People were in the wrong place at the wrong time. . . . You can't tell the troops that they can't shoot back when they're being shot at. . . . The United States wouldn't deliberately kill journalists."[4]

Wrong place, wrong time—in their offices?

The foreign media treated these incidents very differently than their American colleagues. "We can only conclude that the U.S. Army deliberately and without warning targeted journalists," declared the international press watch group Reporters Without Borders. Robert Fisk of the London *Independent* was even more blunt, declaring that the attacks "look very much like murder." After all, the U.S. military was well aware that reporters were working from the Palestine Hotel. And in an interview with the French magazine *Le Nouvel Observateur*, the unit's tank commander made no mention of hostile fire from Iraqi civilians in the area of the hotel.[5]

Journalists who saw the attacks scoffed at the claim that gunfire had come either from the hotel or from Al-Jazeera's offices. Besides, they asked, if people had been shooting from the streets, why had the tank targeted the fifteenth floor? Al-Jazeera noted that on February 24, it had delivered a letter to Pentagon spokesperson Victoria Clarke giving precise coordinates for its bureau.

It might have been the Arab news service's biggest mistake.

Victoria Clarke was unmoved by the evidence. "Our forces

came under fire," the Pentagon flack insisted. The American troops simply "exercised their inherent right to self-defense. . . . [Baghdad] is not a safe place, you should not be there."

That explanation confirmed what many journalists feared: Rather than ensure this would never happen again, the Pentagon was using the journalists' deaths as a pretext to warn other reporters—those who were not embedded with the U.S. military—to leave the battlefield.

"We were targeted because the Americans don't want the world to see the crimes they are committing against the Iraqi people," said Al-Jazeera Baghdad reporter Majed Abdel Hadi. David Chater, Baghdad correspondent for Sky News in Britain, wondered aloud whether unembedded journalists would be able to continue reporting from Iraq. "How are we going to continue to do this," he asked, "if American tanks are targeting us?"[6]

That may be exactly the message the Pentagon wanted to send.

Unilateral Targets

THE PENTAGON WAS eager to accommodate the seven hundred reporters embedded with U.S. troops during the invasion of Iraq. After all, these journalists were virtually hostages. They could report only what they could see, and they could see only what U.S. troops allowed them to see. It was the best PR the Pentagon could buy, and buy it they did. From the quarter-million-dollar Hollywood set that was built in Doha, Qatar, for CENTCOM press briefings to the untold sums spent to jet celebrity journalists such as Ted Koppel and Geraldo Rivera to and from the front, the Pentagon knew this was an investment in their image that would pay dividends for years. Even combative Defense Secretary Donald

Rumsfeld enthused about the embedded reporters: "We've always believed that we are advantaged as a free country by having the press able to report to the extent it's humanly possible what's actually taking place."

But journalists who were not on the military's leash were viewed very differently. These 2,100 so-called unilateral reporters were, after all, on the ground with Iraqis, seeing the war through a different lens.[7] Many of them found out quickly that the U.S. military considered the independent press the enemy. Reporters Without Borders accused the U.S. and British forces in Iraq of displaying contempt for unilateral reporters.

Dan Scemama can testify to that. In late March 2003, he was among a group of four unembedded journalists seized by American troops. All of the men were carrying press credentials issued by the U.S. military. They had been following the troops and staying overnight with U.S. soldiers without incident until they ran into a group of American soldiers who decided they were spying for Iraq. The four journalists were then arrested. Scemama, a correspondent for Israel Channel One, later described the ordeal on *Democracy Now!* He recounted how one of the reporters "lost his patience" after being locked for five and a half hours in the Jeep they had rented. The reporter, who was Portuguese, got out of the Jeep and approached the nearby soldiers. "Please, please, I am begging you, I have a wife and children. Let me just make a call, a telephone call to tell them that we are safe, that we are with you, the Americans, and not with the Iraqis. They might think at home that we are killed by Iraqis. Please just let us tell them that."

"Go immediately to your car," the soldiers replied, according to Scemama. But before the Portuguese journalist could get back to the Jeep, "five soldiers . . . jumped on him and started to beat him and to kick him. We ran to his direction. They all put bullets inside their guns, and they said if we move forward, they would shoot at us."

The soldiers tied the Portuguese reporter's hands behind his back and led him off to the camp. "After half an hour, they let him go, and he came back to us all crying," Scemama recalled. "Then came this Lieutenant Scholl. And he told us, 'Don't mess with my soldiers. Don't mess with them because they are trained like dogs to kill. And they will kill you if you try again.'"

Duly warned, the journalists sat in the Jeep for thirty-six more hours. "They asked us if we need anything," said Scemama. "They came politely, very nice, Lieutenant Scholl, he came again. 'Do you need anything?' And we said, 'Yes, if you can give us a little food.' And he said, 'I don't have enough food for my soldiers. I will not give you food.'

"After about an hour, we saw a soldier going with a bottle of water in our direction. And we said, 'Look! Something human is happening here. Somebody is coming to us with water!' And then we saw that he gave the water to a dog."

After thirty-six hours, the journalists were flown to Kuwait on a helicopter. The next morning, after two days under arrest, "They said, 'Guys, everything is finished. What hotel are you staying at in Kuwait City? We'll take you to your hotel.'"

But their ordeal was not over. "When I arrived in my hotel," Scemama said, "I had time to take a shower. I wanted to eat something, because I did not eat for a long time. And five minutes after I finished my shower, people knocked on my door in my hotel. It was Kuwaiti secret police. And they told me for your own safety, we have to show you out of Kuwait immediately. And they took me to the airport and threw me out of Kuwait. I'm sure the Americans did that."

At least Scemama and his colleagues lived to complain. On August 17, 2003, Mazen Dana, a Palestinian cameraman for Reuters, was killed while filming at a prison outside Baghdad. He had just spoken with American soldiers, making them aware of what he was doing. It didn't matter. Dana ended up filming his own death. As his camera trained on a U.S. tank fifty meters away, the soldiers suddenly opened fire. Dana's camera went out of focus as a high-caliber machine gun bullet tore into his chest.

This time, the explanations were even flimsier than on April 8. U.S. soldiers claimed they mistook Dana's camera for a rocket-propelled grenade launcher. The Pentagon said the soldiers had accidentally "engaged a cameraman." U.S. officials told the Committee to Protect Journalists that Dana's killing was "regrettable," but that the soldiers "acted within the rules of engagement."[8]

It was grimly ironic that Mazen Dana had been awarded the International Press Freedom Award just two years earlier by the Committee to Protect Journalists (CPJ)—for his determination to keep filming in volatile situations. He had been arrested and wounded many times while covering the conflict in the Israeli Occupied Territories. "Mazen was one of the finest conflict cameramen of his generation, enduring bullets and physical violence to report the news," wrote Joel Campagna of CPJ.[9] Thousands marched in Hebron at his funeral, and testimonials poured in from around the world.

"We carry a gift," Dana told his fellow journalists when he accepted the International Press Freedom Award. "We film and we show the world what's going on. We are not part of the conflict."

Mazen Dana concluded, "Words and images are a public trust, and for this reason I will continue with my work regardless of the hardships and even if it costs me my life."[10]

Silencing Al-Jazeera

PENTAGON HAWKS WERE understandably pleased with their ability to keep the media under their talons. Their wrath was reserved for the voice they couldn't dictate to: Al-Jazeera. Deputy Secretary of Defense Paul Wolfowitz said in July 2003, "Our biggest remaining challenges are, number one, electricity; number two, jobs and unemployment; and number three, the domination of the local media by hostile sources, including, from the outside world, from Al-Jazeera and Al-Arabiya and some other unhelpful foreign broadcasts."[11]

Hafez Al-Mirazi, Washington bureau chief of Al-Jazeera, felt a chill wind when he heard Wolfowitz. "When you hear that from someone who's as important in this administration as the information minister was in Iraq, it's really scary."[12]

Al-Mirazi was later asked at a conference, "Whose side is Al-Jazeera on?" He replied: "The sad thing for me is that some of the American networks behaved in similar ways as government-controlled stations in the Arab world before 9/11. They used to call us the Israeli-U.S.-backed network. We were suspected of trying to divide the Arab world. The Americans were so positive about us before 9/11, but afterward, when we gave both sides, they behaved the same way that other government-controlled media in the Arab world did to us."[13]

Al-Jazeera has good reason to be nervous. It has been the target of repeated attacks by the U.S. military:

- In November 2001, despite the fact that Al-Jazeera had given the U.S. military coordinates of its office in Kabul, U.S. war planes dropped two five-hundred-pound bombs on Al-Jazeera's bureau there, destroying it. The United States claimed the office was "a known Al Qaeda facility."[14]

- In Basra, Iraq, in March 2003, the United States dropped four bombs on the Sheraton Hotel, where Al-Jazeera correspondents—the only ones reporting from the embattled city—were the lone guests. Once again, Al-Jazeera had informed the Pentagon of the presence of its reporters in the hotel.

- Near Nasiriya, an Al-Jazeera reporter embedded with the U.S. Marines was threatened with death by a member of the anti-Saddam Free Iraqi Forces attached to the unit. The Marine commander refused to intervene and told the reporter not to file any more reports from the field. The terrified reporter complied.

- An Al-Jazeera staff member driving near Baghdad showed his ID at a Marine checkpoint and was waved through. A Marine then opened fire, badly damaging the car, but the driver was unhurt. Al-Jazeera believed the incident "was meant to send a message."[15]

- The Al-Jazeera reporter covering the Bush-Putin summit meeting in Crawford, Texas, in November 2001 was detained by the FBI because his credit card was found to be "linked to Afghanistan." When the FBI determined that Al-Jazeera and Al Qaeda were two different organizations, the reporter was released.[16]

- The U.S.-picked Iraqi Governing Council ordered a two-week ban on broadcasts from Iraq by Al-Jazeera and Al-Arabiya on September 23, 2003, accusing the Arab TV networks of encouraging political violence. "These sanctions are a bad omen of the council's intentions concerning the speedy establishment of democracy in Iraq," said Robert Ménard, secretary-general of Reporters Without Borders.[17]

I interviewed Tareq Ayyoub's widow, Dima Tahboub, a month after her husband's death. "Hate breeds hate," she told me. "The United States said they were doing this to rout out terrorism. Who is engaged in terrorism now?"

By early 2004, seventeen journalists had died while covering the invasion of Iraq. Six months after Ayyoub's killing, the Pentagon still had not opened an investigation into the matter.

Dark Day for Journalism

THERE HAS HARDLY been a peep from the American mainstream media objecting to the treatment of journalists by the U.S. military. On the contrary, NPR correspondent Anne Garrels reported on the death of Al-Jazeera's Tareq Ayyoub, saying, "In my view, this really was an avoidable tragedy." By working from their bureau, the Arab journalists "insisted on staying near . . . well-known U.S. targets." Garrels added, "It was clear to everyone this was going to be the scene of fierce fighting."[18] In other words, it was Al-Jazeera's fault for reporting from a vantage point other than the hotel favored by Western journalists. Garrels, who, ironically, is on the board of the Committee to Protect Journalists, gave us a classic case of blaming the victim.

Foreign reporters had a very different reaction. In Spain, which lost two reporters in the attack on the Palestine Hotel, media workers went on strike for a day. From the elite journalists right down to the technicians, they laid down their cables, cameras, and their pens. They refused to record the words of Spanish Prime Minister José María Aznar, who joined Blair and Bush in supporting the war. When Aznar came into parliament, they piled their equipment at the front of the room and turned their backs on him.

Photographers refused to take his picture and instead held up a photo of their slain colleagues. At a press conference in Madrid with British Foreign Secretary Jack Straw, Spanish reporters walked out in protest. Later, hundreds of journalists, camera people, and technicians marched to the U.S. embassy in Madrid and stopped traffic in the intersection. "Murderer, murderer," they chanted.[19]

The Egyptian newspaper *Al-Ahrar* called the attack on journalists "a massacre." In Mexico, the daily *El Universal* declared in a front-page story: "The U.S. is now murdering journalists."[20]

By shooting the messenger, the U.S. military was sending a warning to independent reporters: You could be next.

Opposed to War? You're Fired!

MEDIA ORGANIZATIONS LIKE to claim that "objectivity" is sacred. But during the invasion of Iraq, we learned what that really meant: If you're prowar, you're objective. If you're against the war, you're fired.

So NPR's Scott Simon felt safe opining on the op-ed pages of *The Wall Street Journal* in October 2002, "American pacifists have no sane alternative now but to support war."[21] Mara Liasson of NPR didn't hesitate to slam two congressmen who had just returned from Iraq, where they had criticized President Bush. Speaking on *FOX News Sunday* in October 2002, she declared, "These guys are a disgrace. Look, everybody knows it's . . . Politics 101 that you don't go to an adversary country, an enemy country, and badmouth the United States, its policies and the president of the United States. I mean, these guys ought to, I don't know, resign."[22]

And Dan Rather had little to fear when he declared on *Larry King Live* on April 14, 2003: "Look, I'm an American. I never tried to kid anybody that I'm some internationalist or something. And when my country is at war, I want my country to win, whatever the definition of *win* may be. Now, I can't and don't argue that that is coverage without a prejudice. About that I am prejudiced."[23]

Bill O'Reilly of FOX News unashamedly advanced his own military strategy for the war in March 2003—just slaughter the 4.5 million residents of Baghdad: "We should have given the citizens of Baghdad forty-eight hours to get out of Dodge by dropping leaflets and going with the AM radios and all that. Forty-eight hours, you've got to get out of there, and flatten the place. Then the war would be over."[24] O'Reilly champions speaking freely . . . against free speech: "Once the war against Saddam begins, we expect every American to support our military, and if they can't do that, to shut up."[25]

For journalists opposed to war, similar candor has cost them their jobs. The media watch group FAIR kept tabs on the newsroom purges:[26]

- In February 2003, MSNBC canceled Phil Donahue's show. A leaked internal memo claimed that Donahue would present "a difficult public face for NBC in a time of war. He seems to delight in presenting guests who are antiwar, anti-Bush, and skeptical of the administration's motives." The report warned that the Donahue show could be "a home for the liberal antiwar agenda at the same time as our competitors are waving the flag at every opportunity."

- Brent Flynn, a reporter for the *Lewisville Leader* in Texas, was told he could no longer write a column for the paper after attending an antiwar rally and expressing his views in print. He wrote in one of his columns: "I would say that people who hold up the First Amendment as an example of America's greatness but then disparage those who exercise that right to peaceably assemble are the real, useful idiots."

- White House correspondent Russell Mokhiber of the *Corporate Crime Reporter*, known for his "Ari and I" column (later renamed "Scottie and Me") on the Common Dreams website, was banned from attending the White House press briefings for the first month of the invasion. He was allowed back in only after threatening to sue. His first question upon his return: "How many people have been killed in this war?"[27]

- Kurt Houghly, a reporter and columnist for Michigan's *Huron Daily Tribune*, quit the paper after allegedly being told that an antiwar column he'd written would not run because it might upset readers.

- Veteran war correspondent Peter Arnett was fired from NBC after he matter-of-factly stated on Iraqi TV that the war planners had "misjudged the determination of Iraqi forces" and that there was "a growing challenge to President Bush about the conduct of the war." NBC declared on its flag-enshrouded network that "it was wrong for Mr. Arnett to grant an interview to state-controlled Iraqi TV—especially at a time of war."

- Ed Gernon, a veteran TV producer who had just made the CBS miniseries *Hitler*, was fired after he compared the state of U.S. affairs today with that of Nazi Germany. While plugging the miniseries, Gernon said: "It basically boils down to an entire nation gripped by fear who ultimately choose to give up their civil rights and plunge the whole nation into war. I can't think of a better time to examine this history than now."

- Satirist Bill Maher's show *Politically Incorrect* was pulled from ABC in September 2001 after he said, "We have been the cowards, lobbing cruise missiles from 2,000 miles away. That's cowardly. Staying in the airplane when it hits the building, say what you want about it, it's not cowardly." White House press secretary Ari Fleischer warned that Maher's comments and his sacking were "reminders to all Americans that they need to watch what they say, watch what they do. This is not a time for remarks like that; there never is."[28]

- Roxanne Cordonier, cohost of the morning talk show *Love and Hudson* on Clear Channel–owned radio station WMYI-FM in Greenville, South Carolina, was fired on April 17, 2003, after publicly opposing the U.S. invasion of Iraq. Cordonier (her on-air name is Roxanne Walker) says she and other staff were forced to participate in "patriotic rallies." "I was told repeatedly by management and my cohosts to either agree with their point of view or otherwise be silent." Cordonier, who was named 2002 Radio Personality of the Year by the South Carolina Broadcasters Association, sued Clear Channel. The suit is pending.

- Hip-hop artist Michael Franti's record label received an e-mail from MTV in March 2003 stating that no videos could be shown on their network that mentioned the words *bombing* or *war,* or that had protesters in them. Franti said, "MTV has aired videos that show troops saying good-bye to their loved ones and going off to war in a very heroic fashion—troops who are gonna be coming home traumatized, wounded, and dead and then be treated and thrown onto the scrap heap of veterans."

- The *San Francisco Chronicle* fired technology columnist Henry Norr after he took part in an antiwar demonstration in

March 2003. Norr participated in the massive direct-action protest that spread across the Bay Area the day after the U.S. invasion of Iraq began. Defending the *Chronicle,* reader advocate Dick Rogers wrote, "If it were up to me . . . the sign over the entrance to the *Chronicle* would read: 'Check your activism at the door.' "[29]

The day after Henry Norr participated in the antiwar demonstration, his column on computers and technology was pulled. The official line from the *Chronicle* was that Norr was suspended and then fired because he had allegedly falsified his time card. But according to sources within the *Chronicle* interviewed by the *San Francisco Examiner,* there was only one reason for his sacking: politics. Not only had Norr protested the invasion of Iraq, he was also outspoken on the Israeli occupation of Gaza and the West Bank.

Here is what Norr told *Democracy Now!*:

> I had planned to participate with my wife and my daughter in the demonstrations when the war began. The night before when the attack on Iraq began, I sent an e-mail to my supervisors saying that I expected to be arrested the next day and that I wouldn't be in. I went down to Market Street along with thousands of other people and, you know, blocked traffic. And we were arrested pretty early in the day and kept first in a pen on the street and then in the county jail until about 9:30 or 10:00 that night. I didn't go to work that day.
>
> The next day, I returned to work and sat down to write my column for the following week, which had nothing to do with politics. . . . I was working on that and then [my

editor] came by and said, "Hey, never mind. It's not gonna run." I said, "Why?" And he said, "Orders from higher up."

Bruce Springsteen, I think, defined it nicely. He said the pressure coming from the government and big business to enforce conformity of thought concerning the war and politics goes against everything this country is about. But I would amend that myself to say everything this country should be about but often isn't.

And it's scary. I mean, the idea that an employer can dictate political activity and political expression of their employees. You know, there's no reason to think that this is limited to the media. If this trend spreads . . . then we're in a pretty frightening situation.

11

Sanitized

*I must say that I find television very educational. The
minute somebody turns it on, I go to the library and read a
book.*

—GROUCHO MARX

TWO WARS TOOK PLACE in Iraq in 2003. The real war: 8,000
to 10,000 Iraqi civilians killed and 20,000 injured and an undeter-
mined number of Iraqi military killed[1] (speaking of "enemy dead"
in the Persian Gulf War, General Colin Powell remarked, "It's really not a number I'm terribly interested in"). By January 2004,
over 500 American soldiers had died—more than half of them
since President Bush declared an end to "major combat" on May 1,
2003—and more than 11,000 were wounded or medically evacuated.[2] Ninety-six non-U.S. Coalition soldiers died in that same period.[3]

In the real war, there were devastated communities, over-
crowded and underequipped hospitals, dead and dying victims of
U.S. bomb attacks. Anguished families dealt with personal losses.

It was gruesome and heart-wrenching. Pain and suffering starred in this war.

Then there was the fake war—the one Americans saw on TV. In this war, there were almost no victims. The United States overran a whole country, destroyed a foreign army, engaged in street-to-street combat and intense aerial bombing, rescued a brave young woman soldier from enemy hands—and barely saw a victim. The American flag starred in this war.

A study by the Project for Excellence in Journalism of 40.5 hours of prime-time coverage spread over three days by ABC, CBS, NBC, CNN, and FOX examined 108 reports from embedded reporters. Not a single story depicted people hit by weapons.[4]

Not one.

This, despite the fact that about half the reports from the embeds showed combat action. So much for fair and balanced news.

It wouldn't take much to spark a national backlash against war. Just look at what happened in Vietnam. A mere 76 out of 2,300 Vietnam TV reports—that's 3.3 percent—showed actual violence.[5] That was enough to help galvanize many Americans against the war.

If Americans had seen the war in Iraq that the rest of the world saw, it would surely have had an impact: Television viewership skyrocketed during the war, with average daily viewers shooting up 300 percent for MSNBC and CNN and 288 percent for FOX. The most viewed cable news channel, FOX averaged 3.3 million viewers per day. *NBC Nightly News* was tops overall, with over 11.3 million viewers daily.[6]

Too bad it was a case of "the more you watch, the less you know," to quote media critic Danny Schechter.

The U.S. media was engaged in a massive deception. We could devastate Iraq, but the media wouldn't show the results. According to a study published in the *Journal of the American Med-*

ical Association, the typical American child spends twenty-seven hours a week watching television and will witness 40,000 murders and 200,000 other violent acts by the age of eighteen.[7] We can watch Arnold Schwarzenegger blow away and disembowel scores of villains in the movies, but when it comes to showing us the real face of war, the networks suddenly worry about images that are in "poor taste."

"For taste purposes," said Lester Crystal, executive producer for the PBS *NewsHour with Jim Lehrer,* "you don't show people in agony on the air. You don't show a lot of dead bodies."[8]

"We take very seriously our responsibility to tell the story as accurately and comprehensively as we can," CNN spokesman Matthew Furman explained to the *American Journalism Review.* "At the same time, we're mindful of the sensibilities of our audience."[9]

Censorship goes by many names in the United States. Taste is one of the favorite euphemisms. Sensibility is another.

The form good taste would take became clear early in the conflict, when Iraqi TV released footage of dead American soldiers and American POWs being interrogated. Most of the world saw the footage immediately, courtesy of Al-Jazeera—and the U.S. government angrily denounced the network. Donald Rumsfeld called the POW footage "a clear violation of the Geneva Convention," which protects prisoners of war against being publicly humiliated.[10]

Most U.S. networks initially ran either still images from the POW footage or very brief snips. CBS decided to air the POW footage the day it was released, March 23, 2003, on its morning news show, *Face the Nation.* The reason for this bold decision? Defense Secretary Donald Rumsfeld would be there in person to give it the right spin. As a CBS spokesman explained, "We made a real-time decision given that we had the top defense department official live, to immediately put it in appropriate context."[11] CBS quickly fell back into line when the Pentagon requested that they can the footage.

That next week, *The Washington Post* and *The New York Times* featured numerous photos of Iraqi prisoners of war, just like the Americans shown on Al-Jazeera. Other photos showed Iraqi POWs with bags over their heads.

The Geneva Convention was invoked selectively: American POWs mattered; Iraqi POWs did not.

The real issue for the Pentagon was not protecting the dignity of prisoners or the Geneva Convention—international laws that Human Rights Watch suggests the United States has violated in its treatment of prisoners at Guantánamo Bay, Cuba, and in Afghanistan[12]—it was about controlling the media. The Pentagon understood that if the real, grisly images of dead American soldiers and POWs got out, domestic support for the invasion would weaken. That explains why the Pentagon issued orders that all returning caskets from Iraq be off-loaded behind curtains—no press photos allowed—in order to keep images of the grim toll out of the media.

Al-Jazeera's refusal to kowtow to American censors made it the whipping boy of both the Bush administration and the U.S. media pundits—and of their corporate cronies. In late March 2003, two Al-Jazeera financial correspondents were kicked off the trading floors of the New York Stock Exchange and NASDAQ.

"In light of Al-Jazeera's recent conduct during the war, in which they have broadcast footage of U.S. POWs in alleged violation of the Geneva Convention, they are not welcome to broadcast from our facility at this time," said NASDAQ spokesman Scott Peterson. (NASDAQ, with its own atrocious record of enforcing ethical guidelines on its member businesses, later retracted this explanation and said simply that Al-Jazeera's press passes had been pulled for "security reasons.") It was the first time that the exchanges had revoked press accreditation.[13]

But a double standard was at work: The exchanges did not revoke the press credentials of *The New York Times* or *Washington Post* for printing photos of Iraqi prisoners of war. The symbolism of Al-Jazeera's banishment from Wall Street was telling. The captains of industry were about to make a killing in the Iraqi reconstruction effort. They preferred to do their plundering in private.

"Not the Right Time"

THE SANITIZATION OF the news hit a new low when U.S. troops first pushed into Baghdad. Fighting was intense: U.S. military officials declared that between 2,000 and 3,000 Iraqi soldiers were killed—in a *single day*. With even the embedded reporters and cameras capturing blood and death and atrocity, MSNBC announced that it was putting a delay on its live feeds to spare viewers the disturbing images.[14]

Now take a guess: How many Iraqi casualties were shown on U.S. television that day? You guessed it. Not one.[15]

In 2003, the media had far more access to the battlefield than they did during the 1991 Persian Gulf War, but that had little bearing on what viewers saw this time around. Bill Kovach, a veteran editor for *The New York Times* and the *Atlanta Journal-Constitution* and curator of the Nieman Foundation for Journalism at Harvard University, reflected on what the public saw in media dispatches from the first Gulf War. It could just as easily have been written about the 2003 invasion. Kovach wrote that the dispatches from Iraq in 1991 "formed an image of warfare from which the human cost had been surgically eliminated. Film released for television was of 'smart bombs' guided literally through the front doors of military bunkers by laser beams. The language used was equally bloodless. Military targets such as tanks and armored personnel carriers were listed as 'KIAs' (killed in action) when destroyed by bombs, but the toll on human beings inside them was referred to as 'collateral damage.' Unreported were the costs and consequences of the war in human terms. What was transmitted from the Gulf often served to mask reality rather than shed light on what was happening."[16]

CNN: The Network America Trusts?

WE DECIDED TO confront Aaron Brown on the media's sanitizing of the war. Brown's position as anchor of CNN's prime-time *NewsNight* had made him well known to the millions tuning in to war coverage. Behind the scenes, Brown was also one of those directing CNN's war coverage. This was our conversation on *Democracy Now!* on April 4, 2003:

AMY GOODMAN: . . . There are many, many pictures that are now coming out of Iraq of dead children, women, and men. In the foreign press, it is a very different picture that is being shown on the TV screens and in the newspapers—they're showing dead people. We don't see that very much in this country. What are your thoughts on that?

AARON BROWN: . . . The program has . . . discussed whether or not we have oversanitized. This is not, to me, a political question. . . . It is a journalistic question, it is a question of taste. . . . I saw things on the first Sunday of the war that, if you put a gun to my head, I wouldn't have put them on TV because it was just too—it was pornographic, in my view. But it certainly showed the violence of war.

GOODMAN: . . . Many people say that the picture [during the Vietnam War] of the little Vietnamese girl who was napalmed helped to turn the war around.

BROWN: There is no question in my mind that that picture would be shown today. There is no question.

GOODMAN: And yet we are seeing picture after picture—we're broadcasting them here on *Democracy Now!* of children like that—we are not seeing them on CNN.

BROWN: Well, be careful about what you say you've seen, because you're not really right. There are some practical limitations. Let's say because the Iraqi government won't allow it, we do not have in-country correspondents and crews.

GOODMAN: But you've been showing many photographs.

BROWN: You just have to let me finish, then if you want to beat me up, you can beat me up all you want. . . . You want to argue, it seems to me, whether we've shown them enough. Okay, go ahead. I have to make these decisions every day. I try and make them appropriately to where I think the line is between understanding the horror that war is and being pornographic in the use of pictures . . .

I then asked Aaron Brown about the balance of views coming out of CNN. The retired generals were a constant presence. Why?

GOODMAN: Are you bringing as many voices who are opposed to what is going on right now as those who are for it? That is a very serious question.

BROWN: No, we're not.

GOODMAN: If you don't think you're bringing fifty-fifty, what do you think you are bringing, sixty-forty?

BROWN: I don't know.

GOODMAN: Okay, we're not going to count, but do you think you're coming close?

BROWN: I think the degree to which the demonstrations at home and abroad hadn't been covered fairly and thoughtfully is fair. . . . I thought all of us in this organization were a little late in coming to see an antiwar movement develop. . . . If somehow, and perhaps your listeners do expect a kind of fifty-fifty balance at this stage about whether there should or shouldn't be a war or not—in my view, it's just not a relevant question.

GOODMAN: Why not?

BROWN: Because it's over—it's on, it's being done. To talk now, at this moment, about whether it should or not have been is not the right time.

So when is the right time to question war? If it's not before a war and not during it, what's left? After the war? By then, it doesn't matter.

CNN's coverage of the war made the dynamics of news manipulation all too plain to see. CNN has two divisions: CNN International (CNNi) broadcasts to the world, whereas CNN broadcasts to the U.S. audience. They make separate decisions on what images to air—from the same stock of available footage and reports. The result: one war carefully crafted for Americans, another war for the rest of the world.

The difference was never more stark than on the famous day

when U.S. soldiers pulled down a large statue of Saddam Hussein, initially wrapping his head in an American flag. CNN played the triumphal footage in an endless loop: the carefully stage-managed statue-toppling "celebration," in which a small group of Iraqis were allowed into the heavily guarded plaza to cheer for the cameras as Marines, outside the view of the camera, pulled down the edifice. CNNi showed it on a split screen, with images of wounded Iraqis in a hospital sharing half the screen.[17]

Even the websites of the two CNN's conveyed opposite messages. On one typical day during the war, the CNN website featured a photo of people defacing a mural of Saddam Hussein. CNNi went with a picture of an anguished Iraqi being comforted.[18]

"All the American channels are less bloody than most European, Asian, and Arabic channels," said former CNN vice president Frank Sesno.[19]

The Wall Street Journal paraphrased CNN president Chris Cramer, assuring that "rather than politics, the difference in approach between CNNi and the U.S. CNN reflects the practical and commercial need to cater to different audiences."[20]

The difference being that CNN's U.S. audience is served half-truths soaked in spin.

Toppling the Truth

THE FAMOUS STATUE of Saddam Hussein pulled down by U.S. Marines on April 9, 2003, was conveniently chosen as the site for the defining image of the war because of its location—directly across from the Palestine Hotel, the main site of the live-feed television cameras in Baghdad. The Marines established a three-block perimeter around the area, ensuring they could control every angle of this global photo op.

Tom Brokaw compared the event to "all the statues of Lenin [that] came down all across the Soviet Union."

"If you don't have goose bumps now," said FOX News anchor David Asman, "you'll never have them in your life."

While close-up images of the event suggest that throngs of ordinary Iraqis cheered the toppling of the statue, a Reuters long-shot photo showed that Firdos Square was nearly empty, ringed by U.S. tanks and Marines who had moved in to seal off the square before admitting Iraqis.[21] A BBC photo sequence also showed a sparse crowd, comprised mostly of journalists and American soldiers. The BBC reported on its website that only "dozens" of Iraqis were involved.

But these weren't just any Iraqis, as evidenced by two photos published by the Information Clearing House.[22] The first shows the arrival of the CIA's handpicked leader, Ahmed Chalabi, in Nasiriya on April 6, accompanied by several aides. The second photo is a close-up of one of the cheering participants at Firdos Square on April 9. The man celebrating "liberation" in Baghdad in front of the news cameras was one of those accompanying Chalabi into Nasiriya three days earlier.

"It was a rent-a-crowd," chided Reverend Neville Watson, an Australian peace activist who was an eyewitness to the event, in a BBC interview. Robert Fisk of the *Independent,* who was also at Firdos Square, described it as "the most staged photo opportunity since Iwo Jima."

"None That Matter"

THE RULES OF mainstream journalism are simple: The Republicans and Democrats establish the acceptable boundaries of debate. When those groups agree—which is often—there is simply no debate. That's why there is such appalling silence around issues of war and peace. When it came to Afghanistan and Iraq, the majority of Democrats in Congress couldn't rubber-stamp the war fast enough.

So the mainstream media dutifully reported that there was no objection to war. And we're not just talking FOX News. On October 8, 2001, on NPR's *Morning Edition,* Cokie Roberts was asked if there were any dissenters in Congress.

"None that matter," she replied.[23]

"It's a jaw-dropping statement when you think about it," David Potorti wrote of Roberts' comment.[24] Potorti's brother James worked on the ninety-sixth floor of the World Trade Center and was killed on September 11; Roberts' flippant dismissal of dissenters ultimately inspired Potorti to write a book, *September 11th Families for Peaceful Tomorrows.*

"In a larger sense, of course, Roberts is right," wrote Potorti. "In a media universe where you're likely to find right-wing conservatives on ABC, Fox, or NPR, the facts don't matter; only the framing. And in the hands of biased pundits posing as objective journalists, the framing is always going to be the same: promilitary, pro-government, and pro-war."

Potorti suggests that the use of the phrase "none that matter" should be expanded. "It's a handy phrase you can use at home as well," he says. "Will network news divisions, owned by defense contractors, give us any useful insights into the workings of the U.S. military? *None that matter.* Will you hear any coherent news reports from outside of a narrow, statist perspective? *None that matter.* And are there any mainstream media outlets willing to criticize U.S. foreign policy? *None that matter.*"

The media provides a forum for those in power. When there is an establishment consensus—such as during the period leading up to the war—the media just reflects that. The picture changes in an election year, when, for a fleeting moment, the Democrats try to distinguish themselves from the Republicans.

But what about the nonofficial voices around the country and the world who have been consistently opposed to the invasion, the millions of people who took to the streets to say no to war? These voices have been almost completely excluded.

"A Little Left-Wing Cabal"

THE MEDIA'S DEFENSE of war is not limited to Iraq or Afghanistan. We got an ample dose of it in April 2001, when former Senator (and one-time presidential hopeful) Bob Kerrey was the subject of a damning exposé in *The New York Times Magazine* and on the CBS News program *60 Minutes II*.[25] Kerrey was forced to admit that a Navy SEAL combat mission he led during the Vietnam War was responsible for the brutal deaths of more than a dozen unarmed civilians, mostly women and children. He said that he could not militarily or morally justify the mission, for which he was awarded the Bronze Star.

As shocking as the incident was, so too was the media cover-up. *Newsweek* had the story from its national security correspondent, Gregory Vistica, in late 1998, when Kerrey was considering a run for the presidency. But top *Newsweek* editors spiked the story when Kerrey decided not to run. Vistica later quit the magazine and brought the story to *The New York Times Magazine* and *60 Minutes II*.

"We could have run the story," said Evan Thomas, a *Newsweek* assistant managing editor. "We just didn't want to do it to the guy when he wasn't running for president."

Newsweek editor Mark Whitaker added that when Kerrey's

presidential aspirations ended, "the relevance of this story changed a little bit."[26]

Relevance for *whom?* It was still relevant for the families of the unarmed Vietnamese civilians who were slaughtered. *Newsweek* was not concerned about the victims, but about the feelings of the perpetrator, a powerful U.S. senator.

The victims still remember the terror that Kerrey and his comrades unleashed. Pham Di Cu, head of the foreign relations department of the Mekong Delta province of Ben Tre, where the massacre occurred, told Reuters that thirteen children, five women, and an elderly man had been killed in the attack on February 25, 1969. Kerrey has acknowledged that the killing of civilians took place, but he said initially that the squad was returning fire and did not know that civilians had been killed until after the fighting.

Cu quoted surviving witness Pham Thi Lanh, 67, as saying the attack on the hamlet of Thanh Phong began in darkness at about 8:00 p.m. and lasted just twenty minutes. "I think in terms of brutality, this was the worst incident in this province during the war," he told Reuters. "Personally, I think it was inhuman."

Cu also said Lanh had told how the seven-man squad—six masked Americans and a Vietnamese interpreter—moved from bunker to bunker in the hamlet, shooting and stabbing people and slitting their throats. An after-action report said that Kerrey's SEAL unit expended 1,200 rounds of ammunition in the village.[27]

Kerrey decided the best defense was a good offense, launching a preemptive PR strike by helping to leak the story to *The Wall Street Journal* and the *New York Post*. He just wanted to share his anguish over the incident.

"I was so ashamed I wanted to die," he told *The Wall Street Journal* in a story that ran four days before Vistica's magazine article. "This is killing me. I'm tired of people describing me as a hero and holding this inside."[28]

In advance of the April 29 *Times* publication date, Kerrey hired a crisis management PR firm, which orchestrated the effort to spin the media to his side. Kerrey invited members of his Navy SEAL unit to dinner at his house, following which they signed a letter saying they were merely returning fire from Vietcong and were not ordered to shoot civilians. They pilloried the accusing Marine of Vistica's article.

Kerrey, who had recently been named president of the New School University in New York, then held a news conference on April 26 in an attempt to further frame the story on his terms. The New School University was founded in 1919 by pacifists and has long championed human rights and dissent.

At the news conference, I had a chance to ask Bob Kerrey about his actions in Vietnam:

AMY GOODMAN: Senator Kerrey, according to international law, it is not just people like you who pull the trigger and kill civilians who bear differing levels of responsibility, but it is the architects of a war, like in Vietnam, who set up a policy where large areas of the country are free-fire zones that lead to the deaths of, in the case of the Vietnam War, two million Vietnamese, largely civilian. . . . What do you think of setting up a war crimes tribunal that would bring people, perhaps like you, but more important, the architects, like Henry Kissinger, before it?

BOB KERREY: I'm not prepared to talk about where I'm gonna go or where this ought to go. I really am not. And, you know, I think—

GOODMAN: You've had more than thirty years to think about it.

KERREY: Well, I'm sorry, but you know, the first ten years of my life I'm just trying to figure out how to get healthy again.

GOODMAN: But what about the whole country getting healthy again?

KERREY: Well, at some point, I hope to help the whole country get beyond the Vietnam War, but right now, I'm trying to get a private memory public, and I just, I've not gone as far as you're suggesting in trying to figure out where.

I then asked Kerrey a question that came from Father Dan Berrigan, the Jesuit priest who has spent much of his life opposing war and had been jailed repeatedly, beginning during the Vietnam War. I'd called Father Berrigan to see what he'd want to ask Kerrey, given the chance.

Berrigan asked, "Do you think that if you had taken a different path and refused to kill in that filthy war; that if you had chosen to be a refusenik from the beginning, that you wouldn't have any regrets?" Berrigan, I noted, said he had no regrets as he approached his eightieth birthday.

"Well," Kerrey replied. "Well, I just—God bless him for not having any regrets. I mean, I love any eighty-year-old man that doesn't have any regrets. I do, this one included."

"Do you wish you had taken a different path?" I continued.

"No, I do not," he answered. "I'm proud of my service. I'm proud that I volunteered and I don't, I can't wish, I don't wish that I had chosen differently."

I soon discovered that asking inconvenient questions about dead "enemies" is not done. I got slammed—not by Kerrey, but by other so-called journalists.

Over the next two nights, on FOX News Channel's *Special*

Report with Brit Hume, Mort Kondracke of the conservative *Weekly Standard*, Mara Liasson of NPR, and others attacked the questions I and others had asked Senator Kerrey. They questioned the credibility of any journalist who would dare to ask about war crimes and the possibility of war resistance.

Bringing up Father Berrigan's question, Hume asked, "What about that question, and what about the general behavior of our colleagues in that news conference?"

Kondracke piped up. "[T]here was an even worse question where someone said: You're a father. What would you tell the children of the people that you killed, in effect?"

"Yeah, we played that earlier," Hume replied. "I don't know what it was designed . . . it certainly was not designed to get information. It was designed to embarrass him or make him cry or something like that. It was not a journalistic question."

"No," agreed Liasson, "I don't think this kind of press conference would have happened if he was in Washington. . . . I don't know if those people have worked for any publications. I don't know if they really were journalists. They were clearly interested in reliving the war and the antiwar movement."

The next day, a new group of "Foxes" took up the issue. "What was interesting was kind of the tone of the press conference yesterday, the kinds of questions reporters were throwing at him," FOX News' Tony Snow said. "What was your impression of it?"

Kondracke was back. "Well, this struck me as a little left-wing cabal. I don't know who those reporters were, especially the woman who decided that she would cover this by calling up Daniel Berrigan, you know, the left-wing priest—"

"War protester," Snow corrected him.

Fred Barnes of the *Weekly Standard* then added his two cents. "I think there's a political purpose behind this attack on Bob Kerrey, and that is to try to make sure—this is a left-wing attack, obviously—to make sure that people continue to regard the Vietnam War, even though communism has collapsed in most places, the Vietnam War as wrong, that our involvement was wrong. It was immoral. This is a war where the U.S. slaughtered women and children and civilians and so on."

These media personalities are right about one thing: These questions would not be asked by them or their Beltway buddies. By holding Kerrey accountable for his actions, we had broken with their common ideology: The Vietnam War was good. They are trying to rewrite the history of a dark chapter of rights abuses with some new, improved spin. The only way to impose this view is to hit back hard at anyone who breaks their fabricated consensus. These are the media's ideological enforcers. My treatment was supposed to serve as a cautionary lesson to any other journalist who dared step out of line. This is the media version of friendly fire.

In the following week, other leading media personalities weighed in on the issues. By and large, most slammed the *Times* for running the story and criticized those who challenged Kerrey. Jonathan Alter of *Newsweek* described it as "gotcha" journalism. *The Washington Post* suggested it was unfair to "subject a single citizen to such scrutiny."

Kerrey dropped his wounded-warrior pose for a moment to hit back at critics, telling the Associated Press, "The Vietnam government likes to routinely say how terrible Americans were. The *Times* and CBS are now collaborating in that effort."[29]

What lives are valued? That is the main issue here. Kerrey doesn't care about innocent people that he killed. He just cares that he was exposed.

One Year Later . . .

BEFORE KERREY'S CONSCIENCE kicked in, he had one more battle to fight: taking over Iraq. In 2002, the former Democratic senator joined with leading lights of the neoconservative movement to call for a regime change in Iraq.

Kerrey was a member of the Committee for the Liberation of Iraq, a prowar group with close ties to Dick Cheney and Donald Rumsfeld. Its president was Bruce Jackson, former vice president of Lockheed Martin and an adviser to the Bush 2000 election campaign. The committee was a spin-off from the Project for the New American Century, which laid the blueprint for the military and political domination of the Middle East (see Chapter 1, "Blowback").

Here was a leading Democrat joining the top Republicans in advocating and planning for war. No wonder there is so little public debate on issues of war and peace: Bound by the consensus of the establishment elite, the media brands anyone who falls outside the Democrat-Republican "axis of agreement" an "advocate." Kerrey was not just pushing for war, he was using the New School University as a bully pulpit to advocate for it and to legitimize the war industry. Kerrey held a major dinner in January 2003 to honor the CEO of United Technologies, one of the world's largest military contractors.

Students were furious that Kerrey was using his position as university president to misrepresent the values and traditions of their school. They occupied his office in November 2002, called for his resignation, and confronted him in a stormy public debate on December 4, 2002.

The most telling question that evening came from an activist, Mitch Cohen. He noted that the United States estimated that 100,000 to 200,000 Iraqis died during the first Persian Gulf War as a direct result of bombing and as a consequence of the United States having destroyed parts of Iraq's drinking water and sanitation systems. He also noted that half a million Iraqi children had died as a result of twelve years of UN sanctions against Iraq. Cohen asked, "Do you agree with former Secretary of State Madeleine Albright when she says she thinks the price was worth it?"

Kerrey hardly missed a beat. "Yes, I do," he shot back.

Whether it's children massacred in Vietnam or killed in Iraq, this Democrat knows that one position is always safe: supporting war. And he knows the grunts in the media will cover his back.

On December 9, 2003, Kerrey's talent for sanitizing past atrocities earned him a new job: He was appointed to the bipartisan panel investigating the 9/11 attacks. He conveniently replaced former Georgia Senator Max Cleland, the most outspoken member of the commission, who resigned to take a job at the Export-Import Bank. Cleland has accused the White House of engaging in "Nixonian" efforts to conceal pre-9/11 intelligence.

Kerrey, a strong supporter of Clinton/Bush CIA Director George Tenet and a member of a CIA science advisory panel, was tapped by Senate Democratic leader Tom Daschle. "I can think of no individual better suited to look into these issues and aggressively pursue the facts wherever they may lead than Bob Kerrey," said Daschle.[30] Officials with something to hide about 9/11 must have breathed a sigh of relief.

12

Going to Where the Silence Is

For every one torturer, there are a thousand people ready to risk their lives in order to save another. For every soldier who shoots in a neighborhood, there are a thousand compañeros *who help and protect each other.*
—ISABEL ALLENDE

I FIRST TRAVELED TO East Timor with journalist and activist Allan Nairn in 1990. International pressure in the late 1980s had forced Indonesia to open East Timor just a crack, so we were able to visit. The island nation, brutally occupied by the Indonesian military since the 1975 invasion, had been virtually sealed off from the outside world for fifteen years.

What we saw on that first trip was an absolute hell on earth—a totalitarian military dictatorship. The Indonesian military tried to follow us everywhere we went. Troops and military intelligence known as Intel monitored every aspect of Timorese life. Each village had a place where a list of names of villagers was kept. In some villages, people had to sign in and out when they came and went. At times, soldiers would move into a family's house just to make the surveillance complete.

In one marketplace that we visited, a young man came up to us in full view of the police. He wanted to practice his English. Right after we parted, we were taken to the police station and questioned for twenty minutes about our conversation. The young man was arrested and interrogated overnight.

Timorese could be arrested if they were caught listening to a shortwave radio or if they had a newspaper from the outside world. Sometimes, if we were out of view of soldiers, people would dig up newspaper articles that they had buried in their backyard. They were desperate to prove to us what was happening to their country.

Indonesian Repression, American Support

EAST TIMOR WAS a Portuguese colony for more than four hundred years. Following a military coup in 1974, Portugal started pulling out of its colonial empire, and in 1975, Timor began to move toward independence. Indonesia used this as a pretext to invade East Timor on December 7, 1975. The day before the invasion, Secretary of State Henry Kissinger and President Gerald Ford went to Jakarta, the capital of Indonesia, and met with Suharto, the long-reigning dictator. Ford and Kissinger gave the go-ahead for that invasion. Ninety percent of the weapons used were from the United States. As Kissinger and Ford flew back to the United States, U.S. intelligence was monitoring the slaughter through electronic intercepts. Thousands of people were killed in the first days of the invasion. Indonesian troops would drag people out of their houses and shoot them as their family members were forced to count them as they fell into the harbor. The sea was red with blood. Timorese still talk about those awful days.

Kissinger's colleagues at the State Department cabled him as he was flying back from Asia. They warned him that Congress might ask questions and might threaten to cut off military aid to Indonesia. Under a bilateral agreement, Indonesia was allowed to obtain U.S. weapons provided they were not used for aggression—which the invasion clearly was.

Kissinger called his top officials together for a high-level meeting as soon as he returned to Washington. He castigated them for leaving a paper trail. "I know what the law is, but how can it be in the U.S. national interest for us to . . . kick the Indonesians in the teeth?" he told them.[1] L. Paul Bremer III was the note taker for that meeting. He would later go on to join the global consulting firm Kissinger Associates, and in 2003 he became the occupier-in-chief of a devastated Iraq.

From 1975 to 1979, the killing became more and more intense. The Timorese launched an armed resistance that came to be led by Xanana Gusmão. The Timorese were abandoning their villages and heading into the mountains because the Indonesian military had taken to wiping out entire communities. The military tried to bomb and starve the Timorese out of the mountains and place them in military-controlled areas—which were essentially detention camps. Having no access to their subsistence farms, the Timorese were dying in the camps from disease, massacre, and forced starvation. In 1979, some aid workers got into East Timor and reported that the malnutrition there was worse than they'd seen anywhere in the world, comparable to the starvation in Biafra, Nigeria, during the 1960s.

That same year, at the peak of the slaughter, there was hardly a mention in *The New York Times* or *The Washington Post* about the tragedy.

Compare that to Pol Pot's Cambodia, where the genocide was proportionally similar. Hundreds of articles exposing Pol Pot's atrocities appeared in the U.S. media. The difference? Cambodia was an official enemy of the United States. Indonesia was a close ally. The U.S. president and secretary of state regularly denounced Pol Pot's Cambodia, and the press echoed that criticism. But what about when the United States remains silent on atrocities and supports the regime in power?

The 1975 invasion elicited one forty-second news report by Walter Cronkite on CBS. After that, none of the nightly news programs on ABC, NBC, or CBS mentioned East Timor for the next sixteen years. This official silence wasn't broken until November 1991.

WE LEFT EAST TIMOR in 1990 deeply shaken by what we had seen. We decided to go back a year later to cover a UN-sponsored Portuguese parliamentary delegation that was going to investigate the human rights situation. It would be the first real opportunity that Timorese would have to let the outside world know what was happening to them.

In late October 1991, just before the planned Portuguese visit, Allan Nairn and I returned to East Timor. I was doing a documentary for Pacifica, and Allan was writing for *The New Yorker* magazine. On October 28, the day we arrived, we went directly to the Catholic church in Dili, the capital of East Timor. The Motael Church, the main church in Dili, is a prominent white stucco cathedral that overlooks the harbor where so many had died over the years. We walked inside to attend mass. Women were crying. We didn't know if it was just the usual sorrow of Timor or if something terrible had just happened.

After the service, we learned that the Portuguese delegation was not going to come. We later found out that it was canceled at the behest of the United States and Australia, because for the first time word would get out about what was happening inside the country. The United States had good reason to want to keep the Timor story under wraps: It was deeply complicit in the genocide.

The use of U.S. weapons by the Indonesian military in East Timor was a violation of U.S. law. But Ford and Kissinger rewarded Indonesia after the invasion by doubling military aid. Ford's UN ambassador, Daniel Patrick Moynihan, blocked the United Nations from enforcing resolutions against the occupation. Under President Jimmy Carter, the United States sent planes and helicopters to Indonesia that were used to bomb the Timorese. Carter's vice president, Walter Mondale, visited Jakarta in 1978. The Indonesian military asked Mondale for fighter planes because they were having trouble hunting down the Timorese in the rugged terrain of East Timor's mountains. Mondale responded by expediting the shipment of A-4 attack planes to Indonesia.[2] President Reagan sold Suharto $40 million worth of arms per year during his first term, then provided $300 million in weapons in 1986. Under President Bush Sr., General Electric and AT&T, which both invested heavily in Indonesia, helped lobby for increased military aid, but it was ultimately blocked by grassroots activists who lobbied Congress. President Clinton continued support for Suharto and de facto for the Timor occupation.[3]

Back to that October day in 1991. After the church service, we learned that Indonesian troops had surrounded the sanctuary the night before. The military had just learned that the UN delegation was canceled and could now take revenge on those who were organizing to speak out. Young people from around the country who were being hunted by the military had been leaving school and work to take refuge in the Catholic churches so that they could tell the UN delegation what was happening to their country. The church was the only civilian institution left standing in East Timor.

A brave young person climbed up into the steeple and started to ring the bell. That alerted people in Dili that their church was in trouble. There was an unwritten rule in East Timor: Don't go out after dark. That's when the military death squads are out. But the Timorese heard that their church was in need, so they came to surround it. It was too late. Indonesian troops raided the church, dragged out a young man named Sebastião Gomes, and killed him with a point-blank shot into his stomach. His dried blood was still on the church steps.

On October 29, a funeral was led by Roman Catholic Bishop Carlos Ximenes Belo. (In 1996, Belo and Timorese spokesperson Jose Ramos-Horta would win the Nobel Peace Prize for their efforts to liberate East Timor.) Over a thousand people turned out. They attended the funeral mass, and then marched through the streets of Dili to the Santa Cruz cemetery.

In a land where there was no freedom of assembly, no freedom of speech, no freedom of the press, the simple act of a crowd walking through the streets turned out to be one of the largest acts of civil disobedience the Indonesian military occupiers had ever seen. The mourners marched to the cemetery, put up their hands in a V sign, and chanted, "Viva Sebastião! Viva East Timor! Viva independence!" At the cemetery, they buried Sebastião Gomes. It was a courageous act of defiance by a population that had chafed under the boot of Indonesian military repression for sixteen years.

During the following two weeks, Allan and I traveled around East Timor to see how people had been preparing for the aborted Portuguese delegation. Signs of Timor's suffering were seared into the countryside. Terrified community leaders would meet with us in secret. Everywhere we went, we heard the same story: The military warned the people, "If you speak to the UN delegation, we'll kill you after they leave." Bishop Belo told us that the line commonly used by the soldiers was, "We will kill your family to the seventh generation." A nationwide death threat had been issued.

Massacre

ON THE FATEFUL morning of November 12, 1991, Allan and I went to the Motael Church for a mass to commemorate Sebastião Gomes. We had been alerted the night before by Constâncio Pinto, the leader of the civilian underground, that there would be a mass protest of Sebastião's killing. This time, thousands of people turned out. After the mass, the Timorese marched through the streets of Dili; students pulled handmade banners out from beneath their Catholic school blouses that said things like WHY THE INDONESIAN MILITARY SHOOT OUR CHURCH?

Their signs pleaded with President Bush and the UN to do something to help them. They knew that with the cancellation of the UN delegation, all those who had risked their lives to come and speak to the Portuguese were suddenly vulnerable. Those who had taken refuge in the churches were now marked.

When the mourners arrived at the cemetery, the killing began. In the introduction to this book, I described how the soldiers beat us, fracturing Allan's skull. But the experience for the Timorese was far, far worse. The soldiers went on killing for the entire morning. They chased unarmed men, women, and children into houses and through the cemetery and just kept shooting.

The soldiers had dragged an old Timorese man into a sewer ditch behind us. Every time he put up his hands in a prayer sign, they would smash his face with the butts of their rifles. At that point a Red Cross jeep pulled up. The driver picked the old man up and put him into the front of the jeep. Allan and I climbed in the back.

Allan did not know if he would remain conscious, so he told me to remember every number I could to contact people in the outside world. One of the young people had given Allan a list of names of people who were in trouble. Allan wedged it in the crack between the seat cushions in the back of the jeep in case he didn't make it. As we drove off, dozens of Timorese hailed the vehicle and jumped inside of it. They leaped on the roof and hung off the spare tire at the back. We drove like that, as a wounded mass of humanity, to the hospital.

It seemed likely that the military would raid the hospital—this was where some of the survivors were. We clearly couldn't stop the killings inside the country. The only hope for the Timorese now was international pressure, if we could only get word to the outside world.

Although Allan's injuries were serious, after the wounded were dropped off at the hospital, we went into hiding in several places, finally ending up in Bishop Belo's house. There was one plane departing that day. The Indonesian military had stripped us of everything, but if we could get money and get Allan cleaned up, we could make a dash for the plane. As I wiped off Allan's head, the sink turned red with his blood. Bishop Belo gave Allan his shirt. Outside the house, Timorese poured into the compound seeking refuge.

Soldiers had already surrounded our hotel, so we couldn't retrieve anything. We feared the world press would give this story their usual treatment, reporting only the official Indonesian military version of the story, which was usually that nothing happened. So I took Allan's blood-soaked shirt, and Bishop Belo gave me a towel to wrap it up and tie around my waist. A young Timorese man risked his life by racing out of the compound to find film.

When he returned, someone took a dozen photographs of us. We figured this might be the only evidence of the crime, even if it was just what had happened to us.

The whole city was now shut down. Once we had made the decision to leave, Allan went into the street and flagged down a civilian car. It was important to determine if the driver was Timorese. Allan asked in Portuguese if he spoke the language. He responded in Portuguese, "Yes, perfectly." That indicated he was Timorese—Indonesians don't usually speak Portuguese. The man took the incredible risk of driving us to the airport and said he would wait in case we were turned away.

We went inside the airport, which like almost everything else was controlled by the military. Indonesian soldiers immediately stopped us. A heated discussion ensued among several of them. We argued and demanded to get on the plane. I don't know whether it was a communication gap with the military at the massacre site or whether they had consciously decided not to kill us and just wanted us out, but we were able to board the plane and fly out of the country.

We flew from East to West Timor, then to Bali. While in Bali we were able to make one call to a friend in Washington to alert the press that a massacre had taken place in East Timor. As Allan spoke, I would take the handset every few minutes and use our towel to wipe off the blood. We made the next plane to Guam. We avoided the U.S. military hospital there, afraid they would cut off our access to the outside world under the guise of helping us. Instead, we went to a small civilian hospital on Guam, where Allan received emergency treatment and we were able to commandeer the hospital switchboard. They had five phone lines, and media from around the world were calling. For the first time in sixteen years, the international media were interested in what had happened in East Timor. After a doctor sewed up Allan's head, an ambulance brought us to a cable TV studio that linked us to CNN.

But none of the major American TV broadcast networks reported the massacre. Several told us that if there were no pictures, there was no story. Some just told us it wasn't newsworthy. ABC's *Nightline* considered the story for several days, but ultimately dropped it.

For the networks, silence in the face of atrocity is just business as usual. It encourages dictatorships and regimes such as Indonesia's to kill or ban journalists. There has to come a time when eyewitness accounts of atrocities count for something.

Another international reporter at the scene of the massacre, Max Stahl from Yorkshire TV in Britain, was inside the Santa Cruz cemetery. When the soldiers opened fire, he first thought the sound was firecrackers. As young people sprinted through the cemetery, he realized what was happening. He started to film the people fleeing, and every ten minutes he would stop and bury his videotape in the soft dirt of a fresh grave. He knew that he would probably be arrested, and of course he was. He was interrogated for nine hours, then released. He returned to the cemetery that night, dug up the videotape, and had it smuggled out of the country.

Max Stahl's videotape is deeply moving. You see young people running at top speed through the cemetery and then running up into the mountains. But when a friend or family member was shot, others would stop and hold them, even when they knew that they would be taken next or shot. The Timorese didn't want their loved ones to die alone. Max filmed one young man who was shot and was being cradled in a friend's arms. As he lay bleeding to death, the young man pleaded, "Show this to the world."

The videotape was shown first in Japan and Holland, then England. The footage had enormous impact: A poll shortly after the news aired showed that the British wanted to know more about Timor than any other foreign policy issue. That prompted CBS producer Carl Ginsburg to push CBS News to cover the story. He had Allan and me come into CBS's New York headquarters. Allan's head was still wrapped in bandages during his interview. CBS used Max's footage to show what had happened in East Timor. The powerful news report aired on *CBS Evening News* on November 21, 1991.

Finally, nine days after the Santa Cruz massacre, the U.S. broadcast media silence around East Timor was broken. For sixteen years, one of the greatest genocides of the twentieth century had not been considered newsworthy in the United States. The Indonesian military understood how dangerous it was for the world to know what was happening in Timor. Within days of the massacre, the Indonesian military announced that Allan and I were a threat to national security and banned us from ever returning to Indonesia or occupied East Timor.

Only when the media shines a spotlight can people know and decide whether to act. A worldwide movement sprang up in the aftermath of the massacre to demand freedom for East Timor. In the United States, the East Timor Action Network was formed by two longtime human rights activists, Charlie Scheiner and John Miller, together with Allan and many others, with key roles played in later years by Lynn Fredriksson and Kristin Sundell. Chapters formed around the country, drawn from church, peace, student, veterans, and human rights groups. Grassroots efforts resulted in thousands of letters and phone calls to Congress. Military assistance to Indonesia was cut back over its abuses in East Timor against the wishes of successive Republican and Democratic administrations.

Profiting from Repression

WITH ITS LOW wages and iron-fisted political control, Indonesia had long been a cash cow for U.S. multinational corporations. These companies try to preserve their profits by doing the bidding of the Indonesian government. In 1994, there was a growing backlash in the United States from the Santa Cruz massacre. A lobbying group, the United States–Indonesia Society, was launched as a front for Suharto, U.S. multinational corporations, and the U.S. government. According to research done by Allan Nairn, it was backed by Indonesian intelligence, Suharto's son-in-law, the Lippo Group (which had made large donations to the Clinton-Gore campaign), Chevron, Texaco, Freeport-McMoRan, and former State Department and Pentagon officials.[4] The group distributed "educational" materials about Indonesia to 10 million U.S. high school students. The material was intended "to increase understanding of a country that has long been a solid friend of the United States and a nation that offers a great number of opportunities for American business." The group can count among its successes the fact that in 1995, President Clinton welcomed Suharto to the White House and offered to sell him twenty F-16 fighters.

The same military that killed the people of East Timor is in charge of keeping Indonesia safe for foreign investment and unsafe for local workers. For years, footwear companies such as Nike, Reebok, and Adidas thrived in this atmosphere. Reebok was making a substantial proportion of its high-priced athletic shoes in Indonesian sweatshops that pay poverty wages. In the mid-nineties, Reebok workers in Indonesia, most of them young women, were earning about $1.50 per day and working long hours in sweatshop conditions. By 2002, their pay had risen to about $75 per month—barely enough to buy basic goods, which had tripled in price following the Asian economic collapse in the late 1990s.[5]

By contrast, Reebok CEO Paul Fireman was drawing an annual salary of some $3.2 million in 2000, living in a $12 million house, and sailing a $35 million yacht. As one reporter noted, if Fireman sold his yacht, "he could pay his entire Indonesian workforce of 30,000 over a year's worth of wages."[6]

Every year, Reebok gives out four human rights awards, usually to grassroots activists who have been recommended by international panels. In 1992, a year after the Santa Cruz massacre, Reebok decided to honor Fernando de Araujo. Fernando was a Timorese student activist studying in Indonesia who had organized a protest after the Santa Cruz massacre. He was arrested and sentenced to nine years in prison; he was released in 1998.

In 1992, I met the head of the Reebok Human Rights Foundation at a dinner honoring human rights lawyers. Suharto, the former Indonesian dictator, had just been in town, and I heard that the Reebok CEO had met with him. I asked the Reebok representative, "Do you know if they discussed the issue of East Timor? Did Fireman say he would press the United States to stop selling weapons to Indonesia unless they withdraw from East Timor?" He said he didn't know.

To my surprise, soon after, the Reebok Human Rights Foundation called to ask if Allan Nairn and I would speak at the Reebok Human Rights Award ceremony about the massacre, since the honoree, Fernando de Araujo, was imprisoned. Allan and I debated this. We didn't want to seem to be endorsing Reebok, but on the other hand, we saw it as a chance to tell the story of East Timor to a wider audience. We decided to do it.

The event was a two-day affair in Boston in early December 1992. The awards festivities began with a luncheon at the Four Seasons Hotel. As I got my lunch, I saw the singer Richie Havens. I made a beeline to sit next to him, but not before a man slipped in between us. He introduced himself as Michael Stipe.

"Oh, are you an assistant to Richie Havens?" I asked.

"No," he said, smiling, "I have my own band. It's called R.E.M."

Reebok spends millions of dollars on publicity—to launder its image. Even if it cost Reebok $100,000 in prize money for the human rights activists and $1 million to sponsor the event, it was worth it to them. It is also why Reebok has spent millions in the past to underwrite Amnesty International concerts. Why not just pay the workers in Indonesia a nickel more per hour?

That evening there was a dinner. The late great Nigerian drummer Baba Olatunji was playing with Mickey Hart of the Grateful Dead. We met Tabitha Soren from MTV; she would be presenting Fernando's award. We told her not to hand us Fernando's award, because that photograph of us accepting an award from Reebok would go right back to Indonesia. We didn't want that symbolism. Then we explained to her how bad the situation was in East Timor.

The event was held the next morning at the Hynes Auditorium in downtown Boston. Thousands of people attended. We walked out onto a dark stage that had blue neon lights everywhere and the Reebok Human Rights Foundation video logo—a robot breaking through barbed wire—on large screens around the hall. Allan and I sat on the stage alongside singer Peter Gabriel, Tabitha Soren, Joan Baez, Michael Stipe, cellist Yo-Yo Ma, actress Cybill Shepherd, Mickey Hart, Paul Fireman, and Terry Anderson, the AP reporter held hostage for years in Lebanon. The lights came on, the video robot smashed through the barbed wire, and Richie Havens sang his famous song "Freedom."

Paul Fireman rose to speak. As people cheered him, the beaming Reebok boss declared, "If there is hope in 1992, it is in the work [these Reebok award recipients] do, and in our response to join them. It all depends on whether we all become, as Martin Luther King Jr. put it, drum majors for justice."

Fireman continued, "This fifth annual award ceremony is one way that we at Reebok beat that drum. My prayer is that together, we will awaken people everywhere to the cause of human rights. . . . So I welcome you here today not only to celebrate, but to join us as partners in the work and as colleagues in the cause."

Then the awards ceremony began. Each award was preceded by a two-minute video of what the recipients had done. Michael Stipe gave the award to Martin O'Brien, a community mediator from Northern Ireland. Mickey Hart gave the award to Floribert Chebeya Bahizire, a human rights activist from the former Zaire (now Congo). Another award went to Stacey Kabat, an American woman who advocated for battered women. The company basked in the glow of these powerful activists, the Reebok logo everywhere just to ensure that everyone understood who was behind the event.

Tabitha Soren then got up and announced, "This award is for Fernando de Araujo," and his picture appeared around the auditorium. "Amy Goodman and Allan Nairn are here to explain what happened that day because they survived the massacre."

We each had two minutes to speak. I described the massacre and ended with the words of Fernando de Araujo that he had sent from prison: "I shed tears of joy when I learned that I was nominated as a human rights defender. I think the world will not keep quiet. The award is not for me, it is for the East Timorese people. Therefore it must be used for the common interest, above all, for the defense of human rights."

Then Allan Nairn spoke. He described how the United States had collaborated in "one of the greatest genocides of this century." He then directed his message to the people in the room. "Americans who sincerely care about standing up for human rights have to be honest about another fact. The United States has for years supported such repressive regimes in large part on behalf of U.S. corporations. Inside Indonesia, the government suppresses independent unions, which allows companies to pay near-starvation wages. That helps Reebok, Nike, and others make huge profits from Indonesia, paying the workers who make their shoes, many of them young women from the countryside, wages of about one dollar per day. Such companies have an obligation to, at the very least, call on Washington to stop shipping arms to the brutal Indonesian regime."

Allan continued, "Right now in occupied Timor, on the other side of the world, it is about eleven o'clock at night. Chances are, that at this very moment, as we're sitting here in this room, a Timorese is in excruciating pain, being sliced with razor blades or ravaged by electric shock, at the hands of a soldier armed by our own government. . . . Like Fernando de Araujo, they have shown inexpressible courage in standing up for their right to self-determination and a free and decent life. The Timorese cannot vote in American elections. They cannot demonstrate in American streets. They cannot lobby the U.S. Congress. Only we Americans can bring to an end U.S. support for the running slaughter in East Timor."

The auditorium fell totally silent. Then some people started to clap. And then, as they had rehearsed with us, we were to step back and shake Paul Fireman's hand. We weren't going to shake his hand, but we didn't have to worry about that—because he certainly wasn't going to shake ours.

The event ended with Joan Baez singing "Amazing Grace." We were all supposed to sing along, arms linked with the person next to us, and walk through the auditorium to the room where we would have our picture taken. The problem was that we were now positioned so that I would have my arm around Paul Fireman. Allan and I stood back; we let them stand in front of us as they all sang and marched through the audience.

In spite of all the reporters who approached us afterward,

there was nothing in any of the major press accounts following the event. There was an Associated Press story, but we never saw it run in a major publication. *Rolling Stone* ran a brief story about what a fantastic star-studded event it was, with a photo of a number of the celebrities. There was not a word about the situation in East Timor or in the Reebok plants. Over the next decade, despite the lack of corporate press coverage, these corporate labor abuses spawned an antisweatshop movement that swept college campuses.

Reebok has continued to be a flash point for protest. In March 2002, Indonesian labor activist Dita Sari publicly rejected her $50,000 Reebok Human Rights Award. The 29-year-old union activist was arrested and tortured in 1995 for organizing a strike of 5,000 workers at a Reebok factory. Workers were demanding a raise. Dita later spent two years in prison for her activism.

In declining the lucrative prize, Dita declared, "Globalization has divided the world into two sides, which are antagonistic towards each other. There are wealthy creditors and bankrupt debtors, there are super rich countries and underdeveloped countries, super wealthy speculators and impoverished malnourished children. Globalization intensifies . . . the growing gap between the rich and the poor."

She concluded, "We cannot tolerate the way multinational companies treat the workers of the third world countries. And we surely hope that our stand can make a contribution to help change the labor conditions in Reebok companies."[7]

The Timorese Win

IN AUGUST 1999, a UN-backed referendum was finally held in East Timor. I tried to enter the country to cover the historic event, but the Indonesian military caught me twice and deported me. Allan Nairn managed to sneak in and witness what happened. The Timorese voted overwhelmingly for independence from Indonesia. In response, the Indonesian military immediately embarked on a scorched-earth strategy, unleashing militias that burned much of East Timor to the ground, killing more than one thousand Timorese. Allan's vivid reports on *Democracy Now!* documented the final destruction of Timor.

President Clinton initially refused to cut off aid to Indonesia. There was an outcry from grassroots activists and Congressional leaders. Finally, after a quarter century of U.S. backing, Clinton announced he would no longer support the Indonesian military in Timor. Britain followed Clinton's lead. Within days, the Indonesian military announced it would pull out and allow an international peacekeeping force to come in. But before that transition, as the terror intensified, the UN pulled out of Timor, as did the remaining foreign journalists. Allan stayed behind, the only foreign journalist still in Dili. Indonesian soldiers arrested him and threatened to sentence him to ten years in prison. His reports on *Democracy Now!* from the streets to the police station to his jail cell were among the most memorable we have ever aired.

In one of his last dispatches from jail, Allan read the statement that he had prepared in response to the charges that the Indonesian military had made against him: violating the ban and practicing journalism without permission. Here is what he wrote:

> I know that the army has put me on the black list. They did this because I watched their soldiers murder more than 271 people at the Santa Cruz cemetery. This crime was the responsibility of the Indonesian army commander, General Try Sutrisno, and the Minister of Defense, General Benny Murdani.

The murders were committed with American M-16 rifles. The American government also bears some of the responsibility because they have armed, trained, and given money to the TNI-ABRI [Indonesian military], even though they knew the [Indonesian military] is led by murderers and is responsible for the deaths of hundreds of thousands of Timorese, Acehnese, West Papuan, and Indonesian civilians.

Because I survived the massacre and denounced the crime to the outside world, the [Indonesian military] and the Suharto government banned me as a "threat to national security."

I do not think that I am a threat to the Indonesian or Timorese people, but I hope that I am a threat to General Wiranto and General Tanjung, and the other present and former leaders of the [Indonesian military]. I believe that they feel threatened by anyone who would expose their crimes. General Wiranto and Generals Bambang, Zacky, Syafei, Kiki, and many others, for example, are responsible for the current militia terror in occupied East Timor and for the increase in repression against the people of Aceh. This is no secret to the people of Timor or to the people of Indonesia or Aceh. They have suffered for decades under the repression and corruption of the [Indonesian military]. Many brave Indonesians, Timorese, Acehnese, and West Papuans have been killed, arrested, tortured, or raped because they dared to criticize the army and demand their right to freedom.

As a foreigner and a journalist, particularly an American journalist, I know that I enjoy a certain de facto political leeway that enables me to say things that local people would be killed for saying. I have tried to use that privilege to tell the truth about [the Indonesian military]. If, because of this, the army feels they must arrest or jail me, then I know that there is nothing I can do to stop them. But they know that they cannot arrest or kill all the people of Indonesia. That is why they are now so fearful, and that is why I believe they will lose their desperate struggle to retain their hold on power and their police state.

During my most recent detention, I have been interrogated by officials from army Intel, police Intel, Kopassus Group 5, and many other units. They have asked me many questions about my political motives and opinions. I would summarize my opinions this way:

I am pro human rights, pro democracy, and anti-TNI-ABRI [the Indonesian military]. I am a supporter of the people of East Timor, Aceh, West Papua, and Indonesia, and an opponent of the officials who have repressed and exploited them.

As an American citizen who is visiting Indonesia and occupied East Timor, I also want to be clear that I believe in even-handedness. The same political, moral, and legal standards that are applied to the [Indonesian military] officers should also be applied to the officers and political leaders of the United States. So while I support the UN Secretary-General's call for war crimes and crimes against humanity prosecution on East Timor, I think that the prosecution should not be limited to Indonesian officials. Foreign officials who were accomplices to atrocities in East Timor, and provided both murder weapons and the logistics of repression, should also be charged, prosecuted, and if convicted, jailed.

Pragmatically, it is hard to imagine General Wiranto sitting in jail. It is even harder to imagine President Clinton as his cellmate. But justice should be impartial.

It is time for the genocide to end. Untold thousands of Timorese lie slaughtered. Their families are bereft. The victims of Santa Cruz, Liquiça, and Suai can no longer speak. Those of us who can should insist that the killing stop right now. And we should also insist that the killers face justice, regardless of who they are.

These same principles apply of course to atrocities everywhere. I think that this is a simple idea and that most people would agree.

If General Wiranto or any other officials have further questions about my views, I would be glad to answer them personally at a time and place of their choosing. I would also be glad to give details on the crimes referred to above, and on the complicity in them of General Wiranto and other officials.

Allan Nairn was deported from Indonesia several days later.

The Indonesian military's final rampage destroyed more than 80 percent of Timor's buildings. More than 1,000 Timorese were killed.

On May 20, 2002, East Timor celebrated its independence.

13

Not on Bended Knee

Nobody is as powerful as we make them out to be.
—ALICE WALKER

ON ELECTION DAY 2000, I was in the *Democracy Now!* office at WBAI on Wall Street when I received a call minutes before going on the air at 9:00 a.m. The caller said, "Hello, I am calling from White House Communications." Things get very frantic moments before broadcasting, and we get a fair number of unusual calls.

White *Horse?* That's the famous tavern in Greenwich Village where poet Dylan Thomas was said to have drunk himself to death. Even the White Horse has a PR agent?

Then the caller said that the president would like to speak to me. I said, "The president of what?" We were on the air in less than a minute. "The president of the United States." Oh, please. "He'd like to call in to your radio program."

"Yeah, right," I said. "Whatever."

I ran into the studio as the theme music for *Democracy Now!* was playing. Our producers were Brad Simpson, a history grad student, and Maria Carrion. Maria had produced *Democracy Now!* for two years before moving home to Spain, and had flown back just to help out for the election. That was supposed to mean three days, but this was the election of 2000. She ended up staying five weeks—from the night before the election to the day after the final "selection" of George W. Bush.

I could hardly tell Maria and Brad as they were frantically putting the finishing touches on the election show that the president was calling in, especially because I didn't believe it myself. But as the music swelled, I said, "By the way, that was the White House on the phone. They said the president might call in." "Yeah, right," Maria said. I left it at that.

When *Democracy Now!* finished, we were about to head out for coffee when someone began shouting from master control, "President Clinton is on the phone!"

Maria ran in, took the call, and yelled for me to get into master control immediately. Gonzalo Aburto, the host of the Latino music show that followed *Democracy Now!* on Tuesdays, was at the control board.

I ran into the studio and heard, over the blasting Latino beat, the disembodied voice of President Clinton saying, "Hello, hello, is anyone there? Can you hear me?" The faders on our microphones were all the way down, and the music was all the way up. I practically dove over the master control board and pulled down the music, put up all of our mikes, and welcomed the president to WBAI.

"For Clinton it was supposed to be two minutes of get-out-the-vote happy talk with a progressive radio show and then: Gotta go," *The Washington Post* later wrote of the encounter.[1] The story continued, "In this insider media age when oh-so-serious reporters measure status by access to the powerful, Goodman is the journalist as uninvited guest," wrote Michael Powell. "You might think of the impolite question; she asks it. She torments Democrats no less than Republicans."[2]

There was no question this was President Clinton's voice, so we just launched in. Here's an excerpt:

AMY GOODMAN: Mr. President, are you there?

PRESIDENT CLINTON: I am. Can you hear me?

GOODMAN: Yes, we can. You are calling radio stations to tell people to get out and vote. What do you say to people who feel that the two parties are bought by corporations, and . . . at this point feel that their vote doesn't make a difference?

CLINTON: There's just not a shred of evidence to support that. That's what I would say.

. . . The truth is there is an ideological struggle between those who believe that the best way to grow the economy is to give more money to the wealthy, and the Democrats, who believe that the wealthy will make more money if average people do better.

GOODMAN: President Clinton, what is your position on granting Leonard Peltier, the Native American activist, executive clemency?

CLINTON: I know it's very important to a lot of people, maybe on both sides of the issue. And I think I owe it to them to give it an honest look-see. . . . And I pledge to do that.

GOODMAN: And you will give an answer in his case?

CLINTON: Oh, yeah, I'll decide one way or the other.*

---

*Clinton did not act on Peltier's application for clemency. The Native American activist, who is serving two life sentences for the shooting death of two FBI agents, has been imprisoned since 1977. Peltier continues to maintain his innocence. Amnesty International has appealed for his release.

GOODMAN: Do you support a moratorium on the death penalty, given the studies that show the racist way it has been applied?

CLINTON: . . . The disturbing thing to me is that there is not only an apparent racial disparity on death row, but also way over half the cases come from a relatively small number of the U.S. attorneys' offices.

But again, let me just say this. If you are concerned about that, that's a good reason to vote for Al Gore and Joe Lieberman, and Hillary for the Senate. . . . Because we know the Democrats care about these issues, and we know they're not very important to the Republicans. So that's another example of another reason you ought to vote for the Democrats.

GOODMAN: Gore supports the death penalty.

CLINTON: He does, but . . .

GOODMAN: And Lieberman.

CLINTON: Yes, they do. But there is a difference in supporting it and thinking that you would carry it out even if you thought the system was fundamentally unfair.

GOODMAN: But the studies show that . . .

CLINTON: But the studies are not complete. . . . And so I think that if you are interested in having somebody that at least has the capacity to look at the fairness of this, you only have one choice.

GOODMAN: Well, I guess many people were quite disturbed that when you first ran for president, you went back in the midst of your campaign to Arkansas and presided over the execution of a mentally impaired man.

CLINTON: Yeah, but let me . . . let's go back to the facts here. He was not mentally impaired when he committed the crime.

He became mentally impaired because he was wounded after he murdered somebody. And the law says that it is your mental state at the time you committed the crime . . .

GOODMAN: President Clinton, UN figures show that up to 5,000 children a month die in Iraq because of the sanctions against Iraq.

CLINTON: That's not true. That's not true. . . . If any child is without food or medicine or a roof over his or her head in Iraq, it's because [Saddam Hussein] is claiming the sanctions are doing it and sticking it to his own children.

GOODMAN: The past two UN heads of the program in Iraq have quit, calling the U.S./UN policy genocidal. What is your response to that?

CLINTON: They're wrong! . . . Saddam Hussein says, "I'm going to starve my kids unless you let me buy nuclear weapons, chemical weapons, and biological weapons." . . . That's just not right! You know, the truth is, a lot of these people want to start doing business with Saddam Hussein again because they want his money.

GOODMAN: Amnesty International has described what the Israeli forces are now doing in the occupied territories as . . .

CLINTON: Listen, I can't do a whole press conference here. It's Election Day and I've got a lot of people and places to call.

GOODMAN: Well, I guess these are the questions that are very important to our listeners . . .

CLINTON: Well, I've answered them all.

GOODMAN: Right, and we appreciate that. And . . .

CLINTON: I have answered them all. Now let me just tell you, on the Israeli-Palestinian thing . . . which is something that I know more than a little bit about, the only answer to this over the long run is an agreement that covers all the issues that the Palestinians feel aggrieved by; guarantees the Israelis security and acceptance within the region; and is a just and lasting peace. That's the only answer to this in the long run.

GOODMAN: Why not support a UN force in the Middle East for the illegal occupation of the territories? And at this point I think there are around one hundred fifty people who have been killed in the occupied territories, overwhelmingly Palestinian.

CLINTON: You can support it if you want to, but the Israelis won't support it. And there was a war in which that happened. And if you want to make peace, then you have to do things that both sides can agree with. That's what a peace agreement is.

GOODMAN: Many people say that Ralph Nader has the high percentage points he has in the polls because you have been responsible for taking the Democratic party to the right. What do you say to that?

CLINTON: I'm glad you asked that, and that's the last question I've got time for. I'll be happy to . . . answer that.

What is the measure of taking the Democratic party to the right? That we cut the welfare rolls in half? That poverty is at a twenty-year low? That child poverty has been cut by a third in our administration? That the incomes of average Americans have gone up 15 percent after inflation? . . . That the basic standard test scores among African-Americans and other minorities have gone up steadily?

GOODMAN: Can I say that some people . . .

CLINTON: Now, let me just finish.

GOODMAN: Let me just say . . .

CLINTON: Now let me . . . now, wait a minute. You started this, and every question you've asked has been hostile and combative. So you listen to my answer, will you do that?

GOODMAN: They've been critical questions . . .

CLINTON: Now, you just listen to me. You ask the questions, and I'm going to answer. You have asked questions in a hostile, combative, and even disrespectful tone, but I—and you have never been able to combat the facts I have given you. Now, you listen to this. The other thing Ralph Nader says is that, you know, he's pure as Caesar's wife on the environment.

Under this administration, forty-three million more Americans are breathing cleaner air. We have safer drinking water, safer food, cleaner water. We have more land set aside than any administration in history since Theodore Roosevelt. . . . People can say whatever they want to. Those are the facts.

GOODMAN: What people say is that you pushed through NAFTA, that we have the highest population of prisoners in the industrialized world, over two million. That more people are on death row in this country than anywhere else.

CLINTON: Well, all right. Okay, that's fine. But two-thirds of the American people support that. I think there are too many people in prison, too. . . . Nobody ever said America was perfect. The real problem you've got are the . . . this country is in good shape. Now, I've talked to you a long time. It's Election Day. There are a lot of other people that . . .

GOODMAN: We appreciate that.

CLINTON: . . . I've got to go.

GOODMAN: One last question. What about granting an executive order ending racial profiling in this country?

CLINTON: I expect that we will end racial profiling. . . . I'm opposed to it. Al Gore is opposed to it. Here's the deal. Look, I had two people who work for me in the White House who were wrongly stopped, handcuffed, and hassled the other day. I have spoken out against racial profiling and Hillary has made it a big issue in New York.

GOODMAN: Thank you for spending the time, President Clinton.

CLINTON: Thank you.

We were amazed that President Clinton had stayed on the phone for so long. We quickly produced a transcript of the interview, alerted the press, then ran the interview during our regular broadcast the following day.

After the show, I got a call from the White House press office. A staffer let me know how furious they were at me for "breaking the ground rules for the interview."

"Ground rules?" I asked. "What ground rules? He called up to be interviewed, and I interviewed him."

"He called to discuss getting out the vote, and you strayed from the topic. You also kept him on much longer than the two to three minutes we agreed to," she huffed.

"President Clinton is the most powerful person in the world," I replied. "He can hang up when he wants to."

The Clinton administration threatened to ban me from the White House and suggested to a *Newsday* reporter that they might punish me for my attitude by denying me access—not that I had any to lose. White House spokesman Elliot Diringer said, "Any good reporter understands that if you violate the ground rules in an interview, that is going to be taken into account the next time you are seeking an interview."

First of all, we hadn't agreed to any ground rules. Clinton called us.

Second, we wouldn't have agreed to any. The only ground rule for good reporting I know is that you don't trade your principles for access. We were treating the president not as royalty, but as a public servant accountable to the people.

Gingrich Can't Ditch Bitch Comment

NINETEEN NINETY-FOUR WAS a turning point for Republicans in Congress. The House had been Democratic for over thirty years. But two years into Clinton's first presidency, Republicans swept the House, making Newt Gingrich their Speaker. They started to enact the Contract with America: a ten-point plan that included provisions that cracked down on the poor, particularly women and children; called for less money for social programs and more money for prisons; targeted the United Nations; and strengthened the death penalty. Many called it a Contract *on* America.

One of the most effective platforms for Gingrich was the Speaker's conference—a thirty-year-old tradition in which the House leader would meet daily with reporters to lay out his message and strategy. Gingrich was riding high, using the daily gaggles as a way to put his spin on the news.

These daily conferences were quite a phenomenon. The former Speaker, Tom Foley, did not allow cameras. Newt Gingrich, being a master of the mass media, decided to have them. Both CNN and C-SPAN often ran the session live. That was Newt Gingrich's twenty minutes in the limelight every day. It was almost as if he were the conductor of a symphony. For a while, it went very well for him. I attended his Speaker's conference at the fifty-day mark for the new Republican majority, at which he was evaluating all the things Congress had accomplished. He ended by saying that he felt the Speaker's conference was an excellent institution and that he would continue it as long as it worked well.

A number of the reporters seemed to bask in his praise. It was also working well for them. Now they could get their sound bites for their editors and they could say they themselves had asked the Speaker a question.

I considered it a great insult that Newt Gingrich felt this was working well. I do not think that maintaining access is worth the price, where journalists are truly like props for this play being staged every day.

At the Speaker's conference on March 3, 1995, I asked Gingrich about his alleged comment, as Gingrich's mother told then CBS reporter Connie Chung during an interview, that he called First Lady Hillary Clinton a bitch.

> **AMY GOODMAN:** I have a question about tone. You were talking about that earlier. Many people are talking about what's going on in the House as a war on women, the whole issue about reproductive rights that keeps getting raised. But this is a question not about legislation. Some say you really fired the opening salvo against women when you didn't apologize to American women for calling the First Lady a bitch. Why haven't you apologized?
>
> **NEWT GINGRICH:** I never agreed to say anything about that. And I can't imagine you're asking that question.
>
> **GOODMAN:** Why haven't you apologized for it?
>
> **GINGRICH:** I've talked to Mrs. Clinton. She understands exactly where we're at.

GOODMAN: Why haven't you apologized to American women? Because it goes beyond calling . . .

GINGRICH: I never said . . . I never said . . . To the best of my knowledge, I never said what you just said.

GOODMAN: Are you calling your mother a liar, then?

GINGRICH: I'm calling you a remarkably foolish person for having that kind of conversation here, and I am very sorry you have cared to bring what Connie Chung did back into the public arena. Connie Chung lied to my mother. You're now trying to exploit a lie by a professional reporter to my mother. And I'm not going to take any more comment from you. I think it is very embarrassing to you as a reporter to try to make any use of Connie Chung having lied to my mother. I think you should be ashamed . . .

GOODMAN: It's not about Connie Chung . . .

GINGRICH: . . . You should be ashamed. Yes it is.

GOODMAN: Why haven't you apologized to American women for calling her a bitch?

GINGRICH: I'll say it one more time. You are trying to use my mother in a very despicable way. And I think it is very sad. And I have advised my mother to talk to no reporters because of precisely this kind of exploitation by people like you.

This exchange needs to be put in the context of the week that led up to that Speaker's conference. Late one night, the Ways and Means Committee (what some called the "Ways to Be Mean Committee") was debating the issue of welfare funding to the states. They finally decided that if a state's abortion rate increased or the illegitimate births increased, that state would not get a bonus.

Here was a group comprised mainly of white men debating how women get pregnant, particularly young poor women.

This hardly got coverage in the press the next day because it was very complicated, and also happened late at night. The press was hailing the fact that so many decisions were getting passed every day; the premium seemed to be on the speed, rather than on the content, of what was happening.

The next day, a conference was called in the Senate swamp, which is an area outside of the Senate, by two of the twenty-nine women who had charged Oregon Senator Bob Packwood with sexual harassment and assault. The women said that Packwood's assaults ranged from jumping them to, in several cases, ripping their clothes off. The women were quite explicit. They were out there carrying 4,000 letters from Oregonians to the majority leader, Senator Bob Dole, demanding Senate ethics hearings in the case of Robert Packwood. These women, many of them Republicans working for or with Packwood, risked their livelihoods to come forward. Despite their allegations, Bob Packwood was promoted to head of the Senate Finance Committee, one of the most powerful positions in the Senate.

The next evening, I was watching the House Appropriations Committee make their final proposals to the floor. Again, it was eight at night. They were debating an amendment submitted by Congressman Istook from Oklahoma that would bar Medicaid from paying for abortions, even if the woman was a victim of rape or incest. Representative Nita Lowey of New York stood up and said, "You're sending this message to the country that you must have your rapist's child. You must have your father's child."

With that, the assembled members passed the amendment.

While the Contract with America was not explicitly about women's rights, committee after committee was passing legislation around these issues that would have a profound impact on women.

Then there was the language being used by the Republican leadership. Weeks before, there had been a small flap over Majority Leader Dick Armey's slip of the tongue to a group of radio reporters when he called Congressman Barney Frank "Barney Fag." This occurred at a time when a series of brutal gay murders throughout Texas went unsolved. Meanwhile, Congress was refusing to increase the penalties for hate crimes.

It seemed to me that what the leadership said mattered, especially when spoken by the Speaker of the House. From fag to bitch, a message was being sent, a tone set for the new laws being passed. This was the setting for my question to Newt Gingrich.

After the Speaker's conference, I was invited to talk shows around the country. They played my interaction with Gingrich, but they didn't play the first two sentences, where I described the tone set by Gingrich as a war on women. The whole discussion of the poor—most of whom are women—and the discussion about reproductive rights were taken as opportunities to attack women's rights.

The Speaker's conference was fundamentally about control. Who was controlling the discussion? I didn't want to give Newt Gingrich a chance just to hold forth, as he always did. I felt he had to be challenged at each point. That's what a journalist's job is, not to be there to provide him with a comfortable platform. That's why I went back and forth. Some called that badgering. I called that "answer the question."

Two months later, in early May 1995, Newt Gingrich announced he was canceling his weekly Speaker's conference. Gingrich spokesman Tony Blankley told *The Washington Post:* "Some of the questioning was a tad flamboyant and got in the way of serious discussion of the news. It provided an opportunity for obscure journalists to come in and harangue him on their pet points. He was just too juicy a target for some of these folks to resist."[3]

Gingrich was trying to blame me for closing himself off from the press, but that made no sense: If he was reacting to me, he would have ended the Speaker's conference shortly after our exchange, in March 1995.

The real reason Gingrich was trying to hide was something much more damaging: On April 19, 1995, Timothy McVeigh blew up the Alfred P. Murrah Federal Building in Oklahoma City, killing 168 people. McVeigh, an antigovernment extremist, sounded chillingly similar to Gingrich, who railed daily against what he considered to be the evils of big government. The more exposure Gingrich got, the more unpopular he became. The weeks following the bombing were a good time for Gingrich to run for cover.

14

Psyops Comes Home

If you tell a lie big enough and keep repeating it, people will eventually come to believe it.

—JOSEF GOEBBELS (1897–1945), HITLER'S MINISTER OF PROPAGANDA

COLONEL SAM GARDINER IS a warrior of the old school. A retired Air Force colonel and a lecturer at the National War College, Air War College, and Naval War College, he had the utmost respect for the ground rules of his profession. Psychological warfare—psyops, to those in the business—was something that the United States used against its enemies. Foreign enemies, of course, because the CIA and Pentagon have been forbidden since just after World War II from targeting U.S. citizens.

Psyops is the military way of winning the hearts and minds of a population. According to the Department of Defense, psyops is intended to "induce or reinforce *foreign* attitudes and behavior favorable to the U.S. . . . by planning and conducting operations to convey information to *foreign* audiences to influence their emotions, motives, objective reasoning, and ultimately the behavior of *foreign* governments, organizations, groups, and individuals."[1] [emphasis added]

The 1948 Smith-Mundt Act prohibited the domestic dissemination of U.S. government propaganda. The reasoning behind Smith-Mundt was that "Congress wanted to be certain that a U.S. government agency could not brainwash citizens as Hitler had in Germany. On the commercial side, too, the domestic media did not want competition in the marketplace from a nonprofit government-funded entity."[2] This legal firewall is what prevents the Voice of America from broadcasting domestically. And it's why an act of Congress is required to allow a film made by the U.S. Information Agency to be released in the United States.

Like any seasoned military officer, Colonel Sam Gardiner knew the rules. But in the course of lecturing and his frequent appearances as a military analyst in 2003 during the Iraq war on PBS's *NewsHour,* the BBC, and NPR, something began to disturb Gardiner about the news he was seeing and hearing on Iraq. It had a familiar and disturbing ring to it. In fact, it sounded like the work that he once did in the military.

Gardiner came around to a conclusion that horrified him: The Bush administration had turned psychological operations against Americans. No longer were just foreign enemies being targeted for coercion and deception. Now the target was the U.S. public.

"It was not bad intelligence. It was much more. It was an orchestrated effort. It began before the war, was a major effort during the war, and continues as post-conflict distortions," wrote Gardiner in a fifty-six-page self-published report.[3] He had not intended to write the report himself. He had been supplying information to *Los Angeles Times* correspondent Mark Fineman. But

Fineman, 51, unexpectedly died in Baghdad on September 23, 2003. Gardiner released his findings on October 8, 2003.[4]

What Gardiner detailed was blowback on a grand scale. The power of the U.S. military has been deployed to deceive the American public. While the futile search for weapons of mass destruction continued in Iraq, weapons of mass deception were unleashed on an unwitting American population. It was a $200 million PR campaign to deceive the American public.[5]

"In the most basic sense, Washington and London did not trust the peoples of their democracies to come to right decisions," wrote Gardiner. "Truth became a casualty. When truth is a casualty, democracy receives collateral damage."

The issue of whether the Pentagon was waging an orchestrated domestic propaganda campaign was first openly acknowledged in the fall of 2002. Donald Rumsfeld was asked whether the Pentagon was engaged in propagandizing through the Defense Department's Office of Strategic Influence (*strategic influence* is military jargon for propaganda). Military officials said they might release false news stories to the foreign press, but they had to retract that when news organizations expressed concern that the bogus stories could be picked up in the domestic press.

Mocking concerns about propaganda blowback, Rumsfeld informed the media on November 18, 2002, that he would eliminate the program in name only: "And then there was the Office of Strategic Influence. You may recall that. And 'Oh my goodness gracious, isn't that terrible, Henny Penny, the sky is going to fall.' I went down that next day and said fine, if you want to savage this thing, fine. I'll give you the corpse. There's the name. You can have the name, but I'm gonna keep doing every single thing that needs to be done, and I have."

Indeed he did, and the American public became the focus of a high-intensity domestic psyops program. The lies coming out of the Bush administration picked up in frequency and audacity. False claims about the presence of nonexistent weapons of mass destruction were but one thread in this elaborate tapestry of deceit. "Disloyal" allies such as France and Germany were targeted and smeared. The lies took many forms. Sometimes it was an outright official fabrication. At other times, government officials would deliberately not correct a lie gaining currency in the street. There were unofficial leaks and stories planted on background. Finally, there were black operations, where false documents may have been forged in elaborate schemes to smear and deceive.

In total, Gardiner asserts, "There were over fifty stories manufactured or at least engineered that distorted the picture of Gulf [War] II for the American and British people."

The Bush administration recruited some time-tested help for this effort. It retained John Rendon, head of the PR firm The Rendon Group. Rendon is a self-described "information warrior," who has worked on Iraq-related issues for clients including the Pentagon and CIA. Rendon was instrumental in setting up the Iraqi National Congress in 1992, securing the channeling of $12 million from the CIA to the group between 1992 and 1996.[6] The Pentagon's Office of Strategic Influence retained Rendon for the invasion of Iraq.

Rendon spoke at a July 2003 conference in London about the propaganda effort around the invasion. Colonel Gardiner attended the talk and recounts that Rendon "said the embedded idea was great. It worked as they had found in the test. It was the war version of reality television, and for the most part, they did not lose control of the story."

Rendon did note one problem: "He said one of the mistakes they made was that they lost control of the context. The retired people in the networks had too much control of context. That has to be fixed for the next war."

The themes of the invasion propaganda effort were twofold. The war on terror is a fight between good and evil (and it didn't hurt to invoke images of a Christian crusade against Islam). And Iraq was responsible for the 9/11 attacks—"what propaganda theorists would call the 'big lie,'" says Gardiner.

With these two concepts underlying all messages, Gardiner states that the strategic influence campaign around Iraq "distorted perceptions of the situation both before and during the conflict; caused misdirection of portions of the military operation; was irresponsible in parts; might have been illegal in some ways; cost big bucks; will be even more serious in the future."

The media had a starring role in this effort. Propaganda requires a gullible and complacent media in order to thrive. The U.S. corporate media played its part to the hilt.

In his report "Truth from These Podia," Gardiner details a pattern of strategic lies:[7]

THE OFFICIAL LINE

The Poison Factory That Wasn't

Secretary of State Powell showed a picture of a "terrorist poison and explosives factory" in his presentation to the UN Security Council on February 5, 2003.

THE REALITY

From the Los Angeles Times, *September 3, 2003:*

"The 'poison factory' lacked sophistication and was housed in a small cinderblock building bearing brown granules and ammonia-like scents. Tests by U.S. laboratories revealed traces of chemicals including hydrogen cyanide and potassium cyanide, substances usually used to kill rodents."

THE OFFICIAL LINE	THE REALITY

The Missing Terrorist Training Camp

"Former Iraqi military officers have described a highly secret terrorist training facility in Iraq known as Salman Pak, where both Iraqis and non-Iraqi Arabs receive training on hijacking planes and trains, planting explosives in cities, sabotage, and assassinations."

—White House White Paper, *Decade of Deception,* September 12, 2002

No evidence was found of this "secret terrorist training facility."

The Dangerous Dirty Bomb

• "This environment is ideal for countries like Iraq to train and support a terrorist operation using radiation weapons."

—Khidhir Hamza, *Wall Street Journal,* June 12, 2002

• "A few officials speaking on background, have engaged in what-could-go-wrong conversations, saying they are kept awake at night by the prospect of a dirty bomb."

—David Sanger, *International Herald Tribune,* February 28, 2003

There was no credible evidence of Iraq possessing radiation weapons or dirty bombs after UN arms inspections in the 1990s.

THE OFFICIAL LINE

The POW Ruse

"Intelligence officials" leaked information that Lieutenant Commander Scott Speicher, a Navy pilot shot down in the first Gulf War, was alive and being held captive by Iraq. The rumor, which originated with a single defector, was played up by top officials.

September 2002: President Bush mentions the case in a speech to the UN.

March 19, 2003: Wolfowitz says there's "pretty hard evidence he survived the crash."

April 2003: It was reported that his initials had been found on the wall of a cell.

THE REALITY

July 16, 2003—The Washington Times reports there is no evidence that Speicher is or was alive at the time of these reports. "It casts doubt on the credibility of the defector."

THE OFFICIAL LINE

Bombing Baghdad into Darkness

When Baghdad was plunged into darkness, the United States denied targeting the power grid.

- "We did not have the power grid as a target. That was not us."

—DOD news briefing, April 4, 2003, Victoria Clarke

THE REALITY

Colonel Gardiner asserts:

- The United States targeted portions of the power grid in the north during a special operations attack on the dam at Hadithah on April 1 or 2.

- The power grid was attacked two or three times south of Baghdad along Highway 6.

Discovery of Chemical Warheads

- "UN weapons inspectors in Iraq recently discovered a new variety of rocket seemingly configured to strew bomblets filled with chemical or biological agents over large areas, U.S. officials say."

—*New York Times* News Service, March 10, 2003

- "There is no evidence to conclude that Iraq has a warhead with chemical submunitions. No information on testing has been obtained, and experimentation with bursts at relatively high release points has not been seen."

—Office of Secretary of Defense, report on Patriot use during Gulf War I [UN inspections prevented Iraq from developing any major new missile technology in the 1990s]

THE OFFICIAL LINE

Discovery of Chemical Warheads (continued)

- "Inspectors discovered cluster bombs and submunitions that appeared designed to deliver chemical or biological agents. Contrary to initial Iraqi statements, a number of bombs and over a hundred submunitions were found."

—State Department, March 10, 2003

THE REALITY

- [The secretary of defense] had discounted Iraq developing what would be a very complex weapon.

"These rumors were an effort to discredit Hans Blix and UNMOVIC," Gardiner says.

Uniformed Imposter

March 7, 2003: Iraq is acquiring military uniforms "identical down to the last detail" to those worn by American and British forces.

March 26, 2003, Victoria Clarke: "We knew they were acquiring uniforms that looked like U.S. and UK uniforms. And the reporting was that they planned to use them, give them to the thugs, as I call them, to go out, carry out reprisals against the Iraqi people, and try to blame it on coalition forces."

March 28, 2003, Rumsfeld: "They put on American and

Gardiner notes: "The Pentagon had intelligence that Iraq had acquired uniforms, but there is no evidence they were used in any of the ways described."

THE OFFICIAL LINE	THE REALITY
Uniformed Imposter (continued)	

British uniforms to try to fool regular Iraqi soldiers into surrendering to them, and then execute them as an example for others who might contemplate defection or capitulation."

Droning On

October 2002 CIA report: Iraq "attempted to convert some of its J-29 jet trainer aircraft into a [remotely piloted drone aircraft] . . . that can be fitted with spray . . ."

October 2002, President Bush: " . . . Drones that could be used to attack the U.S."

From the Los Angeles Times, *June 15, 2003:*
"They quickly found the 'drones': five burned and blackened nine-foot wings dumped near the front gate. 'It could have been a student project, or maybe a model,' the team's expert, U.S. Air Force Capt. Libbie Boehm, said with a shrug."

Hanging Women

March 23, 2003: "In one case, an Iraqi woman was hanged after she waved to coalition forces."
—General Peter Pace, CNN

There were no other reports of an incident like this and no verification of this story.

THE OFFICIAL LINE	THE REALITY
Punishing France	
France and Germany supplied Iraq with high-precision switches that could be used in a bomb. —*The New York Times*	Iraq had requested these switches, but they were never supplied.

Frenchwhacking Again

May 8, 2003: "France is rumored to have issued passports of Iraqi officials in Syria." —Charleston *Post and Courier*	*May 15 and 16, 2003:* France denies the accusations and accuses the United States of a smear campaign, citing this as one example.
May 9, 2003, Rumsfeld, DOD briefing: "France has historically had a very close relationship with Iraq. My understanding is that it continued right up until the outbreak of the war. What took place after that, we'll find out."	*Colonel Gardiner's analysis:* "When Rumsfeld was questioned, he followed pattern. When something is on the street that is part of the strategic influence campaign, let it linger. . . . He wanted people to believe the stories."

White House press briefing, May 14, 2003, with White House spokesman Scott McClellan:

> Q: Going back to France, the French have denied selling arms to Iraq and issuing passports to Syria to fleeing Iraqi officials. Are those charges valid?

THE OFFICIAL LINE	THE REALITY

Frenchwhacking Again (continued)

MR. McCLELLAN: Well, I think that those are questions you can address to France . . .

Q: Well, no, it's information the U.S. claims to have.

MR. McCLELLAN: I don't have anything for you.

"White Flag" Killings

Allegations swirled that nine Marines were killed on March 23 when they responded to Iraqi soldiers waving a white flag of surrender.

DOD press briefing, Rumsfeld, May 25, 2003: "Some of the biggest losses we have taken are due to Iraqis committing violations of the law of armed conflict . . . by luring us into surrender situations then opening fire on our troops. So this is the plan that is very well thought out, and that will play out, I think, as we expect."

The stories were false.

According to Gardiner: "We know from a lessons-learned report released early in October [2003] that the death of nine Marines is under investigation as a friendly fire accident. From individual reports, we know that at least one of the Marines killed on March 23, reported as having been caught in the ruse, was hit directly in the chest with a round from an A-10 gun. We know at least one of the wives of a Marine killed that day is asking for the truth of her husband's death."

THE OFFICIAL LINE	THE REALITY

"White Flag" Killings (continued)

President Bush, April 5, 2003: "They have executed prisoners of war, waged attacks under the white flag of truce . . ."	Again, the stories were false.

Killing POWs

Iraq was alleged to have executed two British prisoners on March 27, 2003.

"If anyone needs any further evidence of the depravity . . ."

—Tony Blair at joint news conference with President Bush at Camp David

"They have executed prisoners of war."

—General Pace, CNN, *Larry King Live*

"They have executed prisoners of war . . ."

—President Bush

The UK finally pulled away from the story on April 5 when Blair's spokesman said there was no "absolute evidence" that UK servicemen had been executed.

The United States continued pushing the fabricated story until April 7, when Rumsfeld said cagily, "I had said, 'They have executed POWs,' and I did not say from what country."

THE OFFICIAL LINE	THE REALITY

Bombing Civilians, Blaming Iraq

March 29, 2003: Central Command spokesman asserts that an explosion in a Baghdad marketplace killed more than fifty civilians, and suggests the likely cause was Iraqi fire.

April 2, 2003: Correspondent Robert Fisk of *The Independent* (London) newspaper reports finding shrapnel at the bombing site that shows the serial number of a U.S.-made HARM missile built by Raytheon.

Un-Surrendering Division

March 22, 2003, CBS News: "An entire division of the Iraqi army, numbering 8,000 soldiers, surrendered to coalition forces in southern Iraq Friday, Pentagon officials said. The move marked the largest single unit to surrender en masse."

Agence France-Presse, March 23, 2003: "An Iraqi commander near the southern city of Basra said Sunday that his division, which Washington earlier said had surrendered, would continue to resist U.S. and British forces. 'I am with my men in Basra, we continue to defend the people and riches' of the town, Colonel Khaled al-Hashemi, commander of the 51st Mechanized Division, told the satellite television channel Al-Jazeera."

Gardiner says this announcement by the U.S. and UK was a classic psychological warfare operation.

THE OFFICIAL LINE

Uranium from Niger

"The British government has learned that Saddam Hussein recently sought significant quantities of uranium from Africa."
—President Bush, 2003 State of the Union Address

THE REALITY

The claim—repeated by Vice President Cheney in September 2003—was false and is based on forged documents. But who forged them?

Writing in *The New Yorker*, Seymour Hersh reports that while there is no consensus about the origin of the forgeries, it "may have been done by a small group of disgruntled retired CIA clandestine operators [who] had banded together in the late summer of last year and drafted the fraudulent documents themselves. 'The agency guys were so pissed at Cheney,' the former officer said. 'They said, 'Okay, we're going to put the bite on these guys.'" [8]

THE OFFICIAL LINE	THE REALITY
Smearing Antiwar Politician	
April 22, 2003: The London *Daily Telegraph* reports papers retrieved from Iraq's foreign ministry alleged payoffs to British member of Parliament George Galloway, a vocal critic of the war.	*May 11, 2003:* The British paper *The Mail* was reported to have gotten documents from the same source that were forgeries.
April 25, 2003: The Christian Science Monitor reports Saddam Hussein had paid Galloway $10 million over eleven years.	*June 20, 2003: The Christian Science Monitor* reports their analysis revealed their documents were forgeries.
Information was obtained from "an Iraqi general."	"Who had anything to gain? Is this part of the pattern of punishment?" asks Gardiner.

The Bush administration's Big Lie approach works, especially when it is amplified by an unquestioning media. A study done by the Program on International Policy Attitudes (PIPA) at the University of Maryland from June through September 2003 found that 48 percent of Americans believed that there were links between Iraq and Al Qaeda, 22 percent thought that weapons of mass destruction had been found in Iraq, and 25 percent thought that world public opinion favored the United States going to war with Iraq. Overall, 60 percent had at least one of these three misperceptions.[9]

But it turns out that what you believe depends on who you listen to. Viewers of the FOX News Channel were the most misinformed, with 80 percent believing in at least one of the misperceptions. Of those who got their news from print sources, 47 percent held at least one misperception. Among listeners and viewers of NPR and PBS, 23 percent held one of the misperceptions—

about the same percentage of Americans who thought that Iraq was directly involved in the 9/11 attacks.

In other words, we had become victims of our own propaganda.

Colonel Gardiner ultimately ends with questions that he finds deeply troubling—about the media. "Why did *The New York Times* let itself be used by 'intelligence officials' on stories? Why did *The Washington Times* never seem to question a leak they were given? Why were newspapers in the UK better than those in the U.S. in raising questions before and during the war?"

Part of the answer can be found in the symbiotic relationship between the corporate media and the officials they cover. As Vassar College sociology professor William Hoynes explains, "The problem is in the norms and practices of the profession and how news is gathered and produced. Journalists rely upon officials for both professional status and information, which is one of the reasons why news is so heavily tilted toward the views and actions of officials. Add to that the economic structure of the news, the profit orientation of the major media and the power of advertising, the broad ideological climate in the post-9/11 era—a narrow version of patriotism, dissent cast as treason—and the news management/intimidation strategies of officials, and you have a news media that often produces this kind of shameful reporting."[10]

Myth and Reality: The Jessica Lynch Hoax

THE FRONT-PAGE STORY in *The Washington Post* on April 3, 2003, was breathtaking: U.S. special forces had stormed a hospital and rescued a scrub-faced, blond-haired 19-year-old soldier by the name of Jessica Lynch, who the Pentagon said was being held against her will. The military had conveniently filmed the rescue, and grainy footage of the daring night raid was being shown on TV.

The report noted that Private First Class Jessica Lynch, an army clerk from Palestine, West Virginia, had been taken captive by Iraqis following a firefight. She "sustained multiple gunshot wounds" and was stabbed and "fought fiercely and shot several enemy soldiers . . . firing her weapon until she ran out of ammunition."

Lynch had been captured when the 507th Maintenance Company took a wrong turn just outside Nasiriya and was attacked. Eleven of her comrades were killed, and Lynch was taken to the local hospital.

"She was fighting to the death," gushed an unnamed U.S. military official.

Defense Secretary Rumsfeld ran with this theme in a press conference that same day. "We are certainly grateful for the brilliant and courageous rescue of Sergeant—correction—Private First Class Jessica Lynch, who was being held by Iraqi forces in what they called a 'hospital.'"

CENTCOM went further on April 5, stating that Lynch was rescued from a hospital that was an "irregular military headquarters facility that was being used by these death squads in Nasiriya."

The story line was simple: Lynch was an American hero, fighting to the last man, saved from marauding Arabs in a gallant rescue by special forces.

There was just one problem with this riveting drama: It was almost entirely untrue.

The American media was too enchanted with this fairy tale to end it. Some reporters traveled to the hospital where Lynch was treated to speak with doctors and local residents and get the real story of what had happened. But these reports received little play. America wanted a hero, and, by God, Lynch was going to be it.

On April 10, *Democracy Now!* interviewed Andrew Bun-combe, a journalist for the British daily *The Independent,* who had just been at the hospital. "I don't think it was quite the heroic res-cue it was portrayed as," Buncombe said. "A big fuss was made, but the reality was that it was a very benign rescue—I don't think a shot was fired. There were no Iraqi troops there. In terms of be-ing 'liberated,' a big fuss was made to enable the Delta Force to rush in there.

"My sense is that the doctors at the hospital were genuinely concerned for her as a patient," Buncombe said. "She was put in the cleanest room in the hospital; she was given the best bed. The conditions in the hospital were appalling. The situation was wretched and they hadn't had any water for some time—they hadn't had electricity there for several days. The place was pretty wretched and they treated her as best they could."

A news team from the BBC also traveled to the hospital where Lynch was cared for and pieced together the story.

In an exposé on May 15, BBC News declared that Lynch's "story is one of the most stunning pieces of news management ever conceived."[11]

That's the polite British way of saying that they had caught the U.S. military in a bald-faced lie.

The story unraveled when BBC reporters questioned the Iraqi doctor who had treated her. "I examined her, I saw she had a bro-ken arm, a broken thigh and a dislocated ankle," Dr. Harith al-Houssona told the BBC. The injuries were a result of Lynch's vehicle having crashed.

"There was no [sign of] shooting, no bullet inside her body, no stab wound—only road traffic accident," explained the doctor. "They want to distort the picture. I don't know why they think there is some benefit in saying she has a bullet injury."[12]

The reason is simple: There is no propaganda value in saying that a U.S. soldier was "rescued" from a hospital where she was being treated by sympathetic Iraqi doctors for injuries sustained in a traffic accident.

And the fakery gets worse. It turns out that Iraqi doctors had tried to return Lynch to the Americans two days earlier. But when the ambulance with Lynch inside approached a U.S. checkpoint, it was fired upon by American soldiers, forcing the doctors to return Lynch to the hospital.

The military's PR people saw a golden opportunity for myth-making, and an elaborate high-impact rescue was literally staged. As the BBC reported: "When footage of Lynch's rescue was released, General Vincent Brooks, the U.S. spokesman in Doha, said: 'Some brave souls put their lives on the line to make this happen, loyal to a creed that they know that they'll never leave a fallen comrade.'

"The American strategy was to ensure the right television footage by using . . . images from their own cameras, editing the film themselves," said the BBC.

"The Pentagon had been influenced by Hollywood producers of reality TV and action movies, notably the man behind *Black Hawk Down*, Jerry Bruckheimer.

"Bruckheimer advised the Pentagon on the primetime television series *Profiles from the Front Line* that followed U.S. forces in Afghanistan in 2001. That approach was taken on and developed on the field of battle in Iraq," concluded the BBC.

When the hospital staff saw American helicopters approach, they expected a routine pickup of the patient that the Americans had been informed about. But when the choppers touched down, Iraqis thought they were bad guys on a movie location. The special forces, who witnesses said knew that there were no soldiers at the hospital, came out with guns blazing.

"We were surprised. Why do this? There was no military, there were no soldiers in the hospital," said Dr. Anmar Uday, who worked at the hospital, to the BBC.

"It was like a Hollywood film. They cried 'go, go, go,' with guns and blanks without bullets, blanks and the sound of explosions. They made a show for the American attack on the hospital—action movies like Sylvester Stallone or Jackie Chan."

Colonel Sam Gardiner smelled a rat throughout this story. He noted the way it was described as an ambush and how she was held captive by terrorist death squads. "It's not an ambush when you drive a convoy into enemy lines. Terrorists would do something like an ambush," he wrote. And his sources told him that the reference to Iraqi troops as terrorists came on orders from either Donald Rumsfeld or the White House. This was the psyops dimension, recasting the war as something it wasn't to sell it on the home front.

Gardiner's suspicions were also aroused when he read accounts of the "rescue." He was surprised that the first call from the special forces was not to their military commanders, which is the standard procedure, but to Jim Wilkinson, the cagey spin master of CENTCOM.

"This is very strange for a military operation," wrote Gardiner. "When I tell military friends, they often respond, 'Do you suppose they staged it?'"

Then there is the question of how *The Washington Post* got the information about Lynch that resulted in its sensational April 3 story—which it later contradicted. The story was an exclusive— that is, the *Post* was exclusively fed the misinformation by unnamed sources at the Pentagon—and it formed the basis for the sensational accounts that followed. As is often the case, the *Post* simply didn't question the official line at the time. They were pleased to be spoon-fed by propagandists. They were simply doing what they often did, and ended up swallowing the bait hook, line, and sinker.

Washington Post ombudsman Michael Getler, who wrote three crow-eating columns about the incident, observed, "This was the single most memorable story of the war, and it had huge propaganda value. It was false, but it didn't get knocked down until it didn't matter quite so much."[13]

Part of why this story was propped up for so long is that the networks had everything to gain from it. CBS tried to land an exclusive interview with Lynch by dangling everything its multitentacled parent company Viacom—which owns MTV and Paramount Studios—could offer. There was the prospect of a two-hour movie about her, a book deal, and the chance to cohost an hour-long MTV video show and a concert in her hometown featuring either Ja Rule or Ashanti.[14]

"Maybe that went over the line," CBS chairman Leslie Moonves told the BBC. "That was not respecting, possibly, the sanctity of CBS News."[15]

Meanwhile, NBC was reporting the Lynch story while trying unsuccessfully to get the Lynch family to give them an exclusive to make a TV movie. So NBC stood to profit handsomely from the Lynch myth. The movie, *Saving Jessica Lynch,* aired in November 2003.

Then there's the book by Iraqi lawyer Mohammed Odeh al-Rehaief, who claims he told the U.S. Marines of Lynch's location. Al-Rehaief was whisked out of Iraq, granted asylum in the United States, and received $300,000 from Rupert Murdoch's Harper-Collins to write a book about the Lynch rescue. He also was given a job at the Livingston Group, a high-powered D.C. lobby firm run by Bob Livingston, former speaker of the house. Al-Rehaief's book, *Because Each Life Is Precious: Why an Iraqi Man Came to Risk*

Everything for Private Jessica Lynch, was promoted by his Livingston Group colleague Lauri Fitz-Pegado. She is known for her work at the Hill & Knowlton PR firm in 1990, when she arranged the appearance of a 15-year-old Kuwaiti girl called Nayirah on Capitol Hill. Nayirah testified on October 10, 1990, that she had seen Iraqi soldiers pulling 300 premature babies from incubators and throwing them on the floor. Her testimony helped propel the United States to war against Iraq in 1991. The war resolution passed by a mere six votes in the Senate.

The problem is that the baby-killing claims were false. Doctors at the hospital in Kuwait deny that the incident ever occurred. Amnesty International, which originally reported on the baby killings, took the unusual step of retracting its report after further investigating the matter. It turns out that Nayirah was the daughter of the Kuwaiti ambassador to the United States. The embassy never allowed her to be interviewed.

Then there was the "official" book, *I Am a Soldier, Too: The Jessica Lynch Story,* by Pulitzer Prize–winning author Rick Bragg, which also came out in November 2003. (Bragg had some free time on his hands: He had just been forced out of *The New York Times* for having relied on an intern to report a story he took credit for.) The book's publisher, which paid an advance of $1 million for the story,[16] trumpeted it this way: Lynch's "rescue galvanized the nation; she became a symbol of victory, of innocence and courage, of heroism; and then, just as quickly, of deceit and manipulation."

Lynch put it more succinctly in an interview with Diane Sawyer on ABC in November 2003. "They used me as a way to symbolize all this stuff," Lynch said. "It's wrong. I don't know why they filmed [the rescue], or why they say the things" they said.[17]

The Jessica Lynch hoax was a brilliant success by military propagandists. It helped sell the real product: America's war against Iraq.

Media Soldiers

ARMY PSYOPS IS forbidden by law from manipulating U.S. media. So what happens when psyops troops *are* the media? That's exactly what occurred at CNN and National Public Radio.

In February 2000, the Dutch newspaper *Trouw* and France's *Intelligence Newsletter* revealed that officers from the U.S. Army's Fourth Psychological Operations (psyops) Group at Fort Bragg were working in the news division at the Atlanta headquarters of CNN. Five psyops sergeants began working at CNN in the final days of the Kosovo War in 1999: two in radio, two in television, and one in their satellite department. Alexander Cockburn broke the story in the United States in *CounterPunch*.

In April 2000, *TV Guide* broke the news that psyops personnel had also worked at NPR in 1998 and 1999 on flagship programs including *Morning Edition, All Things Considered,* and *Talk of the Nation.* Major Jonathan Withington of the U.S. Army Special Operations Command confirmed to *Current* magazine that the interns had conducted "background research."[18] Several NPR officials stated that the interns had been given only menial tasks such as copying and filing.

CNN news chief Eason Jordan told *Democracy Now!* that "no government or military propaganda expert has ever worked on news at CNN." But Staff Sergeant Jose A. Velasquez insisted to *TV Guide*, "I made calls and researched stories on the internet."[19] And *Trouw* reporter Abe de Vries told Cockburn, "The U.S. Army, U.S. Special Operations Command, and CNN personnel confirmed to me that military personnel have been involved in news production at CNN's news desks. I found it simply astonishing."

As Cockburn wrote in the *Los Angeles Times,* "Maybe CNN was the target of a psyop penetration and is still too naive to figure out what was going on."

The media watchdog group Fairness and Accuracy in Reporting investigated the reasons that psyops soldiers might be interested in gaining access to a major network. FAIR wrote: "Rear
Admiral Thomas Steffens, a psychological warfare expert in the
Special Operations Command, recently told a psyops conference
that the military needed to find ways to 'gain control' over commercial news satellites to help bring down an 'informational cone
of silence' over regions where special operations were taking place."

Quoting an unofficial strategy paper published by the U.S.
Naval War College, FAIR reported that military commanders were
seeking ways to "leverage the vast resources of the fourth estate"
for the purposes of "communicating the [mission's] objective, . . .
playing a major role in deception of the enemy, and enhancing intelligence collection."[20]

Army psyops commander Christopher St. John, whose soldiers
interned at CNN, said the program was an example of the type of
"greater cooperation between the armed forces and media giants
which he hoped to see more of."[21]

Major Thomas Collins of the U.S. Army Information Service
proudly told de Vries that the interns "worked as regular employees of CNN. Conceivably, they would have worked on stories during the Kosovo war. They helped in the production of the news."[22]

While CNN and NPR executives claimed they were unaware
of the interns, blaming the placement on their respective human
resources departments, Sergeant Velasquez says everyone at the
CNN Southeast Bureau, including its chief, knew where he was
from.

Many people within CNN and NPR knew they were working
alongside psyops soldiers. But the revolving door between the media and the military is spinning so fast that media organizations
now have trouble distinguishing between their paid generals and
the spies.

Deck of Death

IN MID-APRIL 2003, CNN announced that U.S. troops had caught a major Iraqi official. When his image appeared on the screen, it was in the form of a photo on a playing card.

The Pentagon's "55 Most Wanted" deck of cards was created by five Army intelligence specialists.[23] They were released by General Vincent Brooks at a news conference in Qatar on April 11. Brooks declared: "The deck of cards is one example of what we provide to soldiers and marines out in the field with faces of individuals and their names."[24]

That wasn't true. Only 1,900 decks were originally printed, and they quickly made the rounds among reporters, who duly adopted and integrated them into their reports. But the U.S. soldiers barely saw them. The *Atlanta Journal-Constitution* reported in late July, "Some frontline soldiers in Iraq said they have seen very few, if any, of the decks. And the ones that they have were sent by friends and families and are kept as mementos. They look at the cards as little more than a Pentagon public relations stunt."

Specialist Matt Larimer of Easton, Pennsylvania, said, "They're not really of much use, because there are a lot of blank cards and the pictures are bad quality."[25]

But it all fit nicely into the Pentagon propaganda effort. Between the grainy target images that look like a video game and the deck of cards, the war was being conveyed as a bloodless game.

The speed with which the U.S. media adopted the cards as their own stunned even the men who created the decks. "As people started to get captured, they wouldn't say who the person was that got captured. They'd say, 'They captured the six of diamonds out of the deck of cards,'" explained card deck cocreator Lieutenant Hans Mumm of the 3404 Military Intelligence unit. Specialist

Joseph Barrios added, "This was the real shock and awe. We were really surprised at how successful they've become."

The Ruckus Society had a different take on this. They came out with a War Profiteers deck of cards. Each card shows the face of a leading Bush administration hawk, oil executive, or major weapons manufacturer. The description of the cards reads, "The War Profiteers Card Deck exposes some of the real war criminals of the U.S.'s war of terror. This is no Sunday bridge club. These are individuals and institutions that stack the deck against democracy in the rigged game of global power."

You may learn more from playing a game of poker with these cards than from watching network news.

15

Things Get Messy with Sally Jessy

*When the operation of the machine becomes so odious . . .
you've got to throw your body upon the wheels, upon the
gears, upon the levers, and upon all the apparatus of the
machine, and you've got to make it stop.*

—MARIO SAVIO, LEADER, FREE SPEECH MOVEMENT (1964), BERKELEY,
CALIFORNIA

DURING THE PERSIAN GULF War in 1991, I was on Pacifica
radio station WBAI in New York, criticizing bombing the cradle of
civilization back to the cradle, when someone ran into the studio to
say that a producer from *The Sally Jessy Raphael Show* was on the
phone.

One of the beautiful things about community media is that all
kinds of volunteers come in. I figured this one was hallucinating.
Sally Jessy Raphael was a popular national TV talk show host—
"the queen of tacky TV talk shows," as the *Houston Chronicle*
dubbed her—known for dealing with issues such as fad diets and
love triangles, but certainly not war.

But when I took the call, a producer from *The Sally Jessy
Raphael Show* was on the other end. She said she was listening to

the radio in her limousine (maybe her chauffeur had tuned in), and she wanted me to come on the program to talk about my opposition to the war. Could I come down to the studio in a couple of days? I was pleasantly surprised—okay, floored. I said I'd be there.

It turned out that Sally Jessy had invited three women who were for the war and three women against. It promised to be an interesting exchange. As we sat offstage before the show, the producers informed us that Sally didn't generally do this kind of show, so when we got out there, we should mix it up. The producer told us not to be afraid to speak our minds. It sounded like Sally Jessy Raphael was going to teach Tom Brokaw and Dan Rather a thing or two about what real diversity of opinion sounds like.

The six of us went out on cue and took our places onstage, and the videotaping began. Sally Jessy started off by wading into the audience and letting someone ask a question: "What do you think about the fact that Saddam Hussein has biological weapons?" a woman asked.

Dr. Yolanda Huet-Vaughn was sitting next to me on the stage. A physician and captain in the army reserves, she refused to serve in the Persian Gulf War because she said she was trained to save lives, not take lives. Wearing glasses and a long black dress, with her hair tied back, the mild-mannered doctor looked as if she could be Amish. "Well, that's an important question," she began. "I think it's important to look at biological weapons that Saddam Hussein might have. And we should also look at the biological weapons that are right here in the United—"

Before Dr. Huet-Vaughn could say "States," Sally whirled around and came charging up to the stage, shouting, "Get out! Get out! Get off my show! You shut up! This is my show!"

I thought she was going to attack Dr. Huet-Vaughn. As she barreled up to the stage, I said, "Whoa! Back off, Sally!"

Not being a regular viewer, I didn't know what to make of this.

I wondered, *Is this how it works? The host goes nuts, and then . . . are we supposed to physically defend ourselves?*

Sally Jessy just kept screaming, "You be quiet! You be quiet!"

People had come from my radio station, WBAI, at the invitation of Sally Jessy's producers. Well, if there's one thing community radio listeners know how to do, it's participate. They started to chant: "Free speech! Free speech! CEN-SOR-SHIP!"

Sally stopped the program.

She was shaking. The producers came out and started rocking her back and forth. "It's okay, Sally. It's okay, Sally," they consoled her. She succeeded in uniting her pro- and antiwar guests—in disbelief at the spectacle in front of us.

The producers finally convinced Sally Jessy to continue with the program. But she came back with a new demand: If any of us wanted to speak, we would have to raise our hands. It was the first show I'd ever seen, apart from *Sesame Street*, on which guests had to raise their hands to participate.

When the program resumed, Sally Jessy played some video footage from antiwar protests. I raised my hand. "I want to congratulate you, Sally," I said. "You're not just showing the images of people protesting. You have actually invited some of us in to have a civilized discussion."

Of course most Americans don't identify with people screaming in the streets. But why *are* they shouting? Because they aren't invited into a corporate media studio to calmly explain their position. The best they can hope for is that if they yell loud enough on a warm day, an executive at one of the networks might have a window open, and their cries of "No war!" will waft into the studio and hit an open mike.

I continued, talking about the oft-repeated claim that Saddam would attack Israel with chemical weapons. I said as the granddaughter of an Orthodox rabbi, I could imagine only one image more horrifying than seeing little Israeli children with gas masks: seeing Palestinian children without them.

That's how the show went. It was interesting. Lively. We disagreed. We argued. The bell rang and it was over. It was an ordinary debate, made extraordinary only because of the lack of such debate in a media world where the range of discussion is defined by questions such as "Which weapons should be used to attack?" As I left the studio, a cameraman gave me a thumbs-up.

Back at WBAI, listeners were calling in to ask when this episode of *The Sally Jessy Raphael Show* would be aired. We waited and waited. I finally called Sally Jessy's producer. She said that there was a "technical problem": When the videos had been sent out to stations around the country, several had complained that there was trouble with the synching of the video and sound tracks. They had pulled the show.

I responded, "I think the trouble was with the sound of our voices."

"Don't be like that," she replied. I asked to speak to the executive producer. She said he was a very busy man and could not talk. But someday, she promised, they would do the show again. I said that would probably be impossible, because Dr. Huet-Vaughn was about to be court-martialed for refusing to serve in the Persian Gulf War and would most likely be imprisoned. (Dr. Huet-Vaughn was sentenced to three years in the maximum-security brig at Fort Leavenworth, in a cell just below Death Row. She was declared a prisoner of conscience by Amnesty International, which helped to persuade the secretary of the army to commute her sentence after eight months. Her husband took care of their three children during her imprisonment. She has waged a long and continuing legal battle to retain her medical license.)

WBAI was flooded with calls. I told listeners that I had no explanation for why the Sally Jessy Raphael episode had been killed.

If they wanted an explanation, I suggested that listeners call her show. Years later, I bumped into one of the producers. She told me that their entire operation was shut down for two days due to the volume of calls.

At the time, all I knew was that I suddenly got a call from the producer. She asked if I would speak to the executive producer. I said I was a very busy woman and really couldn't talk. So she said they were going into a high-level meeting and she wanted to know if I would cry censorship if they edited the show. I said that I was an editor, too; I understood if they wanted to edit out Sally Jessy's tantrum.

Thanks to media activism, they finally aired the show. And it got more attention than it ever would have had Sally Jessy just aired the show as scheduled. One memorable headline ran THINGS GET MESSY WITH SALLY JESSY.

The most interesting response I got afterward was from women on southern military bases who called to thank me. They said that they had never heard someone with my viewpoint before. They shared my skepticism about the reasons for war. They said they didn't want their loved ones to go to war and die for oil. But, they said, they couldn't have these discussions on military bases. They had to rely on civilian society to debate these crucial issues.

War and peace. Life and death. That is the role of media in a democratic society: to provide a forum for this discourse. To do anything less is a disservice to the servicemen and servicewomen of this country.

Muzzled and Manhandled

I DON'T EXPECT serious debate and discussions from shows like Sally Jessy Raphael's but I do expect the news media to examine thoroughly the most important issues of the day. Instead, most of the journalists who reach thousands—and in some cases millions—of readers and viewers do nothing but parrot the government line.

These are the same people who like to accuse me of being an advocacy journalist. I answer by saying that they are my model.

In 1999, I got a lesson in how *their* advocacy journalism—advocating for those in power—is practiced. My colleague Jeremy Scahill and I were pleased to learn that our radio documentary *Drilling and Killing: Chevron and Nigeria's Oil Dictatorship* had received an honor from the Overseas Press Club (OPC). But we weren't so thrilled about attending the awards banquet.

These events are a bit of a scam for the sponsoring organization. You're invited to pay exorbitant fees for the honor of accepting your award. Jeremy and I initially weren't going to go. The event took place in the midst of the bombing of Yugoslavia and we didn't have $250 to spare for dinner and conversation. We finally got the OPC to allow us to attend for free, provided we didn't eat dinner. We figured if nothing else, we could record NBC anchor Tom Brokaw, who was the master of ceremonies, saying the name of our documentary: *Drilling and Killing: Chevron and Nigeria's Oil Dictatorship.* Maybe we could insert his voice reading the title in the documentary and people would find it more believable.

We learned that not paying for dinner meant we hadn't paid for a chair, so we stood in the back and watched our colleagues feast on filet mignon and sip champagne. We picked out the various celebrity journalists who were there. There was Brokaw; Lesley Stahl and Andy Rooney from CBS; CNN vice president Frank Sesno—a constellation of mainstream bigwigs.

According to the program, Richard Holbrooke was the keynote speaker. It's a sad practice at journalistic events to honor by night the powerful people reporters cover by day. It's all about access.

Holbrooke was about to become the U.S. ambassador to the United Nations. As President Clinton's special envoy to Yugoslavia, Holbrooke was the triggerman for the bombing that was under way in that country. So it was quite remarkable to have him address this group of reporters who cover war. Jeremy and I decided to make the most of this: It would be a fine opportunity to gain access to a man who was deeply involved with the bombing of Yugoslavia.

Soon after the lights lowered, it became clear to me that I would have to swallow more than some Perrier to stomach what was going on. An official of the OPC rose to announce that before dinner, he wanted to say that despite the difficulties faced by journalists, there was some good news: Indonesia was treating reporters better.

My jaw dropped. Aside from Indonesia's normal abysmal human rights record, this was the same week in which even *The New York Times* reported that Indonesian troops had massacred a number of East Timorese and beaten up journalists. The club official concluded his remarks by instructing people to enjoy their meals.

Beware of hungry journalists. With nothing to eat and no place to sit, I decided to go over to the official who had just spoken.

"Excuse me," I said. "Where did you get that information that Indonesia was treating journalists better?"

He replied that he had written a letter to the Indonesian foreign ministry expressing concern about the beatings, bannings, and killings of reporters there. He said the foreign ministry wrote him back and assured him that they were treating reporters much better. And that was all it took to allay his concerns.

"Well, I have other information," I replied diplomatically, "so I think you should go back and explain that the Indonesian military is one of the most brutal on earth, and reporters are a target of their wrath."

This gentleman was not about to put down his champagne. "Well, why don't you fax me that information and I'll evaluate it," he said.

When I returned to the back of the bus—I mean ballroom— we spotted Richard Holbrooke heading to the bathroom.

Jeremy and I figured this access was as good as any we would get. We intercepted him and asked him why, if American and NATO planes were bombing Yugoslavia to save the people, they had just obliterated a petrochemical plant on the Danube that could threaten the region with environmental devastation? Wasn't this the old Vietnam notion of "destroying the village to save it"?

Holbrooke said that he had to go (well, we knew that). But we persisted. We asked him about the Rambouillet Accord, which he had delivered to Yugoslav President Slobodan Milosevic two months earlier. This was billed as a plan to avert a bombing of Yugoslavia if Milosevic would accept a NATO occupation of his country. Holbrooke replied that he hadn't been at Rambouillet when the accord was drafted. True, we said, but you *did* deliver the ultimatum to Milosevic—which led to the bombing that's happening now. He brushed us off and moved on.

Suddenly the head of the Overseas Press Club swooped in.

"What do you think you're doing?" she demanded.

"We're asking questions," I said, stating the obvious.

"No, we've made an agreement. Richard Holbrooke said he would come only if we agreed that reporters wouldn't ask questions."

"And you agreed to that?" I asked. "He shouldn't have been invited anyway." But she was done talking. Holbrooke didn't even make it to the bathroom. He quickly returned to his table.

Then an NBC producer rose to introduce Holbrooke, who she said she looked forward to having as "our" ambassador at the United Nations. She talked about how accessible Holbrooke was, saying, "He's here, he's there, he's everywhere!"

Holbrooke got up and thanked all his "friends in the media." "The kind of coverage we're seeing from *The New York Times, The Washington Post*, NBC, CBS, ABC, CNN, and the newsmagazines lately has been extraordinary," Holbrooke said. "You are all doing this on a twenty-four-hour-a-day basis with great skill so far, and I commend you. . . . That kind of reporting can have great impact. . . . I want to say how important it has been."

Holbrooke then continued with a major foreign policy address. Midway through, he made an announcement. "Eason Jordan [then president of CNN International] told me just before I came up here tonight that the air strikes hit Serb TV and took out the Serb television, and at least for the time being they are off the air. That is an enormously important event as Eason reported it, and I believe everything CNN tells me."

Laughter broke out in the room.

"It is an enormously important and I think positive development," Holbrooke added.

Here were hundreds of reporters supposedly upholding the highest principles of journalism, and they chuckled on cue—at a war crime committed against journalists.

Now, what would have been different if Milosevic had stood up to announce "We just bombed CBS!" and a bunch of Serb journalists had laughed? Radio Television Serbia, whatever its faults as a mouthpiece for Milosevic, is not a military target. We went back to our office later that night to see the pictures of body parts being pulled out of the wrecked TV studios in Belgrade. It wasn't soldiers blown to pieces in the rubble. It was the people who apply makeup, the cameramen, and the journalists who were inside.

People like 27-year-old technician Ksenija Bankovic, whose mother
Borka we interviewed on *Democracy Now!* Borka asked how journalists could laugh at the killing of her daughter, whose only crime
was going to work that night. In all, sixteen media workers were
killed in the bombing.

When Holbrooke finished and people applauded, Jeremy approached the podium. He asked the question the media had failed
to ask anyone in power for months.

"Mr. Holbrooke, I'm sure my colleagues would back me up in
asking you a question," Jeremy yelled over the applause. "Mr. Holbrooke, you delivered the ultimatum to President Milosevic following the Rambouillet Accord, and you've said since then that
those accords do not call for an occupation of Yugoslavia. Yet the
text in Appendix B does say that NATO shall enjoy free and unre-
stricted access throughout all of Yugoslavia. Isn't that an occupation that no sovereign country would accept?"

Security men grabbed Jeremy, who continued, "This is a room
full of journalists. We should be able to ask officials questions."

"Not at an awards ceremony," shouted an official of the Overseas Press Club.

Jeremy faced the table where Holbrooke was sitting and said,
"I ask for your support, Tom Brokaw, Lesley Stahl."

Brokaw then stood up from the table where he was dining with
Holbrooke and said, "You go sit down."

"Ambassador Holbrooke will talk to you later," another official
countered from the dais.

I was standing at the back, getting ready to record Brokaw giving us our citation. As security was pushing Jeremy past me at the
back of the ballroom, I said, "Release that man—he's just about to
win an award!" The security people looked confused. They let Jeremy go, and Brokaw came forward to give out the awards.

But first Brokaw announced: "I don't think I have to explain to a room full of journalists that Richard Holbrooke is available. We did in fact identify one person back here in this room tonight who has either never received a call from Richard Holbrooke or who has never called Richard Holbrooke. But only one in the entire room, so far as I know!" The audience broke up laughing.

Actually, two of us hadn't received a call from Holbrooke. It's all about access, and we knew that somehow we wouldn't be getting access to Holbrooke any time soon.

Brokaw then began the awards presentation. I expected to hear him announce awards from the Overseas Press Club. Instead, Brokaw began distributing awards sponsored by Coca-Cola, another by Merrill Lynch, and others by AT&T and the Ford Motor Company. Soon enough, the turn came for the Lowell Thomas Award for Best Radio Reporting (sponsored by ABC). The award went to reporter Sandy Tolan for a fine documentary on the Israeli-Palestinian conflict. Sandy concluded his remarks by saying: "Finally, I want to add my voice to those journalists . . . who have risked their lives to speak truth to power, whose life work is to ask tough questions of those in government, and whose refusal to become cozy with power has cost them immensely. Thank you very much."

We made sure our tape recorders were rolling, and Brokaw announced next, "And the citation goes to Amy Goodman and Jeremy Scahill for *Nigeria's Oil Dictatorship*."

Enough was enough. I walked up onstage and interrupted Brokaw:

AMY GOODMAN: Mr. Brokaw, I'm Amy Goodman and that was Jeremy Scahill who asked the question. We got the honorable mention for *Drilling and Killing: Chevron and Nigeria's Oil Dictatorship*. . . . And on behalf of Jeremy and I, we are sorry to say that we can't accept it tonight, for two reasons. One, it's because we feel it is critical on a night like tonight when we're bombing Yugoslavia, that journalists not agree to not ask questions of Richard Holbrooke, that's number one . . .

TOM BROKAW: But, madam . . .

GOODMAN: And number two . . .

BROKAW: May I just point out that he has agreed to answer the questions after the dinner . . .

GOODMAN: Afterwards, but . . .

BROKAW: That's appropriate. There are ceremonies and there are rituals in everything, including the press.

GOODMAN: But we asked him questions before and we were told that there was an agreement he would not answer questions. But number two, tonight, when the awards began, [the other gentleman] said that "We want to say that there is good news, and that is that Indonesia has apologized for hurting journalists." The fact is that this week in Indonesian-occupied East Timor, journalists have been beaten up, journalists have been brutalized for covering the Indonesian military's arming and supporting of the militias, the death squads that are there. Because the Overseas Press Club was honoring Indonesia, we cannot accept the award, and cannot accept the agreement not to ask Richard Holbrooke questions when we are bombing Yugoslavia. Thank you very much.

I then left the stage.

"It's a great country," Tom Brokaw finally said. "And it is a great First Amendment. . . . And now, with the permission of Pacifica Radio, I will continue with the awards." The rattled NBC anchor made several more joking references to Pacifica during the evening.

But he clearly felt a little uncomfortable. Maybe he was concerned that having security take out an honoree would cause a titter in the gossip press, like what happened the month before when he was pushing his book *The Greatest Generation* and was invited to substitute for Matt Lauer on *Today*.

"I must say some things never change," Brokaw reminisced on air with Katie Couric. The *NBC Nightly News* anchor, who is paid about $7 million per year,[1] continued, "I was coming to work early this morning down Fifth Avenue in predawn darkness and it reminded me of the old days when I was doing the *Today* show because I saw the homeless people in the church shelters and the park benches and so on. And you feel great sympathy for them. But you also envy the extra hour of sleep that they're getting. I mean, you go by and say, 'If I were them, I would still be sleeping.'"[2] His remarks sparked an embarrassing but brief scandal.

When there were no more corporate awards to give out, we went up to Holbrooke for our promised interview. It wasn't to be. Holbrooke dismissed Jeremy's question and was then rescued by Lesley Stahl. "Dick, I'll take you home," she interjected. And off they went, the ambassador and the journalist, safe from any further unscripted queries.

Access of Evil

I AM NOT a fan of partying with the powerful. We shouldn't be sipping champagne with Henry Kissinger, Richard Holbrooke, and Donald Rumsfeld. We should be holding those in power accountable.

As the legendary investigative journalist I. F. Stone once explained about his method (paraphrased by *The Nation* publisher Victor Navasky): "If you didn't attend background briefings you weren't bound by the ground rules; you could debrief correspondents who did, check out what they had been told, and as often as not reveal the lies for what they were."[3]

There aren't many I. F. Stones left in journalism. That point was driven home earlier on the night of the Overseas Press Club banquet. Introducing Tom Brokaw, club president Roy Rowan could do no better than this: "I've known Tom since 1975. We were seatmates together on Henry Kissinger's plane coming back from President Ford's summit meeting in Beijing with Chairman Mao. A couple of times on that flight we were invited to the forward cabin to have canapés and champagne with the secretary of state. . . . On a fourteen-hour flight, you can get to know someone pretty well."

Later that night, I ran into Frank Sesno, the vice president of CNN. I asked about the practice of putting generals on the CNN payroll. "You can get the Pentagon's point of view for free," I pointed out. "Why pay these generals? And have you ever considered putting peace activists on the payroll? Or just inviting them into the studio to respond to the drumbeat for war?"

Sesno said, "We've talked about this. But no, we wouldn't do that. Because generals are analysts, and peace activists are advocates."

I need an *analyst* to analyze that one.

I pressed him. "Would you consider interviewing an antiwar scholar like Noam Chomsky?"

"No, I don't personally know him," he replied.

So that's what it's come to. It's about who these media personalities personally know and dine with. It's why dinners like these matter. I call it the access of evil.

That weekend, there was a story about the Overseas Press Club awards banquet on Page Six of the *New York Post*, the gossip page of the gossip rag. BROKAW SHUSHES KOSOVO CRANK read the headline. When Jeremy read it, he cracked, "That's strange. I didn't see him tell Holbrooke to be quiet!"

At the end of the *Post* piece, Lesley Stahl was asked her opinion. "This was not the time or place for this reporter to ask questions," she declared.

What could be a better time or place to ask hard questions? The time: in the midst of the bombing of Yugoslavia. The place: a gathering of hundreds of journalists who are supposedly honoring the finest in international reporting.

16

Hiroshima Cover-up:
How the War Department's
*Times*man Won a Pulitzer

Governments lie.

—I. F. STONE, JOURNALIST

AT THE DAWN OF the nuclear age, an independent Australian journalist named Wilfred Burchett traveled to Japan to cover the aftermath of the atomic bombing of Hiroshima. The only problem was that General Douglas MacArthur had declared southern Japan off-limits, barring the press. Over 200,000 people died in the atomic bombings of Hiroshima and Nagasaki, but no Western journalist witnessed the aftermath and told the story. The world's media obediently crowded onto the USS *Missouri* off the coast of Japan to cover the surrender of the Japanese.

Wilfred Burchett decided to strike out on his own. He was determined to see for himself what this nuclear bomb had done, to understand what this vaunted new weapon was all about. So he boarded a train and traveled for thirty hours to the city of Hiroshima in defiance of General MacArthur's orders.

Burchett emerged from the train into a nightmare world. The devastation that confronted him was unlike any he had ever seen during the war. The city of Hiroshima, with a population of 350,000, had been razed. Multistory buildings were reduced to charred posts. He saw people's shadows seared into walls and sidewalks. He met people with their skin melting off. In the hospital, he saw patients with purple skin hemorrhages, gangrene, fever, and rapid hair loss. Burchett was among the first to witness and describe radiation sickness.

Burchett sat down on a chunk of rubble with his Baby Hermes typewriter. His dispatch began: "In Hiroshima, thirty days after the first atomic bomb destroyed the city and shook the world, people are still dying, mysteriously and horribly—people who were uninjured in the cataclysm from an unknown something which I can only describe as the atomic plague."

He continued, tapping out the words that still haunt to this day: "Hiroshima does not look like a bombed city. It looks as if a monster steamroller has passed over it and squashed it out of existence. I write these facts as dispassionately as I can in the hope that they will act as a warning to the world."[1]

Burchett's article, headlined THE ATOMIC PLAGUE, was published on September 5, 1945, in the London *Daily Express*. The story caused a worldwide sensation. Burchett's candid reaction to the horror shocked readers. "In this first testing ground of the atomic bomb I have seen the most terrible and frightening desolation in four years of war. It makes a blitzed Pacific island seem like an Eden. The damage is far greater than photographs can show.

"When you arrive in Hiroshima you can look around for twenty-five and perhaps thirty square miles. You can see hardly a building. It gives you an empty feeling in the stomach to see such man-made destruction."

Burchett's searing independent reportage was a public relations fiasco for the U.S. military. General MacArthur had gone to pains to restrict journalists' access to the bombed cities, and his military censors were sanitizing and even killing dispatches that described the horror. The official narrative of the atomic bombings downplayed civilian casualties and categorically dismissed reports of the deadly lingering effects of radiation. Reporters whose dispatches conflicted with this version of events found themselves silenced: George Weller of the *Chicago Daily News* slipped into Nagasaki and wrote a 25,000-word story on the nightmare that he found there. Then he made a crucial error: He submitted the piece to military censors. His newspaper never even received his story. As Weller later summarized his experience with MacArthur's censors, "They won."[2]

U.S. authorities responded in time-honored fashion to Burchett's revelations: They attacked the messenger. General MacArthur ordered him expelled from Japan (the order was later rescinded), and his camera with photos of Hiroshima mysteriously vanished while he was in the hospital. U.S. officials accused Burchett of being influenced by Japanese propaganda. They scoffed at the notion of an atomic sickness. The U.S. military issued a press release right after the Hiroshima bombing that downplayed human casualties, instead emphasizing that the bombed area was the site of valuable industrial and military targets.

Four days after Burchett's story splashed across front pages around the world, Major General Leslie R. Groves, director of the atomic bomb project, invited a select group of thirty reporters to New Mexico. Foremost among this group was William L. Laurence, the Pulitzer Prize–winning science reporter for *The New*

York Times. Groves took the reporters to the site of the first atomic test. His intent was to demonstrate that no atomic radiation lingered at the site. Groves trusted Laurence to convey the military's line; the general was not disappointed.

Laurence's front-page story, U.S. ATOM BOMB SITE BELIES TOKYO TALES: TESTS ON NEW MEXICO RANGE CONFIRM THAT BLAST, AND NOT RADIATION, TOOK TOLL, ran on September 12, 1945, following a three-day delay to clear military censors. "This historic ground in New Mexico, scene of the first atomic explosion on earth and cradle of a new era in civilization, gave the most effective answer today to Japanese propaganda that radiations [sic] were responsible for deaths even after the day of the explosion, Aug. 6, and that persons entering Hiroshima had contracted mysterious maladies due to persistent radioactivity," the article began.[3] Laurence said unapologetically that the Army tour was intended "to give the lie to these claims."*

Laurence quoted General Groves: "The Japanese claim that people died from radiation. If this is true, the number was very small."

Laurence then went on to offer his own remarkable editorial on what happened: "The Japanese are still continuing their propaganda aimed at creating the impression that we won the war unfairly, and thus attempting to create sympathy for themselves and milder terms . . . Thus, at the beginning, the Japanese described 'symptoms' that did not ring true."[4]

But Laurence knew better. He had observed the first atomic

---

*In the course of the press tour, General Groves' driver, a 29-year-old soldier named Patrick Stout, posed in the center of the bomb crater for photographs. A scientist later informed Stout that he had been exposed to high levels of radiation. He died of leukemia in 1969, and was given service-connected disability payments by the Army in apparent recognition that radiation was the cause. [Robert Jay Lifton and Greg Mitchell, *Hiroshima in America: Fifty Years of Denial* (New York: Putnam, 1995), pp. 51–52.]

bomb test on July 16, 1945, and he withheld what he knew about radioactive fallout across the southwestern desert that poisoned local residents and livestock. He kept mum about the spiking Geiger counters all around the test site.

William L. Laurence went on to write a series of ten articles for the *Times* that served as a glowing tribute to the ingenuity and technical achievements of the nuclear program. Throughout these and other reports, he downplayed and denied the human impact of the bombing. Laurence won the Pulitzer Prize for his reporting.

It turns out that William L. Laurence was not only receiving a salary from *The New York Times*. He was also on the payroll of the War Department. In March 1945, General Leslie Groves had held a secret meeting at *The New York Times* with Laurence to offer him a job writing press releases for the Manhattan Project, the U.S. program to develop atomic weapons.[5] The intent, according to the *Times*, was "to explain the intricacies of the atomic bomb's operating principles in laymen's language."[6] Laurence also helped write statements on the bomb for President Truman and Secretary of War Henry Stimson.

Laurence eagerly accepted the offer, "his scientific curiosity and patriotic zeal perhaps blinding him to the notion that he was at the same time compromising his journalistic independence," as essayist Harold Evans wrote in a history of war reporting.[7] Evans recounted: "After the bombing, the brilliant but bullying Groves continually suppressed or distorted the effects of radiation. He dismissed reports of Japanese deaths as 'hoax or propaganda.' The *Times*' Laurence weighed in, too, after Burchett's reports, and parroted the government line." Indeed, numerous press releases issued by the military after the Hiroshima bombing—which in the absence of eyewitness accounts were often reproduced verbatim by U.S. newspapers—were written by none other than Laurence.

"Mine has been the honor, unique in the history of journalism, of preparing the War Department's official press release for worldwide distribution," boasted Laurence in his memoirs, *Dawn Over Zero*. "No greater honor could have come to any newspaperman, or anyone else for that matter."[8]

"Atomic Bill" Laurence revered atomic weapons. He had been crusading for an American nuclear program in articles as far back as 1929. His dual status as government agent and reporter earned him an unprecedented level of access to American military officials—he even flew in the squadron of planes that dropped the atomic bomb on Nagasaki. His reports on the atomic bomb and its use had a hagiographic tone, laced with descriptions that conveyed almost religious awe.

In Laurence's article about the bombing of Nagasaki (it was withheld by military censors until a month after the bombing), he described the detonation over Nagasaki that incinerated 100,000 people. Laurence waxed: "Awe-struck, we watched it shoot upward like a meteor coming from the earth instead of from outer space, becoming ever more alive as it climbed skyward through the white clouds. . . . It was a living thing, a new species of being, born right before our incredulous eyes."

Laurence later recounted his impressions of the atomic bomb: "Being close to it and watching it as it was being fashioned into a living thing, so exquisitely shaped that any sculptor would be proud to have created it, one . . . felt oneself in the presence of the supranatural."[9]

Laurence was good at keeping his master's secrets—from suppressing the reports of deadly radioactivity in New Mexico to denying them in Japan. The *Times* was also good at keeping secrets, only revealing Laurence's dual status as government spokesman and reporter on August 7, the day after the Hiroshima bombing—and four months after Laurence began working for the Pentagon.* As Robert Jay Lifton and Greg Mitchell wrote in their excellent book *Hiroshima in America: Fifty Years of Denial,* "Here was the nation's leading science reporter, severely compromised, not only unable but disinclined to reveal all he knew about the potential hazards of the most important scientific discovery of his time."[10]

Radiation: Now You See It, Now You Don't

A CURIOUS TWIST to this story concerns another *New York Times* journalist who reported on Hiroshima; his name, believe it or not, was William Lawrence (his byline was W. H. Lawrence). He has long been confused with William L. Laurence. (Even Wilfred Burchett confuses the two men in his memoirs and his 1983 book, *Shadows of Hiroshima.*) Unlike the War Department's Pulitzer Prize winner, W. H. Lawrence visited and reported on Hiroshima on the same day as Burchett. (William L. Laurence, after flying in the squadron of planes that bombed Nagasaki, was subsequently called back to the United States by the *Times* and did not visit the bombed cities.)

W. H. Lawrence's original dispatch from Hiroshima was published on September 5, 1945. He reported matter-of-factly about the deadly effects of radiation, and wrote that Japanese doctors worried that "all who had been in Hiroshima that day would die as a result of the bomb's lingering effects." He described how "persons who had been only slightly injured on the day of the blast lost

---

*The *Times* sometimes identified William L. Laurence as a special consultant to the War Department, beginning with his article about the bombing of Nagasaki on September 9, 1945.

86 percent of their white blood corpuscles, developed temperatures of 104 degrees Fahrenheit, their hair began to drop out, they lost their appetites, vomited blood and finally died."[11]

Oddly enough, W. H. Lawrence contradicted himself one week later in an article headlined NO RADIOACTIVITY IN HIROSHIMA RUIN. For this article, the Pentagon's spin machine had swung into high gear in response to Burchett's horrifying account of "atomic plague." W. H. Lawrence reported that Brigadier General T. F. Farrell, chief of the War Department's atomic bomb mission to Hiroshima, "denied categorically that [the bomb] produced a dangerous, lingering radioactivity."[12] Lawrence's dispatch quotes only Farrell; the reporter never mentions his eyewitness account of people dying from radiation sickness that he wrote the previous week.

The conflicting accounts of Wilfred Burchett and William L. Laurence might be ancient history were it not for a modern twist.* On October 23, 2003, *The New York Times* published an article about a controversy over a Pulitzer Prize awarded in 1932 to *Times* reporter Walter Duranty. A former correspondent in the Soviet Union, Duranty had denied the existence of a famine that had killed millions of Ukrainians in 1932 and 1933. The Pulitzer Board had launched two inquiries to consider stripping Duranty of his prize. The *Times* "regretted the lapses" of its reporter and had published a signed editorial saying that Duranty's work was "some of the worst reporting to appear in this newspaper." Current *Times* executive editor Bill Keller decried Duranty's "credulous, uncritical parroting of propaganda."[13]

On November 21, 2003, the Pulitzer Board decided against rescinding Duranty's award, concluding that there was "no clear

---

*Wilfred Burchett died in 1983. William L. Laurence died in 1997.

and convincing evidence of deliberate deception" in the articles that won the prize.[14]

As an apologist for Joseph Stalin, Duranty is easy pickings. What about the "deliberate deception" of William L. Laurence in denying the lethal effects of radioactivity? And what of the fact that the Pulitzer Board knowingly awarded the top journalism prize to the Pentagon's paid publicist, who denied the suffering of millions of Japanese? Do the Pulitzer Board and the *Times* approve of "uncritical parroting of propaganda"—as long as it is from the United States?

It is long overdue that the prize for Hiroshima's apologist be stripped.

17

The People's Airwaves

Power concedes nothing without a demand. It never did and it never will.

—FREDERICK DOUGLASS

ON A COLD MARCH morning in 2002, a small group of people gathered outside the Federal Communications Commission in Washington, D.C. They were protesting the aggressively procorporate agenda being put forth by FCC chairman Michael K. Powell, the son of Secretary of State General Colin Powell, himself a board member of media giant America Online until his appointment to the Bush cabinet.[1]

Michael Powell's role as chief regulator of the media in the United States includes protection of the public interest. The protesters were reacting to Michael Powell's assertion before an American Bar Association audience on April 5, 1998, when he declared: "The night after I was sworn in, I waited for a visit from the angel of the public interest. I waited all night, but she did not come. And in fact, five months into this job, I still have had no divine awakening and no one has issued me my public interest crystal ball."[2]

To help Chairman Powell awaken, this group donned cardboard wings as angels of the public interest to pay him a visit. It was another of a growing number of direct actions in the global movement for media democracy.

There has been a complete abdication by the federal government of its responsibility to genuinely regulate the airwaves and the broadcast industry. Much of the current problem dates to the 1996 Telecommunications Act (TCA), which effected the single largest giveaway of public assets in history.

The New America Foundation estimates the value of the electromagnetic spectrum—the real estate of the airwaves—at $782 billion.[3] This is a public resource, owned by the people. Most of that bandwidth is handed over to corporate interests, used in broadcasting and newsgathering for profit, data transmission for profit, and cellular and wireless services, again for profit. The pieces of the radio spectrum that are not ceded to corporations are reserved for use by the military and other government agencies. Limited, low-power regions are reserved for the public's garage door openers, microwave ovens, and cordless phones—for the people's gadgetry, not their democracy.

The 1996 TCA was signed into law by the Clinton-Gore administration with much fanfare. The TCA revealed a bipartisan willingness by elected officials to serve the powerful media and telecommunications industry at the expense of the public. When President George W. Bush appointed Michael Powell to be FCC chair, the FCC dramatically accelerated its giveaways to corporate interests. The already highly concentrated media would now

experience sweeping rules changes that would lead to unprecedented mergers. This is exacerbating the trend toward having a
media cartel of just a few corporate giants.

Among the regulations Powell slated to be scrapped were thirty-
year-old rules that limited the reach of any television network to no
more than 35 percent of the national population, and limits on
cross-ownership that, for example, prevented newspapers from buying television or radio stations in the same city. The new rules would
allow a broadcast network to buy up stations that together reached
45 percent of the national population. The attack on the existing media ownership rules came from predictable corners: Both Viacom,
which owns CBS, and Rupert Murdoch's conservative FOX News
Channel were already in violation, and would be forced to sell off
stations to come into compliance with the 35 percent limit.

It looked like Powell, backed by the Bush White House and
with Republican control of Congress, would have no trouble ram-
ming through these historic rule changes. His work would be aided
by the fact that the telecommunications industry is numbingly
complex and dominated by lobbyists and technocrats speaking a
language incomprehensible to the common citizen.

Michael Powell did everything he could to ensure that few
people would find out about the FCC's stealth agenda. He was required to hold public hearings, so he did: He held exactly one hearing, in February 2003 in the middle of a snowstorm in Richmond,
Virginia. According to *The Washington Post*, 195 people showed
up—"119 of them were white men in suits"—and just 22 people
were scheduled to testify.[4]

Meanwhile, the FCC held seventy-one closed-door meetings
with corporate media industry lobbyists.[5] That was just the start of
the coziness between the FCC and the people it supposedly regulates. From 1995 to 2003, FCC officials took more than 2,500

trips worth nearly $2.8 million, all paid for by companies and trade groups from the telecommunications and broadcasting industries.[6]

This would normally be called bribery. At the FCC, it's just business as usual.

Powell figured the rule changes would be easy payback to the corporations that had been supporting his career for so long. He and his cronies tried to hijack the FCC from being a body that *regulates* the media into one that *de*regulates the media and gives away the public airwaves to the highest bidder. His lone hearing went largely unnoticed by the corporate media. But in a hint of the brewing opposition, the public meeting, despite the snowstorm and minimal publicity, revealed vocal opposition to his plan.

Things soon started to get out of Powell's control. Two of the five FCC commissioners, Michael Copps and Jonathan Adelstein, broke publicly with Powell and launched a series of unofficial public hearings around the country to alert the public to the radical rule changes and to mobilize opposition. They were responding to the growing public demand for accountability from the FCC and the media corporations. The dissident commissioners had no budget, so they put out a call for grassroots organizations to host these informal hearings. The ragtag angels of the public interest were already at work mobilizing, educating, and protesting.

The first unofficial FCC hearing—which preceded the official hearing in Richmond—was held in January 2003 at Columbia University in New York. *Democracy Now!* covered the event, pulling speakers aside to interview them live via cell phone. The meeting had generated sufficient prominence that Michael Powell was compelled to make an appearance. He declined our invitation to speak on air, but he went before the public with what became his mantra in the coming months: The FCC was mandated by Congress and the courts to conduct biennial rule reviews (a product of the 1996 TCA), and his charge was to do away with any rule that he could not justify.

Simply put, Powell would just toss out any rules to which the industry objected. There was no talk of expanding regulation. An executive from CBS came to the hearing to speak in favor of the proposed rule changes, which they were supporting jointly with the other major networks. While these networks made sure to send their executives, they failed to send any reporters.

Democracy Now! cohost and New York *Daily News* columnist Juan Gonzalez testified in his role as president of the National Association of Hispanic Journalists. "As Latino journalists, we are painfully aware of the historical failings of our industry when it comes to serving the public interest and preserving diverse voices," said Gonzalez. "A few weeks ago, the NAHJ released our seventh annual network 'brown-out' report, which found that in 2001, less than one percent of all news stories on the network evening newscasts of ABC, CBS, NBC, and CNN were about anything related to Latino issues." He noted wryly, "We are experts on nothing, as far as the networks are concerned, but crime and immigration."

Gonzalez added, "Journalism is not just some consumer product like cornflakes or cars. At its best, it is a noble profession and a public service. It helps to right wrongs, it gives strength to the powerless, it informs and enlightens readers, viewers, and listeners about events outside their direct experience. But at its worst, journalism becomes the bait for the commercials. It distorts reality, inflames passions, reinforces stereotypes, marginalizes dissenting views, and functions as a mouthpiece for the powerful."

The groundswell of opposition, the likes of which the FCC had never confronted, grew. Powell's attack on local media brought together groups from both the right and the left. The National Rifle Association joined the activist women's group Code Pink in a broad coalition opposed to media deregulation.

Additional unsanctioned hearings were held in Phoenix and Atlanta. Pacifica Radio broadcast the Atlanta hearing nationally. The FCC and congressional leaders were subsequently deluged by constituents about this issue. The FCC and Congress received over three million e-mails, phone calls, and letters, almost all of which were opposed to media consolidation.[7]

The fight over media consolidation is critical at this moment because the media moguls are getting more and more power and gobbling up small local stations that are the backbone of a functioning democracy. That was dramatized on a freezing cold morning in January 2002 in Minot, North Dakota. A train derailed in Minot, and ammonia gas began leaking. Authorities needed to alert residents to what had happened. Naturally, they turned to the radio stations to get out the word.

There are nine radio stations in Minot, six of them owned by Clear Channel Communications. Dick Leavitt, the owner of Christian station KHRT in Minot, told *Democracy Now!* that he was out at the accident site shortly after it happened, around 2:00 a.m., reporting via cell phone to his stations and feeding reports to the Associated Press radio desk in Minneapolis. KHRT won an AP award for its reporting that day. Leavitt and his son were the only radio reporters covering the event at that point.

Texas-based Clear Channel, which owns more than 1,200 radio stations nationwide, happens to own almost all the stations in Minot, including KCJB, designated as the local emergency broadcast station. When the authorities tried to reach people at the six stations, they could not find a single news employee. The six stations were simply clear-channeling music from another state. Three hundred people ended up going to the hospital that day. One died. Clear Channel insists that the blame lay with local officials who did not alert them properly.

You would think that the FCC deregulation, affecting millions of Americans, would get major play in the media, but the national networks knew that if people found out about how one media mogul could own nearly everything you watch, hear, and read in a city, there would be a revolt. The solution for them was simple: They just didn't cover the issue for a year. The only thing the networks did was to join together—and you thought they were competitors?—in a brief filed with the FCC to call for media deregulation.

But people said *no*. They started to learn, not through the major networks, but through alternative media.

On June 2, 2003, despite mountains of public opposition, the Republican-appointed majority of three FCC commissioners cast their yea votes and attempted a massive violation of the public interest. Commissioners Michael K. Powell, Kathleen Q. Abernathy, and Kevin J. Martin, in voting down long-standing media ownership regulations in favor of rules that strengthen corporate media conglomerates, acted to silence the voices of millions.

Medea Benjamin and another Code Pink member were in the chamber that day. They rose up singing, "Media consolidation is a threat to the nation." *Democracy Now!* was broadcasting the hearing via a video webstream subscription service. The FCC also provided a free live video webstream, which we monitored as a backup. Not surprisingly, the FCC's feed cut off before the Code Pink protesters began singing, but our alternate feed kept on streaming. These two singers symbolized the millions of people who opposed the FCC's actions. They were *singing* truth to power.

In Michael Powell's world, the voices of protesters are never heard, the public interest is ignored, and the public commons are sold to the highest bidder. By ignoring the FCC's campaign to roll back the regulations, the major news media in the United States were willing accomplices in this grand theft.

But the protesters—and the angels—were ultimately heard. In

a rare move in July 2003, the Senate Commerce Committee over-ruled the FCC and voted to turn back the worst of the media consolidation rules. Then, on September 4, a U.S. Appeals Court issued a stay against the implementation of the rules changes the day before they were to take effect. The court case was brought by lawyers with the Media Access Project on behalf of the Prometheus Radio Project, an activist organization based in Philadelphia that promotes low-power FM radio and grassroots media activism. Pete TriDish, a member of Prometheus, was one of those cardboard-winged angels—now delivering the divine awakening that Michael Powell had been pining for.

The debate over media ownership raged in Congress into 2004. That there was *any* debate—no less a battle in Congress—over what was to be a stealth corporate giveaway is testimony to the dedicated grassroots organizing, creative use of alternative media, appeals to elected officials and the courts, and the direct action of groups like Code Pink and the Angels of the Public Interest.

A blow against media ownership consolidation—now or in the future—will have far-reaching implications, as critical information gains exposure to a caring, active public. Instead of fake reality TV, maybe the media will start to cover the reality of people struggling to get by and of the victories that happen every day in our communities.

When people get information, they are empowered. We have to ensure that the airwaves are open for more of that. Our motto at *Democracy Now!* is to break the sound barrier. We call ourselves the exception to the rulers. We believe all media should be.

18

Conclusion: Free the Media

Another world is not only possible, she's on her way. Maybe many of us won't be here to greet her, but on a quiet day, if I listen carefully, I can hear her breathing.

—ARUNDHATI ROY[1]

WE NEED TO FREE the media—and we are.

Media should not be a tool only of the powerful. The media can be a platform for the most important debates of our day: war and peace, freedom and tyranny. The debate must be wide-ranging—not just a narrow discussion between Democrats and Republicans embedded in the establishment. We need to break open the box, tear down the boundaries that currently define acceptable discussion. We need a democratic media.

A democratic media gives us hope. It chronicles the movements and organizations that are making history today. When people hear their neighbors given a voice, see their struggles in what they watch and read, spirits are lifted. People feel like they can make a difference.

Social change does not spring forth from the minds of generals or presidents—in fact, change is often blocked by the powerful. Change starts with ordinary people working in their communities. And that's where media should start as well. The role of the media isn't to agree with any person or group—or with the government or the powerful. But the media does have a responsibility to include all voices in the discourse. Then let the people decide. This is a new kind of power politics. Instead of backroom deals, it's open-air rallies, public, transparent, and full of lively debate. That is what democracy looks like.

It's what Seattle looked like in 1999. The occasion was the first ministerial conference in the United States of the World Trade Organization (WTO).

The *who?*

Exactly. People had barely heard of this powerful institution. It's an unelected secretive body, established in Geneva in 1995 with strong support from President Bill Clinton, that has the power to overrule local laws in the name of free trade. In closed-door meetings, nameless trade bureaucrats from 146 countries and multinational corporations were now saying, in effect, you can pass your laws in your democratically elected legislatures to protect workers or the environment. We'll just overturn them at the WTO.

Ordinary people were not supposed to know about this. It was all supposed to fly under the radar. The WTO was barely mentioned in the U.S. press. The corporate media—whose parent companies had everything to gain from secret trade deals—decided on our behalf that we just wouldn't understand. It was much too complicated for an eight-second sound bite.

But to the dismay of the powerful, tens of thousands of people from around the world *did* understand. They descended on Seattle to show this shadow corporate government how people feel when their democracy—and their jobs, environment, and right to participate—is stolen from them.

They were religious people, trade unionists, doctors and nurses, environmentalists, students, and steelworkers in a global uprising against corporate power.

As all this was about to unfold, activists confronted a dilemma: What media would cover their actions? Protesters knew that the corporate media would belittle or misrepresent them—or completely ignore them.

A new kind of media rose up in response. People came together with pens and pencils, tape recorders and video cameras. An independent media center (IMC) was established in the heart of downtown Seattle, with powerful computers that would feed the world with reports from radio, video, and print reporting teams set up in the streets. Rather than allow this uprising against corporate power to be viewed through a corporate lens, they were determined to get as close to the story as possible. They would *become* the media.

Tens of thousands of marchers were tear-gassed and shot with rubber bullets and pepper spray. The mayor of Seattle declared martial law for the first time since World War II. The city established "no-protest zones."

As the onslaught unfolded in the streets—and the networks in New York and Atlanta scrambled to buy plane tickets and book hotel rooms from which to cover it—this new independent media movement swung into action. When one person carrying a video camera would be tear-gassed and arrested, they would hand that video camera on to the next person. My colleagues and I from *Democracy Now!* spent many long hours in the streets, with journalists from the IMC, being gassed and harassed by police dressed in black futuristic body armor as we attempted to report what was happening to the world.

While the networks were quoting the police saying that they

weren't using rubber bullets, independent media reporters were uploading minute-by-minute images as we all picked up the bullets off the street by the handful. While the networks caricatured protesters, showing an endless loop of a single smashed store window, the IMC reporters were interviewing the mothers, fathers, daughters, and sons who had come together to protest against the threat that the WTO posed to their communities. In the IMC dispatches, these people had real names, real jobs, and real concerns.

Compare that to the edict issued by the news director of Seattle's ABC affiliate, KOMO-TV. The station "will not devote coverage to irresponsible or illegal activities," wrote news director Joe Barnes. "KOMO 4 News is taking a stand on not giving some protest groups the publicity they want."[2]

Some stand. If this policy had been applied in the fifties, we might never have heard the names Rosa Parks or Martin Luther King Jr.

People are hungry for unfiltered, real-time coverage from real people's perspectives. So hungry that during the "Battle of Seattle," there were more hits on the brand-new website indymedia.org than on cnn.com.

Even some in the mainstream media were forced to acknowledge that they had been scooped. "The fact of the matter," wrote *The Christian Science Monitor,* "is that people who really wanted to learn about the WTO, and why it upsets so many people, were far better served by these small independent sites than they were by the traditional media, particularly television." While independent media provided "edgy, fresh, dramatic video of the events," noted the *Monitor,* traditional media countered with "repeated footage of a couple of incidents and interviews with establishment talking heads that the network and cable-news operations favored."[3]

The article ended with a bold prediction: "It wouldn't be surprising for one or two of these 'independent' media centers to develop into a major media source, especially if they continue to function on the sort of 'open source' reporting model seen in Seattle.

"After all, the open-source movement is reshaping the business world. Who says it couldn't happen to us in the media as well."[4]

A People's Media

CORPORATIONS HAVE BEEN gaining unprecedented power through globalization. Of the hundred largest economies right now, more than half of them are not countries—they are corporations. The whole concept of the nation-state is being called into serious question. What the corporations fear most is that grassroots activists and independent journalists will utilize the same model that companies have used to grab power: globalization. Grassroots globalization.

It's already happening. Inspired in part by Seattle, a media democracy groundswell has grown up to challenge the concentration of media ownership that freezes out independent voices. IMCs are cropping up all the time, all over the world. Today, there are more than a hundred IMCs across the globe. People are educating one another, learning to use the Internet to fill the vast voids left by the corporate media. This media and democracy movement is a budding revolution. It is a bold, new grassroots media for a new millennium of resistance. It's also a natural outgrowth of the spirit that inspired Lew Hill to start Pacifica in 1949—and inspired us to start *Democracy Now!* in 1996.

Democracy Now! has now become the largest public media collaboration in the United States. We use all means of getting to people: broadcasting on hundreds of radio and television stations, audio and video streaming on the Internet, satellite TV, and broadcasting internationally on shortwave radio.

A key outlet for us is a much underutilized resource: public access TV. Many people don't even know they have public access channels; the cable companies, which are required to provide the channels in exchange for local monopolies on cable services, certainly don't publicize it. So *Democracy Now!* goes to communities and informs people that they have these channels to use, much as Pacifica did with the FM dial fifty years ago.

By doing this, *Democracy Now!* does what the IMC in Seattle did: show the mainstream media there's a market for real people's news. Every community can model their own human rights, grassroots news shows to bring together the local and the global. It's all part of a continuum. Pacifica, NPR, and PBS aren't the only media outlets that use the public airwaves; CBS, ABC, NBC, and FOX use the public airwaves, too. They have just as much responsibility to represent the full diversity of views in this country and not just beat the drums of war or provide cover for the powerful and their governments and corporations.

Hope and Victories

"NEVER DOUBT FOR a moment that a small group of committed, thoughtful people can make a difference. Indeed, it's the only thing that ever has." Margaret Mead said this more than half a century ago. In the troubled times in which we now live—when corporate power sometimes seems invincible, the silence in mainstream media seems deafening, and true democracy seems like a far-off dream—where do we look for hope?

Try death row in Illinois. In January 2003, Governor George Ryan, a conservative Republican who co-chaired the 2000 Bush presidential campaign in Illinois, commuted the sentences of 163 death row inmates and pardoned 4 more. "Because the Illinois death penalty system is arbitrary and capricious—and therefore immoral—I no longer shall tinker with the machinery of death," declared this rock-ribbed conservative.

Ryan did not take this brave and controversial action on a whim. It grew out of years of lonely and thankless grassroots activism against the death penalty. It happened because mothers of men on death row never gave up the struggle to exonerate their sons. It happened because Northwestern University students, led by an impassioned professor named Dave Protess, began investigating the cases of men on death row, sometimes tracking down the actual murderers. And it happened because a pair of crusading investigative reporters, Steve Mills and Ken Armstrong, at an influential mainstream paper, the *Chicago Tribune,* painstakingly exposed the racist and fraudulent bases of one case after another.

Together, the mothers, the activists, the students, and the reporters completely changed the way the death penalty was viewed in Illinois—even by the governor. It was a powerful confirmation of what Jane Bohman of the Illinois Coalition Against the Death Penalty had been saying all along: "The only way that the death penalty can survive," she said, "is if no one tells the truth about it."[5]

The same could be said of Henry Kissinger. While many in the United States still see Nixon and Ford's former secretary of state as an elder statesman, the rest of the world sees him as a war criminal, responsible for the deaths and suffering of millions in Chile, Vietnam, Laos, Argentina, East Timor, and Cambodia, to name a few. When he wants to travel internationally, Kissinger now checks with the State Department to see if he'll be safe. He fears he could meet the same fate as his old crony, Chilean dictator General Augusto Pinochet, who was arrested on war crimes charges during a medical visit to England.

Even in the United States, Kissinger has begun to feel the heat—thanks in large part to reporters such as Seymour Hersh, who has doggedly chronicled the abuses of the old war criminal for thirty years. When President George W. Bush named the former secretary of state to head a commission investigating the 9/11 attacks, there was a public outcry. At long last, Kissinger's sordid human rights record came back to haunt him, and he was forced to resign from the commission in disgrace. Kissinger's lifelong contempt for human rights was finally coming back to dog him.

We can also find hope in Tulia, Texas. *Democracy Now!* and WBAI covered this incredible story from early on: Forty-six innocent people, thirty-nine of them black, had been arrested for drug dealing, solely on the word of a corrupt, racist undercover agent named Tom Coleman. Many of these innocent citizens spent *four years* in jail on bogus charges. One person was sentenced to over three hundred years. Their only real offense, as Elaine Jones of the NAACP Legal Defense Fund said, was "being black and living in Tulia."[6]

Thanks to media publicity, and galvanized by the unrelenting grassroots activism of the William Moses Kunstler Fund for Racial Justice, Tulia's wrongly convicted African-American citizens were freed and pardoned in late 2003. Coleman, the officer who fingered them, was indicted for perjury.

There's also hope in East Timor. On May 20, 2002, Allan Nairn and I went back, eleven years after we survived the Santa Cruz massacre. We returned to witness the founding of a new nation. Standing with some 100,000 Timorese at the stroke of midnight, we watched Xanana Gusmão, the rebel leader turned founding president, raise the new flag of the Democratic Republic of East Timor.

We watched the light of the fireworks glint off the tear-streaked faces of the Timorese. We did not know, on that terrible day when we lay on the ground helpless to stop the slaughter of innocent people, that we would return to celebrate their independence. Yet thanks to the resistance, determination, and persistence of the Timorese and the activists around the world who refused to look the other way, a nation of survivors was celebrating its freedom.

I thought back to when Allan and I made it to the hospital in Dili after the massacre. The doctors and nurses started to cry when they saw us. It wasn't because we were in worse shape than the Timorese. It was because of what Americans represent—not just in East Timor, but in so many places. People around the world see the United States in two ways:

The sword . . . The United States provides so many of the weapons that repressive regimes use to kill their own people. In East Timor, as in Guatemala, Nigeria, El Salvador, Iran, Iraq, and Chile—to name a few—immoral policies of successive U.S. administrations have tragically placed this nation on the wrong side of justice.

. . . *And the shield.* They know we have the power to stop attacks instead of mounting them, and to fight injustice, brutality, and tyranny. On that day of the Santa Cruz massacre in East Timor, they saw that shield bloodied.

Today, millions of people around the world tremble at the might of the greatest superpower on earth. But the true power of this country does not lie in its military, government, or corporations. It lies with individual people struggling every day to better their communities. We must build a trickle-up media that reflects the true character of this country and its people. A democratic media serving a democratic society. We have to make a decision every day: whether to represent the sword or the shield.

Notes

Introduction: The Silenced Majority

1. "In Iraq Crisis, Networks Are Megaphones for Official Views," *FAIR Action Alert*, March 18, 2003.

2. Mark Benjamin, "Medical Evacuations from Iraq Near 11,000," United Press International, December 19, 2003.

3. Michael Ratner, "The War on Terrorism: Guantanamo Prisoners, Military Commissions, and Torture," in Cynthia Clarke, *Lost Liberties: Ashcroft and the Assault on Personal Freedom* (New York: W.W. Norton, 2003), p. 133.

1. Blowback

1. George Santayana, *Life of Reason: Reason in Common Sense* (New York: Scribner's, 1905), p. 284.

2. Kissinger was national security advisor under President Richard Nixon until September 22, 1973, when he was sworn in as secretary of state.

3. Christopher Hitchens, "Why Has He Got Away With It?" *The*

Guardian, February 24, 2001. http://www.guardian.co.uk/pinochet/Story/ 0,11993,448749,00.html.

4. Peter Kornbluh, "Chile, 9/11/73," *The Nation,* September 29, 2003.

5. "Kissinger to Argentines on Dirty War: 'The Quicker You Succeed the Better,'" National Security Archive, December 4, 2003.

6. Mary Anne Weaver, "The Real bin Laden," *The New Yorker,* January 24, 2000. http://www.newyorker.com/printable/?archive/010924fr_archive03.

7. Steve Coll, "Anatomy of a Victory: CIA's Covert Afghan War," *Washington Post,* July 19, 1992.

8. Ahmed Rashid, "Osama bin Laden: How the U.S. Helped Midwife a Terrorist," *The Public I* special report, Center for Public Integrity, September 13, 2001. http://www.publici.org/excerpts_01_091301.htm.

9. Tim Weiner, "Afghan Taliban Camps Were Built by NATO," *New York Times,* August 24, 1998.

10. "The CIA's Intervention in Afghanistan: An Interview with Zbigniew Brzezinski, President Jimmy Carter's National Security Advisor," *Le Nouvel Observateur,* January 15–21, 1998, p. 76. English translation by Bill Blum posted on http://globalresearch.ca/articles/BRZ110A.html.

11. Weaver, "The Real bin Laden."

12. Jeremy Scahill, "The Saddam in Rumsfeld's Closet," commondreams. org, August 2, 2002, and *Democracy Now!,* August 5, 2002.

13. Ibid.

14. Ibid.

15. *Democracy Now!,* August 27, 2002.

16. CNN Transcript, September 21, 2002. http://www.cnn.com/ TRANSCRIPTS/0209/21/cst.01.html.

17. Henry Weinstein and William C. Rempel, "Iraq Arms: Big Help from U.S. Technology Was Sold with Approval—and Encouragement—from the Commerce Department but Often over Defense Officials' Objections," *Los Angeles Times,* February 13, 1991.

18. Cited in Scahill, "The Saddam in Rumsfeld's Closet."

19. Coll, *Washington Post,* "Anatomy of a Victory."

20. Mark Strauss, "On the Dole: Saddam Hussein Had at Least One Friend in 1990," *Washington Monthly,* June 1, 1996.

21. Samantha Power, *"A Problem from Hell": America and the Age of Genocide* (New York: Basic Books, 2002), p. 221.

22. Weinstein and Rempel, "Iraq Arms."

23. Sheldon Rampton and John Stauber, *Weapons of Mass Deception* (New York: Penguin, 2003), p. 77.

24. Jonathan Steele, "It Was Punishment Without Trial," *The Guardian,* August 15, 2003. http://www.guardian.co.uk/g2/story/0,3604,1019096,00.html.

25. The information about anthrax and plague comes from Michael Dobbs, "U.S. Had Key Role in Iraq Buildup; Trade in Chemical Arms Allowed Despite Their Use on Iranians, Kurds," *Washington Post,* December 30, 2002.

26. *Democracy Now!,* December 18, 2002. Russell Mokhiber, "Interview with Andreas Zumach," *Corporate Crime Reporter,* February 3, 2003. http://dc.indymedia.org/newswire/display/49451.

·27. James Cusick and Felicity Arbuthnot, "America Tore Out 8000 Pages of Iraq Dossier," *Sunday Herald* (Scotland), December 22, 2002. http://www.sundayherald.com/30195.

28. Russell Mokhiber, "Interview with Andreas Zumach."

29. *Democracy Now!,* September 17, 2003.

30. *Rebuilding America's Defenses: Strategies, Forces, and Resources for a New Century,* Project for the New American Century, September 2000, p. 63.

31. John Pilger, "John Pilger Reveals the American Plan," *New Statesman,* December 16, 2002.

32. *Rebuilding America's Defenses,* p. 26.

33. Bob Woodward, *Bush at War* (New York: Simon & Schuster, 2002), p. 49. Cited in Pilger.

34. Pilger, "John Pilger Reveals."

35. William Arkin, "The Secret War," *Los Angeles Times,* October 27, 2002.

36. Michael Meacher, "This War on Terrorism Is Bogus," *The Guardian,* September 6, 2003.

37. Ben Smith, "Iraq Media Guy Rebuilds Qatar at the Garden," *New York Observer,* October 27, 2003.

2. OILYgarchy

1. Microsoft Encarta Reference Library, 2003.

2. The girl blogger of Baghdad—aka Riverbend—cited in Tom Englehart, "Missing Words, Legacy Corporations, and a Sheep of Fools," tomdispatch. com, September 29, 2003. http://www.nationinstitute.org/tomdispatch/index. mhtml?emx=x&pid=980.

3. Craig Unger, "Saving the Saudis," *Vanity Fair,* October 2003.

4. Ibid.

5. Ibid.

6. Warren King, "Plane Ban Nearly Cost Patient His New Heart," *Seattle Times*, September 13, 2001.

7. Eric Lichtblau, "White House Approved Departure of Saudis After Sept. 11, Ex-Aide Says," *New York Times*, September 4, 2003.

8. Jean-Charles Brisard and Guillaumie Dasquie, *Forbidden Truth: U.S.- Taliban Secret Oil Diplomacy, Saudi Arabia, and the Failed Search for bin Laden* (New York: Nation Books, 2002).

9. Lichtblau, "White House Approved Departure of Saudis."

10. Daniel Golden, James Bandler, and Marcus Walker, "Bin Laden Family Could Profit," *Wall Street Journal*, September 27, 2001.

11. Robert Baer, *Sleeping with the Devil: How Washington Sold Our Soul for Saudi Crude* (New York: Crown, 2003), p. 51.

12. *Democracy Now!* broadcast of Rubenstein's speech, July 3, 2003.

13. Baer, p. 64.

14. Ibid.

15. Baer, p. 51.

16. Julian Borger, "An Axis of Junkies," *The Guardian*, August 6, 2003.

17. Brian Whitaker, "Spoils of War," *The Guardian*, October 13, 2003. http://www.guardian.co.uk/print/0,3858,4773441-105806,00.html.

18. *Democracy Now!*, December 8, 2003.

19. Michael Scherer, "K Street on the Tigris," motherjones.com, September 2003. http://www.motherjones.org/cgibin/print_article.pl?url=http://www.motherjones.org/news/outfront/2003/40/ma_556_01.html.

20. Ibid.

21. "Contracts With Provisional Authorities," *Windfalls of War*, Center for Public Integrity, October 20, 2003. http://www.publicintegrity.org/wow/default.aspx.

22. Paul Krugman, "Who's Sordid Now?," *New York Times*, September 30, 2003.

23. Steven Pizzo, "A Band of Brothers: The Rebuilding of Iraq," MoveOn. org, p. 21.

24. Joshua Chaffin, James Drummond, Stephen Fidler, Roula Khalaf, Nicolas Pelham, and Demetri Sevastopulo, "Reconstruction on Hold: How the Contest for Iraq's Mobile Telephone Contracts Sank into Disarray," *Financial Times*, September 26, 2003.

25. André Verlöy and Daniel Politi, "Advisers of Influence: Nine Members of the Defense Policy Board Have Ties to Defense Contractors," *Public I*, Center for Public Integrity, March 28, 2003.

26. "Winning Contractors," *Windfalls of War*, Center for Public Integrity, October 20, 2003. http://www.publicintegrity.org/wow/default.aspx.

27. For the section on contracts and corporate connections, we relied heavily on the report *Windfalls of War,* Center for Public Integrity.

28. For each company listed, contract value covers January 1, 2002 through September 30, 2003. *Windfalls of War.*

29. Ibid.

30. Walter Pincus, "Army's Iraq Media Plan Criticized; Lugar Wants to Transfer Project's Funds to State Department," *Washington Post,* October 16, 2003.

31. Brian Whitaker, "Voice of Free Iraq Walks Out on US," *The Guardian,* August 6, 2003.

32. Bob Williams, "Anatomy of a Contract," *Windfalls of War.*

33. *Windfalls of War.*

34. Project on Government Oversight (pogo.org) and News Release, Fluor Corp., June 19, 1997.

35. *Windfalls of War.*

36. *Los Angeles Times,* cited in ibid.

37. "Postwar Profits," *Capital Eye,* March 12, 2003. http://www.capital eye.org/inside.asp?ID=69.

38. Robert Capps, "Outside the Law," Salon.com, June 26, 2002. http://archive.salon.com/news/feature/2002/06/26/bosnia/.

39. Cited in William D. Hartung, "Mercenaries Inc.: How a U.S. Company Props Up the House of Saud," *The Progressive,* April 1996.

40. Ibid.

41. *Windfalls of War.*

42. Cited in "A Band of Brothers," p. 15.

43. *Windfalls of War.*

44. NBC *Meet the Press,* September 16, 2003.

45. Katty Kay, "Analysis: Oil and the Bush Cabinet," BBC News, January 29, 2001. http://news.bbc.co.uk/1/hi/world/americas/1138009.stm.

46. Molly Ivins, "Cheney's Mess Worth a Close Look," *Baltimore Sun,* June 10, 2002.

47. Center for Responsive Politics, *Rebuilding Iraq: The Contractors,* April 28, 2003. http://www.opensecrets.org/news/rebuilding_iraq/index.asp.

48. Robert Scheer, "Dick Cheney's Slimy Business Trail," Salon.com, July 17, 2002. http://archive.salon.com/news/col/scheer/2002/07/17/cheney/.

49. Michael Dobbs, "Halliburton's Deals Greater Than Thought," *Washington Post,* August 28, 2003.

50. Colum Lynch, "Firm's Iraq Deals Greater Than Thought," *Washington Post,* June 23, 2001.

51. Scheer, "Dick Cheney's Slimy Business Trail."

52. Dobbs, "Halliburton's Deals Greater Than Thought."

53. Ibid.

54. Pratap Chatterjee, "Halliburton Makes a Killing on Iraq War," *Corp-Watch*, March 20, 2003. http://www.corpwatch.org/issues/PRT.jsp?articleid=6008.

55. Neela Banerjee, "Rivals Say Halliburton Dominates Iraq Oil Work," *New York Times*, August 8, 2003.

56. Ruth Rosen, "As Ordered, It's About Oil," *San Francisco Chronicle*, August 8, 2003.

57. Robin Wright and Dana Milbank, "Bush Defends Barring Foes of War from Iraq Business," *Washington Post*, December 12, 2003.

3. Drilling and Killing

1. Erin Bartels, "Condoleezza Rice's Chevron Service Could Pose Conflict," *The Public I*, Center for Public Integrity, March 7, 2001. www.publicintegrity.org/story_01_022801.htm.

2. Steven Mufson, "For Rice, a Daunting Challenge Ahead," *Washington Post*, December 18, 2000.

3. Bartels, "Condoleezza Rice's Chevron Service."

4. Mufson, "For Rice, a Daunting Challenge."

5. John Stauber and Sheldon Rampton, "Race-Baiting Strategy Helps Keep Shell Pumping in Nigeria," *PR Watch* 3(2), 1996.

6. Meredith Turshen, "It's About Oil," *Association of Concerned African Scholars Bulletin*, Fall 2001.

7. "U.S. Senator Shows Nigerian Dictator's Letter Endorsing Clinton," Associated Press, September 12, 1996.

8. Human Rights Watch World Report, 1999.

9. Bartels, "Condoleezza Rice's Chevron Service."

10. Carla Marinucci, "Chevron Redubs Ship Named for Bush Aide; Condoleezza Rice Drew Too Much Attention," *San Francisco Chronicle*, May 5, 2001.

4. Crackdown

1. David Cole, personal communication, December 2003.

2. Warren Richey and Linda Feldmann, "Has Post-9/11 Dragnet Gone Too Far?" *Christian Science Monitor*, September 12, 2003.

3. "Surveillance Under the USA PATRIOT Act," ACLU, n.d. http://www.aclu.org/SafeandFree/SafeandFree.cfm?ID=12263&c=206.

4. "The USA PATRIOT Act and Government Actions That Threaten

Our Civil Liberties, ACLU, n.d., http://www.aclu.org/SafeandFree/Safeand Free.cfm?ID=11813&c=207.

5. Diana Jean Schemo, "Electronic Tracking System Monitors Foreign Students," *New York Times*, February 17, 2003.

6. "International Students in the U.S." International Institute of Education, November 3, 2003. http://opendoors.iienetwork.org/?p=36523.

7. Catharine Stimpson, "Foreign Students Need Not Apply," *Los Angeles Times*, August 27, 2003.

8. "International Students in the U.S."

9. John M. Broder with Susan Sachs, "Facing Registry Deadline, Men from Muslim Nations Swamp Immigration Office," *New York Times*, December 17, 2002.

10. Michael Powell, "An Exodus Grows in Brooklyn," *Washington Post*, May 29, 2003.

11. Testimony of Attorney General John Ashcroft Before the Senate Judiciary Committee, December 6, 2001.

12. "Sept. 11, 2001: Pakistani Family Mourns Loss of Son Who Went from Terror Suspect to 9/11 Hero," *Democracy Now!*, September 11, 2003.

5. Smackdown

1. "Ashcroft's Matronly Nemesis," *MetroTimes*, September 17, 2003. http://www.metrotimes.com/editorial/story.asp?id=5415.

2. *Democracy Now!*, April 10, 2002.

3. Elaine Cassel, "Vengeance, Thy Name Is Ashcroft," *City Pages/Twin Cities Babelogue*, November 20, 2003.

4. Jason Halperin, "Patriot Raid," alternet.org, April 28, 2003. http://www.alternet.org/story.html?StoryID=15760. Used by permission of the author.

5. *Of Civil Rights and Wrong*, film transcript, P.O.V., July 10, 2001. http://www.pbs.org/pov/pov2001/ofcivilwrongsandrights/.

6. Eric Lichtblau, "Justice Department Lists Use of New Power to Fight Terror," *New York Times*, May 21, 2003.

7. Eric Lichtblau, "Ashcroft Mocks Librarians and Others Who Oppose Parts of Counterterrorism Law," *New York Times*, September 16, 2003.

8. William Safire, "You Are a Suspect," *New York Times*, November 14, 2002.

9. "Pentagon Releases Report on Cyber-Surveillance System's Privacy Threat; Right-Left Groups Urge Continued Oversight," ACLU news release, May 20, 2003. http://www.aclu.org/SafeandFree/SafeandFree.cfm?ID=12673 &c=206.

10. Eric Lichtblau, "Administration Creates Center for Master Terror Watch List," *New York Times,* September 17, 2003.

11. *Democracy Now!,* September 18, 2003.

12. David Goodman, "No Child Unrecruited: Should the Military Be Given the Names of Every High School Student in America?" *Mother Jones,* December 2002.

13. Bob Keeler, "Letting the Troops Through the School Door," *Newsday,* September 15, 2003.

14. White House Transcripts, September 26, 2001. http://www.white house.gov/news/releases/2001/09/20010926-5.html.

15. Ariel Dorfman, "Lessons of a Catastrophe," *The Nation,* September 29, 2003. Used by permission of the author.

6. Lockdown

1. Mumia Abu-Jamal, edited by Noelle Hanrahan, *All Things Censored* (New York: Seven Stories Press, 2000), p. 55.

2. "Another One Bites the Dust . . . ," Society of Professional Journalists *FOI Alert,* January 10, 1997.

3. *Democracy Now!,* September 21, 1999.

4. Marc Fisher, "Pacifica Stations Bolt Over Convicted Killer's Commentary," *Washington Post,* February 25, 1997.

5. *Facts About Prisons and Prisoners,* The Sentencing Project, October 2003.

6. Ibid.

7. "How Do Prisons Profit from Immigrant Detainees?" *Democracy Now!,* September 12, 2003.

8. Ibid.

9. Death Penalty Information Center, www.deathpenaltyinfo.org.

10. Cited in "Death Penalty Facts: Racial Disparity," Amnesty International, 2003. http://www.amnestyusa.org/abolish/racialprejudices.html.

11. Ibid.

12. Innocence Project, 2003. http://innocenceproject.org/.

13. David Hinckley, "Pa. Stations Scrap 'Democracy' and Mumia," New York *Daily News,* February 25, 1997.

14. Interview with Noelle Hanrahan, director of the Prison Radio Project.

15. Associated Press, "Public Radio Hires Officer's Killer as a Death Row Commentator," *New York Times,* May 15, 1994.

16. Lois Romano, "Cancel That Call," *Washington Post,* May 17, 1994.

17. Jenifer B. McKim, "A Case of Poetic Injustice?" *Boston Globe*, July 30, 1997.

18. Ibid.

19. Martin Espada. *Zapata's Disciple* (Boston: South End Press, 1998) pp. 133–135. Reprinted with permission of the author.

7. Lies of Our *Times*

1. Elisabeth Bümiller, "Bush Aides Set Strategy to Sell Policy on Iraq," *New York Times*, September 7, 2002.

2. Michael R. Gordon and Judith Miller, "U.S. Says Hussein Intensifies Quest for A-Bomb Parts," *New York Times*, September 8, 2002.

3. *Meet the Press*, September 8, 2002.

4. John R. MacArthur, "The Lies We Bought," *Columbia Journalism Review*, May/June 2003, pp. 62–63.

5. Jack Shafer, "The *Times* Scoops That Melted: Cataloging the Wretched Reporting of Judith Miller," *Slate*, July 25, 2003. http://slate.msn.com/id/2086110/.

6. Richard Norton-Taylor, "Atomic Agency: Doubt Cast on PM's 'Nuclear Threat' Claim," *The Guardian*, September 9, 2002.

7. Howard Kurtz, "Intra-Times Battle Over Iraqi Weapons," *Washington Post*, May 26, 2003.

8. Sheldon Rampton and John Stauber, *Weapons of Mass Deception* (New York: Penguin, 2003), p. 43.

9. Eduardo Galeano, "The Finest Liars in the World," *The Progressive*, August 2003. Online at http://www.nationinstitute.org/tomdispatch/index.mhtml?emx=x&pid=886].

10. Kurtz, "Intra-Times Battle."

11. Dafna Linzer and Tarek Al-Issawi (AP), "U.S. Finds No Sign of Smallpox in Iraq: 'Team Pox' Reports Only Empty Labs, Disabled Equipment," *Ottawa Citizen*, September 19, 2003.

12. *The NewsHour with Jim Lehrer*, April 22, 2003.

13. Quoted in Harold Evans, "Reporting in the Time of Conflict," The Newseum. www.newseum.org/warstories/essay/.

14. Howard Kurtz, "Embedded Reporter's Role in Army Unit's Actions Questioned by Military," *Washington Post*, June 25, 2003.

15. Ibid.

16. William E. Jackson Jr., "Miller's Star Fades (Slightly) at NY Times," *Editor & Publisher*, October 2, 2003.

8. State Media, American Style

1. Dana Milbank, "The Iraq Truth Is Out: It's All About Oil: U.S. Military's Penchant for Strike Names Finally Trips over Slick—Too Slick—Acronym," *Washington Post*, August 14, 2003.

2. *On the Record with Greta Van Susteren*, FOX News Channel, March 24, 2003.

3. Chris Hedges, "The Press and the Myths of War," *The Nation*, April 21, 2003.

4. Ina Howard, "Power Sources," *FAIR Extra!*, May/June 2002. http://www.fair.org/extra/0205/power_sources.html.

5. John Dunbar and Aron Pilhofer, "Big Radio Rules in Small Markets," The Center for Public Integrity, October 1, 2003. http://www.openairwaves.org/telecom/report.aspx?aid=63.

6. John Schwartz and Geraldine Fabrikant, "War Puts Radio Giant on the Defensive," *New York Times*, March 31, 2003.

7. Michael Moore, "Tears Down the Westside Highway," michaelmoore.com, November 27, 2001.

8. Max Walsh, "The Murdoch Interview," *The Bulletin* (Australia), February 12, 2003. http://bulletin.ninemsn.com.au/bulletin/EdDesk.nsf/All/87D6BE4ACBB673C4CA256CC5007E11E2#9msnshared_top.

9. Poynter Online, October 31, 2003. http://poynter.org/column.asp?id=45&aid=53018.

10. Bob Woodward, *Bush at War* (New York: Simon & Schuster, 2002), quoted in *Washington Post*, November 16, 2002.

11. Paul Farhi, "The Day We Dropped the Bomb," *Washington Post*, August 6, 2003.

12. Howard Kurtz, "Chief Orders 'Balance' in War News; Reporters Are Told to Remind Viewers Why U.S. Is Bombing," *Washington Post*, October 31, 2001.

9. In Bed with the Military

1. "Dispatches: Slices of the War," *Columbia Journalism Review*, May/June 2003, pp. 32–44.

2. Howard Kurtz, "For Media After Iraq, A Case of Shell Shock; Battle Assessment Begins for Saturation Reporting," *Washington Post*, April 28, 2003.

3. Chantal Escoto, "Military, Media Benefit from 'Embed,'" *The Leaf-Chronicle*, June 22, 2003. http://www.theleafchronicle.com/news/troops/516446.html.

4. Kurtz, "For Media After Iraq."

5. Ibid.

6. Bill Kovach, "The Media and the Gulf War," *Colliers Year Book 1992*.

7. John R. MacArthur, *Second Front: Censorship and Propaganda in the Gulf War* (New York: Hill & Wang, 1992), pp. 12–17.

8. Ibid., p. 35.

9. Cited in Kovach, "The Media and the Gulf War."

10. Chris Hedges, "The Press and the Myths of War," *The Nation,* April 21, 2003.

11. "Veteran CBS News Anchor Dan Rather Speaks Out on BBC Newsnight Tonight," BBC press release, May 16, 2002. http://www.bbc.co.uk/press office/pressreleases/stories/2002/05_may/16/dan_rather.shtml.

12. From a conference held at the New School on July 24, 2003, reported in Michael Wolff, "The Media at War," *New York,* August 11, 2003.

13. Ibid.

14. Jules Crittenden, "Embedded Journal: 'I Went Over to the Dark Side,'" Poynter Online, April 11, 2003. http://poynteronline.org/content/ content_view.asp?id=29774.

15. F. Marshall Maher, "When Journalists Attack," *FAIR Extra!,* May/June 2003. http://www.fair.org/extra/0305/journalists.html.

16. All preceding quotes in box from "Dispatches: Slices of the War."

17. Bill Katovsky and Timothy Carlson, *Embedded: The Media at War in Iraq* (Guilford, Conn.: Lyons Press, 2003), p. 131.

18. Jules Crittenden, "Embedded Journalist Returns Home, Searched by Customs," Poynter Online, n.d. http://www.poynter.org/content/content_ view.asp?id=31187.

19. Ibid.

20. Wolff, "The Media at War."

21. *Topic A With Tina Brown,* CNBC, September 10, 2003.

22. Peter Johnson, "Amanpour: CNN Practiced Self-Censorship," *USA Today,* September 14, 2003.

10. Killing the Messenger

1. Robert Fisk, "Does the U.S. Military Want to Kill Journalists?" *Independent* (London), April 8, 2003.

2. Joel Campagna and Rhonda Roumani, "Permission to Fire," Committee to Protect Journalists, May 27, 2003. http://cpj.org/Briefings/2003/palestine_ hotel/palestine_hotel.html.

3. Ibid.

4. *Larry King Live,* April 8, 2003.

5. "Permission to Fire."

6. Hugh Dellios, "Three Journalists Are Killed in U.S. Attacks," *Chicago Tribune,* April 9, 2003.

7. Bill Katovsky and Timothy Carlson, *Embedded: The Media at War in Iraq* (Guilford, Conn.: Lyons Press, 2003), p. xiv.

8. "Journalists Killed in 2003," Committee to Protect Journalists. http://www.cpj.org/killed/killed03.html.

9. Joel Campagna, "CPJ Remembers: Mazen Dana," *Dangerous Assignments,* Committee to Protect Journalists, Fall/Winter 2003, p. 7.

10. "Covering a Dangerous Beat: Mazen Dana," Committee to Protect Journalists, n.d. http://www.cpj.org/awards01/dana.html.

11. Department of Defense press briefing, July 23, 2003. http://www.defense.gov/transcripts/2003/tr20030723-depsecdef0441.html.

12. Michael Wolff, "The Media at War," *New York,* August 11, 2003. www.newyorkmetro.com/nymetro/news/media/features/n_9067/index.html.

13. Ibid.

14. "U.S. Airstrike Destroys Al-Jazeera Office in Kabul," *News Alert,* Committee to Protect Journalists, November 13, 2001.

15. Michael Massing, "The Bombing of Al-Jazeera," *Columbia Journalism Review,* May/June 2003, p. 37.

16. *New York Times,* November 14, 2001.

17. "Iraqi council's ban on Al-Jazeera and Al-Arabiya condemned," press release, Reporters Without Borders, September 23, 2003. http://www.rsf.org/article.php3?id_article=8064.

18. *NPR Morning Edition,* April 8, 2003.

19. Reuters, "Journalists Protest Around Globe over Deaths of Their Colleagues," *Toronto Star,* April 10, 2003.

20. Ibid.

21. Scott Simon, "Even Pacifists Must Support This War," *The Wall Street Journal,* October 11, 2002.

22. Mike Janssen, "When Reporters Sound Off, Eyebrows Rise," *Current,* September 8, 2003.

23. Quoted in Steve Rendall and Tara Broughel, "Amplifying Officials, Squelching Dissent," *FAIR Extra!,* May/June 2003. www.fair.org/extra/0305/warstudy.html.

24. Peter Hart, "O'Reilly's War," *FAIR Extra!,* May/June 2003. www.fair.org/extra/0305/o'reilly.html.

25. Ibid.

26. Following accounts cited in "Some Critical Media Voices Face Censorship," *FAIR Media Advisory*, April 3, 2003. www.fair.org/press-releases/iraq censorship.html.

27. Russell Mokhiber, "Ari and I," Common Dreams, April 10, 2003. www.commondreams.org/ari/0410-12.htm.

28. White House press briefing, September 26, 2001. http://www. whitehouse.gov/news/releases/2001/09/20010926-5.html.

29. Dick Rogers, "Credibility at Stake," *San Francisco Chronicle*, April 3, 2003. http://www.sfgate.com/cgi-bin/article.cgi?file=/chronicle/archive/2003/04/03/ED288989.DTL.

11. Sanitized

1. Civilian casualties from Iraqbodycount.org, as of January 16, 2004.

2. Mark Benjamin, "Medical Evacuations from Iraq Near 11,000," UPI, December 19, 2003.

3. "U.S. and Coalition Casualties," cnn.com, January 16, 2004.

4. "Embedded Reporters: What Are Americans Getting?" Project for Excellence in Journalism, n.d. http://journalism.org/resources/research/reports/war/embed/numbers.asp.

5. Jacqueline E. Sharkey, "Airing Graphic Footage," *American Journalism Review*, May 2003.

6. Jacqueline E. Sharkey, "The Television War," *American Journalism Review*, May 2003.

7. 1992 *JAMA* study cited in Scott Stossel, "The Man Who Counts the Killings," *The Atlantic*, May 1997.

8. Sharkey, "The Television War."

9. Ibid.

10. Ibid.

11. Bill Carter with Jane Perlez, "Channels Struggle on Images of Captured and Slain Soldiers," *New York Times*, March 24, 2003.

12. "Iraq Must Not Parade POWs," *Human Rights Watch News*, March 24, 2003. http://hrw.org/press/2003/03/iraq032403.htm.

13. "Al-Jazeera Banned from Two Wall Street Exchanges," *NewsHour Online Report*, March 26, 2003.

14. Michael Massing, "The Unseen War," *New York Review of Books*, May 29, 2003.

15. Ibid.

16. Bill Kovach, "The Media and the Gulf War," originally published in *Colliers Year Book 1992*.

17. Joe Flint, Charles Goldsmith, and Gabriel Kahn, "CNN Gives U.S., World Audiences Different Views," *Wall Street Journal*, April 11, 2003.

18. Ibid.

19. Ibid.

20. Ibid.

21. Sheldon Rampton and John Stauber, "How to Sell a War," *In These Times*, August 4, 2003.

22. "A Tale of Two Photos," informationclearinghouse.info/article2838.htm, April 15, 2003.

23. David Potorti, "I Lost My Brother on 9-11; Does He Matter?" Alternet.org, October 10, 2001. http://www.alternet.org/story.html?StoryID=11686.

24. Ibid.

25. Gregory L. Vistica, "What Happened in Thanh Phong," *New York Times Magazine*, April 29, 2003.

26. Howard Kurtz, "Newsweek Spiked Kerrey Story in '98; Editors Cite Dropped Presidential Bid," *Washington Post*, April 27, 2001.

27. Vistica, "What Happened in Thanh Phong."

28. Cited in Howard Kurtz, "Kerrey Tells of Role in Vietnam Civilian Deaths; Ex-Senator Calls '69 Killings by Navy SEAL Unit Accidental," *Washington Post*, April 26, 2001.

29. John Hess, "The Uncovering and Reburial of a War Crime," *FAIR Extra!*, August 2001.

30. Philip Shenon, "Ex-Senator Kerrey Is Named to Federal 9/11 Commission," *New York Times*, December 10, 2003.

12.   Going to Where the Silence Is

1. Christopher Hitchens, "The Case Against Henry Kissinger," *Harper's*, March 2001.

2. "Mondale in Indonesia Says U.S. Appreciates Freeing of Prisoners," *Washington Post*, May 7, 1978.

3. Allan Nairn, Foreword, in Constâncio Pinto and Matthew Jardine, *East Timor's Unfinished Struggle: Inside the Timorese Resistance* (Boston: South End Press, 1996), pp. xx–xxi.

4. Ibid., p. xxii.

5. Leslie Dwyer, "A Reprimand for Reebok," Salon.com, March 25, 2002. http:/archive.salon.com/tech/feature/2002/03/25/dita_sari/.

6. Ibid.

7. Dita Sari, "Why I Rejected the Reebok Human Rights Award," *Counterpunch*, February 2, 2002. http://www.counterpunch.org/ditasari.html.

13. Not on Bended Knee

1. Michael Powell, "Peace Correspondent: 'Democracy Now!' Host Amy Goodman Is Making Her Voice Heard on Iraq," *Washington Post*, March 10, 2003.

2. Ibid.

3. Howard Kurtz, "Gingrich Plans to End Daily News Briefings," *Washington Post*, May 3, 1995.

14. Psyops Comes Home

1. Annual Report to the President and Congress, Department of Defense, 1998.

2. The Annenberg Washington Program in Communications Policy Studies of Northwestern University, *U.S. Foreign Affairs in the New Information Age: Charting a Course for the 21st Century* (Washington, D.C.: The Annenberg Washington Program in Communications Policy Studies of Northwestern University, 1994). http://www.annenberg.nwu.edu/pubs/usfa/usfa4.htm.

3. Samuel Gardiner, "Truth from These Podia," October 8, 2003. http://www.usnews.com/usnews/politics/whispers/documents/truth.pdf.

4. Ibid.

5. Ibid., p. 6.

6. Sheldon Rampton and John Stauber, *Weapons of Mass Deception* (New York: Penguin, 2003), p. 43.

7. The chart on pages 255–266 is based on and quotes extensively from Samuel Gardiner, "Truth from These Podia," October 8, 2003. Used by permission of the author.

8. Seymour M. Hersh, "The Stovepipe," *The New Yorker*, October 27, 2003.

9. Steven Kull, "Misperceptions, the Media, and the Iraq War," Program on International Policy Attitudes/Knowledge Networks, October 2, 2003. http://pipa.org/OnlineReports/Iraq/Media_10_02_03_Report.pdf.

10. Professor William Hoynes, personal interview, October 2003.

11. John Kampfner, "Saving Private Lynch Story 'Flawed,'" BBC News, May 15, 2003. http://news.bbc.co.uk/1/hi/programmes/correspondent/3028585.stm.

12. Ibid.

13. Michael Getler, "A Long, and Incomplete, Correction," *Washington Post*, June 29, 2003.

14. David Usborne and Andrew Buncombe, "Private Jessica's Public Turnout for a Woman They Regard as a Hero," *Independent* (London), June 23, 2003.

15. "CBS Backs Down on Lynch Movie," BBC News, July 21, 2003. http://news.bbc.co.uk/2/hi/entertainment/3083235.stm.

16. Linton Weeks, "Jessica Lynch Biography Hits Racks in November," *Washington Post*, September 2, 2003.

17. "Too Painful," *Primetime Special Edition*, ABC News, November 6, 2003. http://abcnews.go.com/sections/Primetime/US/Jessica_Lynch_031106.html.

18. Mike Janssen, "NPR News Chiefs Deny They Knew of Army Interns," *Current*, April 17, 2000.

19. J. Max Robins, "Military Interns Booted from CNN, NPR," *TV Guide*, April 15–21, 2000.

20. "Why Were Government Propaganda Experts Working On News at CNN?" *FAIR Action Alert*, March 27, 2000.

21. *Intelligence Newsletter*, February 17, 2000. Cited in Ibid.

22. Alexander Cockburn, "CNN and PSYOPS," *Counterpunch*, March 26, 2000.

23. Doug Sample, "The Faces Behind the Faces on the 'Most Wanted' Deck," *American Forces Press Service*, May 6, 2003. http://www.defenselink.mil/news/May2003/n05062003_200305062.html.

24. Donald MacIntyre, "Targeting the Regime—US Issues Cards to Their Troops Showing Iraq's Most Wanted," *Independent* (London), April 12, 2003.

25. Moni Basu, "Playing Cards Featuring Saddam, 51 Top Iraqi Lieutenants Were Seen by Few Soldiers, but Became a Hit at Home," *Atlanta Journal-Constitution*, July 27, 2003.

15.   Things Get Messy with Sally Jessy

1. *USA Today*, March 11, 1999.

2. NBC News transcript, *Today*, March 8, 1999.

3. Victor Navasky, "I. F. Stone," *The Nation*, July 21, 2003.

16.   Hiroshima Cover-up

1. Wilfred Burchett, *Shadows of Hiroshima* (London: Verso, 1983), p. 34.

2. Robert Jay Lifton and Greg Mitchell, *Hiroshima in America: Fifty Years of Denial* (New York: Putnam, 1995), p. 50.

3. William L. Laurence, "U.S. Atom Bomb Site Belies Tokyo Tales," *New York Times,* September 12, 1945.

4. Ibid.

5. Lifton and Mitchell, *Hiroshima in America,* p. 12.

6. "War Department Called *Times* Reporter to Explain Bomb's Intricacies to the Public," *New York Times,* August 7, 1945.

7. Harold Evans, "Reporting in the Time of Conflict," Newseum, n.d. http://www.newseum.org/warstories/essay/firstdraft.htm.

8. William L. Laurence, *Dawn Over Zero: The Story of the Atomic Bomb* (New York: Knopf, 1946), p. 224.

9. Laurence, *Dawn Over Zero,* p. 224.

10. Lifton and Mitchell, *Hiroshima in America,* p. 52.

11. W. H. Lawrence, "Visit to Hiroshima Proves It World's Most Damaged City," *New York Times,* September 5, 1945.

12. W. H. Lawrence, "No Radioactivity in Hiroshima Ruin," *New York Times,* September 13, 1945.

13. Jacques Steinberg, "*Times* Should Lose Pulitzer from 30's, Consultant to Paper Says," *New York Times,* October 23, 2003.

14. Pulitzer Prize Board, "Statement on Walter Duranty's 1932 Prize," November 21, 2003. http://pulitzer.org/Resources/Whats_new/Duranty/duranty.html.

17. The People's Airwaves

1. John Tarleton, "Public Interest Angels Descend on FCC," http://dc.indymedia.org, March 24, 2002.

2. Mark Cooper, *Media Ownership and Democracy in the Digital Information Age: Promoting Diversity with First Amendment Principles and Market Structure Analysis,* Center for the Internet and Society, Stanford Law School, 2003, p. 5.

3. J. H. Snider Sr., *The Citizens Guide to the Airwaves,* New America Foundation, 2003. www.spectrumpolicy.org.

4. Marc Fisher, "FCC Tests Reception for Lifting Owner Limits," *Washington Post,* February 28, 2003.

5. Bob Williams, "Behind Closed Doors: Top Broadcasters Met 71 Times with FCC Officials," Special Report, Center for Public Integrity, May 21, 2003. http://www.publici.org/dtaweb/report.asp?ReportID=526&L1=10&L2=10&L3=0&L4=0&L5=0.

6. "Well Connected: FCC and Industry Maintain Cozy Relationship on Many Levels," Center for Public Integrity, May 22, 2003. http://www.publici.org/dtaweb/report.asp?ReportID=524&L1=10&L2=10&L3=0&L4=0&L5=0.

7. Robert W. McChesney and John Nichols, "Up in Flames," *The Nation*, November 17, 2003.

18. Conclusion: Free the Media

1. Arundhati Roy, Speech for Lannan Foundation, Santa Fe, New Mexico, September 18, 2002.

2. Mike Carter, "KOMO Announces It Won't Cover 'Irresponsible or Illegal' Activities," *Seattle Times*, November 30, 1999.

3. Tom Regan, "News You Can Use from the Little Guys," *Christian Science Monitor*, December 9, 1999.

4. Ibid.

5. David Goodman, "The Conversion of Gov. Ryan," *Amnesty Now*, Spring 2003.

6. Margaret Kimberly, "The Truth About Tulia," *The Black Commentator*, October 10, 2003, cited on AlterNet.

Index